# Fodor's 90 Washington, D.C.

Fodor's Travel Publications
New York and London

ISBN 0-679-01848-4

Grateful acknowledgment is made to the following for permission to reprint previously published material:

Random House, Inc.: Excerpt from *The Power Game: How Washington Works* by Hedrick Smith. Copyright © 1988 by Hedrick Smith. Reprinted by permission of Random House, Inc., and Julian Bach Literary Agency, Inc.

---

**Fodor's Washington, D.C.**

**Editor:** Christopher Billy
**Contributors:** Suzanne Brown, Tom Carter, Michael J. Dolan, John F. Kelly, Deborah Papier, Jan Ziegler
**Art Director:** Fabrizio La Rocca
**Cartographer:** David Lindroth
**Illustrator:** Karl Tanner
**Cover Photograph:** Steve Weber/UniPhoto

**Design:** Vignelli Associates

---

**Special Sales**

# Contents

**Maps**

# Foreword

This is an exciting time for Fodor's, as we continue our ambitious program to rewrite, reformat, and redesign all 140 of our guides. Here are just a few of the new features:

★ Brand-new computer-generated maps locating all the top attractions, hotels, restaurants, and shops

★ A unique system of numbers and legends to help readers move effortlessly between text and maps

★ A new star rating system for hotels and restaurants

★ Restaurant reviews by major food critics around the world

★ Stamped, self-addressed postcards, bound into every guide, give readers an opportunity to help evaluate hotels and restaurants

★ Complete page redesign for instant retrieval of information

★ FODOR'S CHOICE—Our favorite museums, beaches, cafés, romantic hideaways, festivals, and more

★ HIGHLIGHTS—An insider's look at the most important developments in tourism during the past year

★ TIME OUT—The best and most convenient lunch stops along the shopping and exploring routes

★ Exclusive background essays create a powerful portrait of each destination

★ A mini-journal for travelers to keep track of their own itineraries and addresses

While every care has been taken to assure the accuracy of the information in this guide, the passage of time will always bring change, and consequently, the publisher cannot accept responsibility for errors that may occur.

All prices and opening times quoted here are based on information available to us at press time. Hours and admission fees may change, however, and the prudent traveler will avoid inconvenience by calling ahead.

Fodor's wants to hear about your travel experiences, both pleasant and unpleasant. When a hotel or restaurant fails to live up to its billing, let us know and we will investigate the complaint and revise our entries where the facts warrant it.

Send your letters to the editors of Fodor's Travel Publications, 201 E. 50th Street, New York, NY 10022.

# Highlights '90 and Fodor's Choice

# Highlights '90

Eighty-three years after the laying of its foundation stone, taken from a field near Bethlehem, the **Washington National Cathedral** is being completed. The final stone is to be set on September 29, 1990, an occasion being marked by a year-long series of concerts, festivities, and services of thanksgiving and dedication. The English Gothic–style building has more than 100 gargoyles, 320 stone angels, and 200 stained-glass windows.

In 1988, seven years after Congress ordered that something be done to eliminate one embarrassment on Capitol Hill, **Union Station** had its grand opening. The landmark 1907 beaux arts train station, which had a short-lived incarnation as a National Visitor Center, has been turned into a complex of over 100 shops, 25 food stands and restaurants, and a nine-screen movie house. The largest adaptive re-use project ever attempted in the United States, the restoration cost $160 million, a half million of which was spent on gold leaf.

The **Warner Theatre** is now closed for renovation. The 1924 building is having its ceiling re-gilded, and its drapes and curtains replaced. When it reopens at the end of 1991, the Warner will continue to present an eclectic mix of performance events, but with more of an emphasis on Broadway plays.

A few recent developments on the local nightlife scene are worth mentioning. One is that in Washington, as in New York and Los Angeles, much of the club action is at places that can't be found in the telephone book. You have to read the listings in *The City Paper* and watch for billboards to find these fly-by-nightspots—Chinese restaurants that metamorphose into discos, warehouses that are jumping one weekend, somnolent the next.

Speaking of jumping, swing dancing has hit Washington in a big way. There's a **Washington Area Swing Dance Committee** that sponsors dances with live music in local high school auditoriums; various clubs and restaurants, ballrooms, and studios also hold dances.

For those who'd rather dine to music than dance to it, there's the new **Hard Rock Cafe.** This worldwide chain, which began in London in 1971, features American food (hamburgers, club sandwiches, milk shakes) served amidst rock music (played by a dj) and rock memorabilia (on sale and on display).

The **Smithsonian Castle** building, which was closed for two years, reopened in the fall of 1989 with an expanded **visitors center.** With film, video, and electronic information—as well as information desks manned by real, live human beings—the center provides a much-needed orientation to the Smithsonian's 13 museums in Washington. At the moment, however, only 12 of these are open. The **Freer Gallery** of art from Asia is under renovation until 1992.

Outside the Smithsonian complex, the most important news is the renovation and expansion of the **Phillips Collection.** The nation's first museum of modern art, the Phillips is now able to provide a proper home to its matchless collection of paintings by such artists as Cezanne, Klee, Braque, and Rothko. The renovation, which also has entailed enlarging the space devoted to temporary exhibits, has been accomplished without losing any of the intimacy that makes the Phillips the city's best-loved museum.

Finally, 1990 brings still another museum to Washington: **Techworld 2000.** The exhibition space of **Techworld Plaza,** the new high-tech trade center/office building at 8th and I streets NW, Techworld 2000 is a showcase for interactive video. This is the emerging technology that allows users to manipulate video images to create their own infotainment experiences. While it may not be the hands-on experience of the future promised by the promotional literature, it is certainly different from the look-but-don't-touch encounter with the past offered by most museums.

During the mid-'80s, 18 hotels were built in Washington by developers scrambling to get a piece of the Convention Center action, and to take advantage of tax-reform incentives. The amount of construction is now at a more realistic level. Only one new hotel will be constructed in 1990: an **Embassy Suites** on upper Wisconsin Avenue. It is scheduled to open at the end of the year.

While new construction has slowed, renovations are proceeding apace. Closed for most of 1988, the deluxe **Sheraton Carlton Hotel,** two blocks from the White House on 16th Street, has re-opened with 16-million dollars' worth of improvements. The Italian palazzo facade was restored, and the guest rooms, meeting areas, restaurant, and lobby were refurnished. Meanwhile, a renovation is also planned for another old luxury hotel, the **Ritz Carlton** on Massachusetts Avenue.

Another, even more significant renovation project is the **Morrison-Clark Inn Hotel,** on Massachusetts Avenue. One of 31 hotels in America recognized for their historic significance by the National Trust for Historic Preservation, the Morrison-Clark dates from approximately 1865. The building was originally two townhouses; these were combined into one structure that was used as a military barracks until 1980. In 1988, it was opened as an inn. The Morrison-Clark contains 54 rooms decorated with period furniture.

# Fodor's Choice

No two people will agree on what makes a perfect vacation, but it's fun and helpful to know what others think. We hope you'll have a chance to experience some of Fodor's Choices yourself while visiting Washington. For detailed information about each entry, refer to the appropriate chapters (given in parentheses) within this guidebook.

## Sights

The view of Washington from Arlington House in Arlington National Cemetery

The view of the White House from the steps of the Jefferson Memorial

The Washington skyline from the roof of the Kennedy Center for the Performing Arts

## Buildings and Monuments

The White House (Tour 3: The White House)

The East building of the National Gallery of Art (Tour 1: The Mall)

The Jefferson Memorial (Tour 2: The Monuments)

Union Station (Tour 4: Capitol Hill)

The Vietnam Veterans Memorial (Tour 2: The Monuments)

Washington Cathedral (Churches, Temples, and Mosques)

## Activities

Strolling the streets of Georgetown on a weekend morning before 10 (Tour 6: Georgetown)

Bicycling along the C&O Canal (Excursions)

Visiting the Aviary at the National Zoo (Tour 9: Cleveland Park and the National Zoo)

Taking a boat ride to Mount Vernon (Excursions)

Exploring the city with Scandal Tours (Essential Information)

Seeing a movie at the Air and Space Museum (Tour 1: The Mall)

## Museums

The Phillips Collection (Tour 7: Dupont Circle)

The National Air and Space Museum (Tour 1: The Mall)

The Corcoran Gallery of Art (Tour 3: The White House)

The National Museum of African Art (Tour 1: The Mall)

The National Museum of American History (Tour 1: The Mall)

Capital Children's Museum (Museums and Galleries)

## Parks and Gardens

Rock Creek Park

Dumbarton Oaks Garden

Lafayette Square

The National Arboretum

## Restaurants

Prime Rib (American, *Very Expensive*)

Jean-Louis at the Watergate (French, *Very Expensive*)

Twenty-One Federal (New American, *Very Expensive*)

i Ricchi (Italian, *Expensive*)

Las Pampas (Argentinian, *Moderate*)

Marrakesh (Moroccan, *Moderate*)

Austin Grill (Tex-Mex, *Inexpensive*)

## Hotels

Hay-Adams Hotel *(Very Expensive)*

The Willard Inter-Continental *(Very Expensive)*

Morrison-Clark Inn Hotel *(Expensive)*

Omni Shoreham Hotel *(Expensive)*

Georgetown Marbury Hotel *(Moderate)*

Hotel Tabard Inn *(Inexpensive)*

Kalorama Guest House *(Inexpensive)*

## Nightlife

Blues Alley

Comedy Cafe

Gross National Product

The Dubliner

F. Scott's

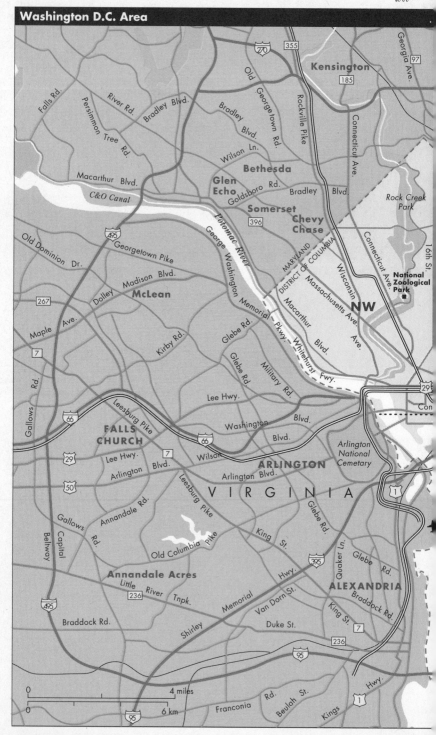

# Washington D.C. Area

Georgia Ave.

97

270   355

**Kensington**

185

Connecticut Ave.

Falls Rd.

River Rd.

Bradley Blvd.

Old Georgetown Rd.

Rockville Pike

Persimmon Tree Rd.

Bradley Blvd.

Wilson Ln.

**Bethesda**

**Glen Echo**

Goldsboro Rd.

Bradley   Blvd.

Macarthur Blvd.

C&O Canal

**Somerset**

396

**Chevy Chase**

Rock Creek Park

16th St.

MARYLAND

DISTRICT OF COLUMBIA

Wisconsin Ave.

Connecticut Ave.

**National Zoological Park**

495

Georgetown Pike

Potomac River

George Washington Memorial Pkwy.

Massachusetts Ave.

Macarthur Blvd.

**NW**

Old Dominion Dr.

267

Madison Blvd.

Dolley

**McLean**

Maple   Ave.

7

Kirby Rd.

Glebe Rd.

Glebe Rd.

Military Rd.

Whitehurst Fwy.

29

Con

Gallows   Rd.

66

Leesburg Pike

Lee Hwy.

Washington   Blvd.

Blvd.

**Arlington National Cemetary**

**FALLS CHURCH**

29

Lee Hwy.

7

Wilson

**ARLINGTON**

50

Arlington   Blvd.

Arlington Blvd.

**V I R G I N I A**

Glebe Rd.

1

Gallows   Rd.

Annandale Rd.

Leesburg Pike

Old Columbia Pike

King   St.

395

Quaker Ln.

Glebe   Rd.

Capital   Belway

**Annandale Acres**

Little River Tnpk.

236

Hwy.

**ALEXANDRIA**

Braddock Rd.

495

Braddock Rd.

Shirley

Memorial

Van Dorn St.

Duke St.

King   St.

7

236

95

0                    4 miles

0              6 km

95

Franconia   Rd.

Beulah St.

Kings   Hwy.

1

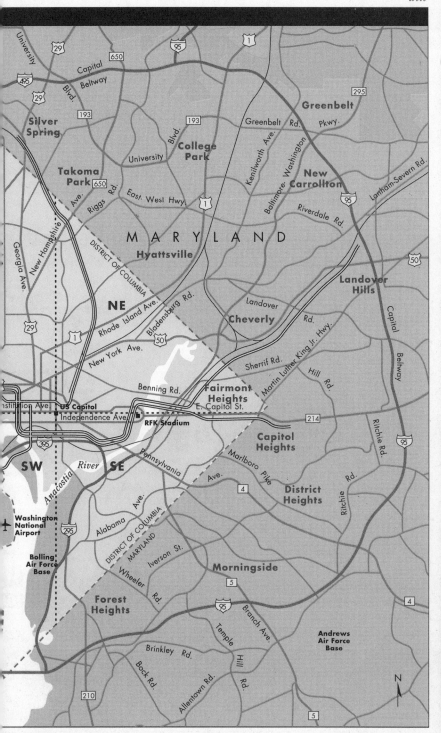

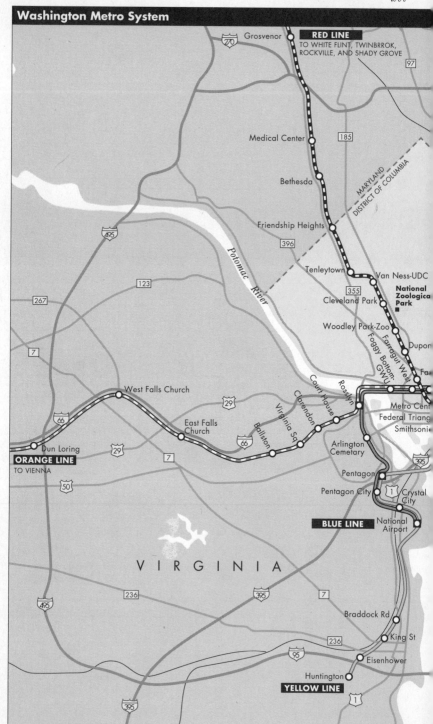

**Washington Metro System**

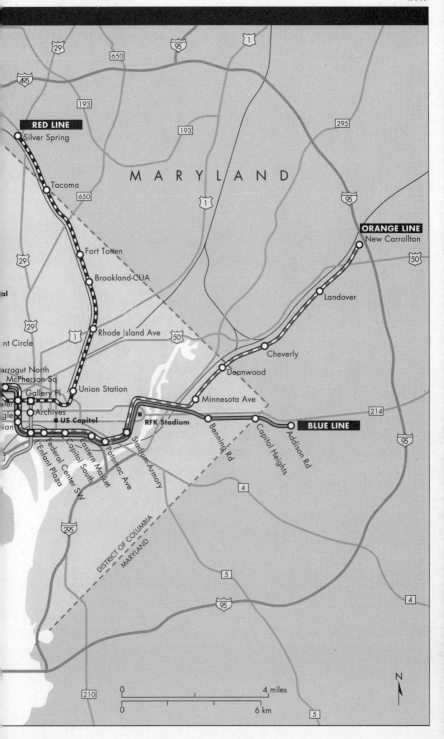

RED LINE
Silver Spring
Tacoma
Fort Totten
Brookland-CUA
Rhode Island Ave
Union Station
rragut North
McPherson Sq
Gallery Pl
Archives
US Capitol
L'Enfant Plaza
Federal Center SW
Capitol South
Eastern Market
Potomac Ave
Stadium-Armory
RFK Stadium
Minnesota Ave
Deanwood
Cheverly
Landover
ORANGE LINE
New Carrollton
Benning Rd
Capitol Heights
Addison Rd
BLUE LINE

M A R Y L A N D

DISTRICT OF COLUMBIA
MARYLAND

N

0        4 miles
0        6 km

# World Time Zones

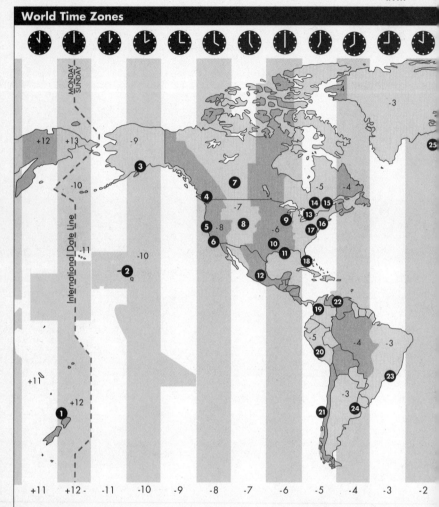

Numbers below vertical bands relate each zone to Greenwich Mean Time (0 hrs.).
Local times may differ, as indicated by lightface numbers on the map.

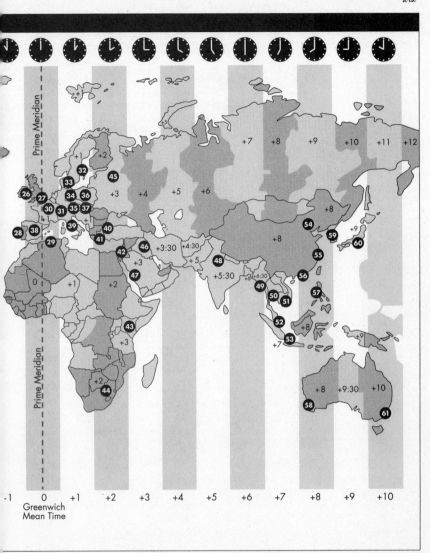

# Introduction

*by Deborah Papier*

*Deborah Papier is a native Washingtonian who has worked as an editor and writer for numerous local newspapers and magazines.*

To a surprising degree, Washington is a city much like any other. True, it does not have a baseball team, that sine qua non of an urban identity. But in most other respects, life in the nation's capital is not that different from life elsewhere in the nation. People are born here, grow up, get jobs—by no means invariably with the federal government—and have children who repeat the cycle. Very often, they live out their lives without ever testifying before Congress, being indicted for influence peddling, or attending a state dinner at the White House.

Which is not to say that the federal government does not cast a long shadow over the city. Among Washington's 630,000 inhabitants are an awful lot of lawyers, journalists, and people who include the word "policy" in their job titles. It's just that DC—to use the vernacular—is much more of a hometown than most tourists realize.

Just a few blocks away from the monuments and museums on the Mall are residential and business districts whose scale is very human. The houses are a crazy quilt of architectural styles, kept in linear formation by rows of lush trees. On the commercial streets, bookstores and ethnic groceries abound.

It is often said that Washington does not have any "real" neighborhoods, the way nearby Baltimore does. While it's true that Washingtonians are not given to huddling together on their front stoops, each area of the city does have a clearly defined personality.

Sometimes, this personality is a split one. Take Georgetown, for example. One of the city's most in-bred, exclusive communities—its residents successfully fought to keep out the subway—Georgetown is a magnet for the young and the restless from miles around.

On any day of the week the streets are full of teenagers with dripping ice cream cones. Friday and Saturday nights it's almost impossible to make your way through the crowds of tourists and natives. Halloween in Georgetown is as close as Washington gets to Mardi Gras, though things aren't quite as weird and wild as they were a few years ago.

Another distinctive neighborhood is Dupont Circle. Insofar as there is a bohemian Washington, it can be found here. This is where the artists and activists used to live, before the rents got too high, and where the hippies hung out, back at the dawning of the New Age. Now Dupont Circle is home to the most visible segment of Washington's gay community.

Adjacent to Dupont Circle is Adams-Morgan, long the city's most intensely ethnic neighborhood. In recent years Adams-Morgan has begun to lose some of its Hispanic flavor, as New American restaurants have begun to crowd out the Latin places. But you're still likely to hear more Spanish than English on the streets here.

As different as Georgetown, Dupont Circle, and Adams-Morgan are, they have one thing in common. They are all on the same side of the line that divides white from black Washington. With the exception of Capitol Hill, whites live west of 16th Street, while blacks—who make up the majority of the population—live to the east of it.

That's a long-standing demographic pattern, unchanged despite the supposed advent of integration. Whites and blacks now work together in the downtown offices, but they go off in different directions when they head home, and rarely encounter one another when they go out for the evening. At the Kennedy Center, for example, there are few black faces to be found.

Meanwhile, there is no comparable center for black culture. The riots of 1968 wiped out most of the black clubs and businesses, and while the area around 14th and U streets where they once flourished is finally being rebuilt, its vitality is unlikely to be re-created.

Further down on 14th Street, another aspect of Washington life is breathing its last: The 14th Street red-light district is almost gone. The city was determined to clean up the strip, and to everyone's surprise it succeeded.

**N**or is much left of the tacky commercial district around 9th and F streets. This was Washington's original downtown, which deteriorated when the city's center shifted to the west, to the "new" downtown of Connecticut Avenue and K Street. But the "old" downtown is being rejuvenated. The department stores that once drew crowds with their window displays have been renovated; there are new hotels and office buildings; and as the construction dust clears, the area is looking pretty good.

There is still work to be done, however. Seventh Street, for example, is a particular eyesore. It was hoped that this street would develop into a downtown arts district. But the gallery row that was envisioned for it has not materialized as planned, leaving the future of the street in doubt.

But the success or failure of an urban renewal project is probably not a matter of the utmost concern to the visitor. What many people who come here are worried about is crime. Crime is certainly a major problem here, as it is in other big cities, but Washington is not nearly as dangerous as its well-publicized homicide rate might lead you to believe. Most visitors have relatively little to fear. The drug-related shootings that have made Washington the murder capital generally take place in remote sections of the city. Unless you go seeking out the drug markets, there isn't much chance you'll get caught in the crossfire of rival drug gangs. Crimes against property are more widespread, but still far from ubiquitous. Unlike New York, Washington is not full of expert pickpockets; nor is it plagued by gold-chain snatchers.

The city's Metro is generally safe, even at night. However, if you're going to have to walk from your stop in a neighborhood that isn't well-lit and trafficked, you probably should invest in a taxi. Of course, even exercising normal prudence, it is still possible that you will have an encounter with someone who believes that what's yours ought to be his. If that happens, don't argue.

Your attachment to the contents of your wallet is certain to be tested in another way, however. Panhandlers are now a fixture of the cityscape, and there is no avoiding their importunities. How you respond to them is a matter only your conscience can advise you on. Some Washingtonians start the day with a pocketful of quarters, which they dispense to anyone who approaches them—until the money runs out. Other people sometimes give, sometimes don't, presumably according to some moral yardstick invisible to anyone else. Still others, overwhelmed or outraged by the incessant requests for a handout, feign deafness.

Whether or not you choose to dig into your pocket, you needn't feel threatened by the beggers. While they can be quite unsavory-looking, they are almost never aggressive or abusive. They ask for money; they don't demand it. And they accept a refusal, particularly one prefaced with an "I'm sorry," with considerable grace.

But they are changing the face of the city. Wealth and poverty have always coexisted here, but until recently poverty kept its distance. It's now omnipresent, wearing a very human face.

# 1 Essential Information

# Before You Go

## Visitor Information

For free brochures, an up-to-date calendar of events, and other general information about the District of Columbia, contact the **Washington Convention and Visitors Association** (1212 New York Ave. NW, Washington, DC 20005, tel. 202/789–7000).

If you're planning to visit sites in the surrounding areas of Maryland, contact the **Maryland Department of Economic and Community Development** (Office of Tourist Development, 45 Calvert St., Annapolis, MD 21401, tel. 301/269–3517). For tourist information on Virginia, contact the **Virginia Division of Tourism** (202 N. 9th St., Suite 500, Richmond, VA 23219, tel. 804/786–4484).

## Tour Groups

Joining a tour group has some advantages: Someone else worries about travel arrangements, accommodations, and baggage transfer; you are likely to save money on airfare, hotels, and ground transportation; and you will probably cover a lot of territory. The major disadvantages are that you'll have to adjust to someone else's time schedule and pacing, and you won't be as free for independent explorations. Listed below are the major companies that serve the Washington area; many of them offer packages that include trips to sites in Virginia and Maryland as well. Consult your travel agent or the Washington Convention and Visitors Association (*see* Visitor Information, above) for additional resources.

When considering a tour, be sure to find out (1) exactly what expenses are included—particularly tips, taxes, side trips, additional meals, and entertainment; (2) ratings of all hotels on the itinerary and the facilities they offer; (3) cancellation policies for both you and the tour operator; (4) the number of travelers in your group; and (5) if you are traveling alone, the cost of the single supplement. Most tour operators request that bookings be made through a travel agent, and in most cases there is no additional charge for doing so.

**General-Interest Tours** **American Express Vacations** (100 Church St., New York, NY 10007, tel. 800/241–1700), **Maupintour** (Box 807, Lawrence, KS 66044, tel. 913/843–1211 or 800/255–4266), **Cosmos/Globus Gateway** (150 S. Los Robles Ave., Suite 860, Pasadena, CA 91101, tel. 818/449–0919 or 800/556–5454) and **Domenico Tours** (751 Broadway, Bayonne, NJ 07002, tel. 201/823–TOUR or 800/554–TOUR) all offer escorted tours of Washington and its environs. For a change of pace, consider touring by rail: **Amtrak** (tel. 800/USA–RAIL) offers several escorted tours as well as independent rail/hotel tours.

**Special-Interest Tours** *Art/Architecture* Study Washington's treasures while aiding the **Smithsonian Associates** (1100 Washington Dr. SW, Washington, DC 20560, tel. 202/357–4700) and their research efforts. Past programs have included helping to inventory works of sculpture and observing Memorial Day ceremonies at key monuments.

**A Tour de Force** (Box 2782, Washington, DC, 20013, tel. 703/525–2948) promises unconventional outings led by a fourth-generation Washingtonian and local historian.

*Holiday* **Maupintour** (*see* General-Interest Tours, above) has special Thanksgiving and Christmas tours.

*Music* **Dailey-Thorp** (315 W. 57th St., New York, NY 10019, tel. 212/307–1555) offers excellent programs, including the best of operas, ballet, and other performing arts, along with a walking tour of the city. Tours are scheduled around major performance events.

## Package Deals for Independent Travelers

**American Express** (*see* General-Interest Tours, above) offers "Washington à la carte," with several options for hotels, sightseeing, and shows. **Firstours** (12755 State Hwy. 55, Minneapolis, MN 55441, tel. 800/556–5660) offers a "Supercities" package that includes hotel, a choice of tours, and entertainment. **Amtrak** (*see* General-Interest Tours, above) offers rail/hotel packages as well as an independent sightseeing package. Also check with **American Fly AAway Vacations** (tel. 800/443–7300 or 817/1234) and **Delta Airlines** (tel. 800/221–6666 or 404/765–2952).

## Tips for British Travelers

Tourist Information   Contact the **United States Travel and Tourism Administration** (22 Sackville St., London W1X 2EA, tel. 01/439–7433) for brochures and tourist information.

Passports and Visas   You will need a valid 10-year passport (cost £15). You do not need a visa if you are staying for less than 90 days, have a return ticket, and are flying with a major airline. There are some exceptions to this, so check with your travel agent or with the **United States Embassy** (Visa and Immigration Department, 5 Upper Grosvenor St., London W1A 2JB, tel. 01/499–3443). No vaccinations are needed for entry into the United States.

Customs   Visitors 21 or over can take in 200 cigarettes or 50 cigars or 3 pounds of tobacco; 1 U.S. quart of alcohol; duty-free gifts to a value of $100. You may not take in meat or meat products, seeds, plants, or fruits. Avoid illegal drugs like the plague.

Returning to the United Kingdom, you may bring home, if you are 17 or older: (1) 200 cigarettes or 100 cigarillos or 50 cigars or 250 grams of tobacco; (2) two liters of table wine and (a) one liter of alcohol over 22% by volume (most spirits, (b) two liters of alcohol under 22% by volume (fortified or sparkling wine), or (c) two more liters of table wine; (3) 50 grams of perfume and ¼ liter of toilet water; and (4) other goods up to a value of £32.

Insurance   We recommend that you insure yourself to cover health and motoring mishaps with **Europ Assistance** (252 High St., Croydon, Surrey CR0 1NF, tel. 01/680–1234).

It is also wise to take out insurance to cover lost luggage if such loss isn't already covered in any homeowners' policies you may already have). Trip-cancellation insurance is also a good idea. **The Association of British Insurers** (Aldermary House, Queen St., London EC4N 1TT, tel. 01/248–4477) will give you comprehensive advice on all aspects of vacation insurance.

**Tour Operators** The on-again, off-again price battle over transatlantic fares has meant that most tour operators now offer excellent budget packages to the United States. Among those you might consider are:

**Albany Travel (Manchester) Ltd.** (190 Deansgate, Manchester M3 3WD, tel. 061/833–0202).
**American Airplan** (Marlborough House, Churchfield Rd., Walton-on-Thames, Surrey KT12 2TJ, tel. 0932/246166).
**American Connections** (294 High St., Slough, Berks SL1 1NB, tel. 0753/692525).
**North American Vacations** (Acorn House, 172/174 Albert Rd., Jarrow, Tyne & Wear NE32 5JA, tel. 091/483–6226).
**Poundstretcher** (Airlink House, Hazelwick Ave., Three Bridges, Sussex RH10 1YS, tel. 0293/518241).
**Premier Holidays America** (Westbrook, Milton Rd., Cambridge CB4 1YQ, tel. 0223/355977).
**Speedbird Holidays** (Alta House, 152 King St., London W6 0QU, tel. 01/741–8041).
**Thomas Cook Faraway Holidays** (Thorpe Wood, Box 36, Peterborough, Cambs PE3 6SB, tel. 0733/503202).

**Airlines and Airfares** Airlines flying to Washington DC include **British Airways, TWA, Continental,** and **Virgin Atlantic.** At press time, a low-season APEX return fare was £353.

**Thomas Cook Ltd** can often book you on inexpensive flights. Phone the Cook Branch nearest you and ask to be put through to the "Airfare Warehouse." Be sure to call at least 21 days in advance of when you want to travel.

Also check out the small ads in magazines such as *Time Out* and *City Limits* and in the Sunday papers, where flights are offered for as low as £250.

## When to Go

Washington has two delightful seasons: spring and autumn, each with its own best features. In spring the city's ornamental fruit trees are budding, and its many gardens are in bloom. The Cherry Blossom Festival is held every April—whether or not the pink flowers choose to grace the city with their presence. The Smithsonian Kite Flying Contest behind the Washington Monument and the White House Easter Egg Roll are other popular spring activities. By autumn most of the summer crowds have left and visitors can enjoy the museums, galleries, and timeless monuments in peace.

Summers can be uncomfortably hot and humid (local legend has it that Washington was considered a "tropical hardship post" by some European diplomats), but that doesn't stop thousands of people from converging on the Mall for the annual Smithsonian Festival of American Folklife. Winter witnesses the lighting of the National Christmas Tree and countless historic-house tours, but the winter months are often bitter, with a handful of modest snowstorms that somehow bring this "southern" city to a standstill.

Visitors interested in government will want to visit Washington when Congress is in session. When lawmakers break for recess (for Christmas, Easter, July 4, and other holiday periods), the city seems a little less vibrant.

What follows are the average daily maximum and minimum
temperatures for Washington.

| Climate | | | | | | | | | |
|---|---|---|---|---|---|---|---|---|---|
| **Jan.** | 47F | 8C | **May** | 76F | 24C | **Sept.** | 79F | 26C |
| | 34 | −1 | | 58 | 14 | | 61 | 16 |
| **Feb.** | 47F | 8C | **June** | 85F | 29C | **Oct.** | 70F | 21C |
| | 31 | −1 | | 65 | 18 | | 52 | 11 |
| **Mar.** | 56F | 13C | **July** | 88F | 31C | **Nov.** | 56F | 13C |
| | 38 | 3 | | 70 | 21 | | 41 | 5 |
| **Apr.** | 67F | 19C | **Aug.** | 86F | 30C | **Dec.** | 47F | 8C |
| | 47 | 8 | | 68 | 20 | | 32 | 0 |

Current weather information for over 500 cities around the
world may be obtained by calling the WeatherTrak information
service at 900/370–8728, or in Texas 900/575–8728. A taped
message will ask you to dial a three-digit access code for your
chosen destination. The code is either the area code (in the
United States) or the first three letters of the foreign city. For
a list of all access codes, send a stamped, addressed envelope to
Cities, Box 7000, Dallas, TX 75209. For further information,
phone 214/869–3035 or 800/247–3282.

## Festivals and Seasonal Events

Washington has a lively calendar of special events; listed below
are some of the most important or unusual. For further information, contact the Washington Convention and Visitors
Association (*see* Visitor Information, above) or call the contact
number noted at the end of some listings.

**Jan. 15: Martin Luther King's Birthday** is celebrated with
speeches, dance, choral performances, and special readings
throughout the area. (Tel. 202/727–1186 or 202/357–2700. For
Arlington, Virginia, celebrations, tel. 703/358–5920.)
**Mid-Jan.: Washington Antiques Show** at the Omni Shoreham
Hotel is an established, high-quality presentation for buyers
and browsers. (Tel. 202/234–0700.)
**Feb.: Black History Month** features special events, museum exhibits, and cultural programs. (Tel. 202/357–2700 or 202/727–
0321.)
**Feb. 12: Lincoln's Birthday** celebrations include a wreath-
laying ceremony and a reading of the Gettysburg Address at
the Lincoln Memorial. (Tel. 202/485–9666.)
**Mid-Feb.: The Chinese New Year's Festival** explodes in Chinatown, amid hails of firecrackers and a dragon-led parade. (Tel.
202/638–1041 or 202/338–3888.)
**Feb. 19: George Washington's Birthday** is celebrated with a parade down Washington Street in Old Town Alexandria, a
historic-homes tour, and Revolutionary War reenactments.
(Tel. 703/838–4200.)
**Early Mar.: The Spring Antiques Show** hosts more than 185
dealers from 20 states, Canada, and Europe, at the D.C. Ar-
mory. (Tel. 301/924–2551 or 202/547–9215 during show.)
**Early to mid-Mar.: St. Patrick's Day and Festival** begins with a
parade down Constitution Avenue at 1 PM on March 11th. (tel.
202/424–2200). The following days feature theater, folk music,
and dance concerts (tel. 202/347–1450). For Old Town Alexandria
festivities, tel. 703/838–4200. Arlington, VA, goes green as well
(tel. 703/557–0613).
**Mar. 11: Annual Bach Marathon** honors Johann Sebastian's

birthday. Ten organists each play the massive pipe organ at Chevy Chase Presbyterian Church (1 Chevy Chase Circle NW, tel. 202/363–2202) from 1 to 6. Boxed lunches and refreshments are available.

**Mar. 24–Apr. 22: The U.S. Botanic Gardens' Easter Flower Show** presents a different flower theme each year. (Tel. 202/225–8333.)

**Mar. 31: Smithsonian Kite Festival,** a treat for kite makers and kite flyers of all ages, is held at the Washington Monument grounds from 10–4. Rain day is April 1. (Tel. 202/357–3030.)

**Apr.–May: The D.C. International Film Festival** premieres dozens of international and American films. Tickets are required. (Tel. 202/727–2396.)

**Apr. 1–8: The National Cherry Blossom Festival's** highlights are a VIP-led parade, a marathon run, a fashion show, and a Japanese Lantern Lighting ceremony. (For parade information, tel. 202/293–0480 or 202/485–9666. For general information, tel. 202/737–2599 or 202/789–7000.)

**Apr. 2–15: Imagination Celebration,** an annual festival of the performing arts for young people, hosts some of the best national children's theater companies, at the John F. Kennedy Center for the Performing Arts. Hours and performances vary. (Tel. 202/254–3600.)

**Apr. 13: Thomas Jefferson's Birthday** is marked by military drills and a wreath-laying at his memorial.

**Mid–Apr.: White House Spring Garden Tour** offers walks around the Jacqueline Kennedy Rose Garden and the West Lawn; public rooms within the White House can also be visited. (Tel. 202/456–2200.)

**Apr. 16: The White House Easter Egg Roll** welcomes children ages 8 and under (accompanied by an adult) to the White House lawn. (Tel. 202/456–2200.)

**Apr. 19–22: Smithsonian's Washington Craft Show** presents a sales exhibition of one-of-a-kind, handcrafted objects of original design by 100 of the country's best artisans. (Tel. 202/357–2700.)

**Apr. 21: The Georgetown Garden Tour** offers the opportunity to see the private gardens of one of the city's loveliest and most historic neighborhoods. (Tel. 202/338–1796. Noon–5.)

**Apr. 28–29: Georgetown House Tour** affords the same opportunity to view private homes. Admission includes high tea at historic St. John's Georgetown Parish Church. (Tel. 202/338–1796. Noon–5; tea 2–6.)

**Mid-May–Aug.: The Big Band Concert Series** offers performances at the Sylvan Theatre on the Washington Monument grounds every Wednesday evening from 8 to 10. (Tel. 202/485–9666.)

**Mid-May–Aug.: The Marine Corps Tuesday Evening Parades** present the U.S. Marine Drum and Bugle Corps and Silent Drill team at the Iwo Jima Memorial, every Tuesday evening at 7:30. Free shuttle bus service is available from Arlington Cemetery Visitors Center starting at 6. (Tel. 202/485–9666.)

**May 20: Malcolm X Day** pays tribute to the slain civil-rights leader. Concerts and speeches are held in Anacostia Park. (Tel. 202/546–7100.)

**May 26: The Memorial Day Weekend Concert,** performed by the National Symphony Orchestra at 8 PM on the West Lawn of the U.S. Capitol, officially welcomes the summer to Washington. (Tel. 202/485–9666.)

**May 27: Memorial Day Jazz Festival** marks the 13th annual jazz festival in Old Town Alexandria and features big-band music performed by local bands. (Tel. 703/838–4844. Noon–6 *PM*.)

**May 28: Memorial Day** is recognized with a wreath-laying ceremony at the Vietnam Veterans Memorial and a concert by the National Symphony.

**Late May–Early Sept.:** The **Military Band Summer Concert Series** runs from Memorial Day to Labor Day, beginning at 8 PM. (For schedules: Navy, tel. 202/433–6090; Army, tel. 202/696–3647; Marine, tel. 202/694–3502; Air Force, tel. 202/767–9253.)

**Early June: The Potomac River Fest** boasts free concerts, a tall-ship regatta, an arts and crafts fair, ethnic foods, boat rides, and fireworks. (Tel. 202/387–8292.)

**Early June: The Alexandria Waterfront Festival** is a family-oriented weekend designed to promote the American Red Cross and to recognize Alexandria's rich maritime heritage. Activities include visiting tall ships, arts and crafts displays, a 10K run, and the blessing of the fleet. (Tel. 703/549–8300.)

**July–Aug.: Washington Cathedral's Summer Festival of Music** is part of the Cathedral's year-long celebration of its formal dedication. (Tel. 202/537–6200.)

**Early July: The Mostly Mozart Festival** is held at the John F. Kennedy Center for the Performing Arts. (Tel. 202/254–3600.)

**July 4: D.C. Free Jazz Festival** showcases the city's most accomplished and innovative musicians in free concerts (Freedom Plaza, 1300 Pennsylvania Ave., tel. 202/783–0360).

**July 4: The Independence Day Celebration** includes a grand parade that follows a route past many of the capital's historic monuments. In the evening the National Symphony Orchestra performs for free on the steps of the Capitol building; this is followed by a fireworks display over the Washington Monument. (Tel. 202/485–9666.)

**July 11–Aug. 29: The Twilight Tattoo Series** features the 3rd U.S. Infantry and the U.S. Army Band on the Ellipse grounds, between the White House and the Washington Monument, every Wednesday evening at 7. (Tel. 202/696–3647.)

**July 28–29: The Virginia Scottish Games,** one of the largest Scottish festivals in the United States, features traditional Highland dance, bagpipes, a national professional heptathlon, animal events, and fiddling competitions (Episcopal High School grounds, 3901 W. Braddock Rd., Alexandria, VA, tel. 703/838–4200).

**Late July: Hispanic-American Cultural Festival** spotlights Washington's large Latino community in the Adams-Morgan and Mt. Pleasant neighborhoods. (18th and Columbia Rd., NW, tel. 202/265–2659.)

**Sept. 1: The National Frisbee Festival** is the largest noncompetitive assembly of frisbee-lovers. The disc-catching canines almost steal the show from the two-legged pros (National Mall near the Smithsonian's National Air and Space Museum, tel. 301/645–5043).

**Sept. 2: The Labor Day Weekend Concert** features the National Symphony Orchestra on the West Lawn of the U.S. Capitol, beginning at 8 PM. (Tel. 202/785–8100.)

**Sept. 9: Adams-Morgan Day** celebrates that neighborhood's Hispanic community with colorful arts and crafts, lively music, ethnic foods, and dancing. (Tel. 202/745–0179.)

**Mid–Sept.: The Washington National Cathedral Consecration and Dedication** is scheduled for September 29, 1990, exactly 83 years from the start of its construction. (Tel. 202/537–6247.)

**Sept. 17: The Constitution Day Commemoration** observes the anniversary of the signing of the United States Constitution. Events include a naturalization ceremony, speakers, and band concerts (National Archives, tel. 202/523–3097).

**Sept. 29: Rock Creek Park Day** celebrates the park's 100th birthday, with international and national music, children's activities, foods, and arts and crafts. (Tel. 202/426–6832. Noon–dusk.)

**Mid-Oct.: The Capitol City Jazz Festival** offers a dazzling array of jazz concerts by longtime masters and today's leading-edge artists. (Tel. 202/832–4272.)

**Mid–Oct.: White House Fall Garden Tours** provide an opportunity to see the splendid gardens of the White House, including the famous Rose Gardens and the South Lawn. (Tel. 202/426–6700 or 202/472–3669.)

**Oct. 21–28: The Washington International Horse Show** is D.C.'s major equestrian event, held at the Capital Centre in Landover, Maryland. (Tel. 301/840–0281.)

**Oct. 31: Halloween** brings crowds of native and visiting revelers to the streets. Block parties in the residential neighborhoods of Georgetown and Dupont Circle are especially boisterous and last until the wee hours of the morning.

**Nov. 4: The Marine Corps Marathon** attracts thousands of world-class runners. It begins at the Iwo Jima Marine Corps Memorial in Arlington, Virginia. There is a registration fee. (Tel. 703/690–3431.)

**Nov. 11: Veteran's Day** activities include a service at Arlington National Cemetery and a wreath-laying ceremony at the Tomb of the Unknown Soldier, led by the President or other ranking official. (Tel. 202/475–0843.)

**Dec.: Christmas** celebrations start early in the month. Major events include carol singing with the U.S. Marine Band, the Smithsonian Museum's annual display of Christmas trees, the Capitol Tree Lighting (done by the President himself), and the Pageant of Peace.

**Early Dec.: The Winter Antiques Fair** draws dealers from around the country, Canada, and Europe. (Tel. 301/924–2551.)

**Dec. 8–9: Old Town Christmas Candlelight Tours:** Visit historic Ramsay House, Gadsby's Tavern Museum, the Lee-Fendall House, and the Carlyle House in Old Town Alexandria. Included in the tour are music, colonial dancing, and light refreshments. (Tel. 703/838–4200.)

**Dec. 12: The People's Christmas Tree Lighting** on the west side of the U.S. Capitol precedes the city's Pageant of Peace. Military bands perform. (Tel. 202/224–3069.)

**Dec. 13–Jan. 1: The National Christmas Tree Lighting/Pageant of Peace** is accompanied by seasonal music and caroling. The National Christmas Tree (on the Ellipse just south of the White House) is lighted by the President at 5:30 PM on the 13th. For the next few weeks the Ellipse grounds are the site of nightly choral performances, a Nativity scene, a burning yule log, and a display of lighted Christmas trees representing each state and territory in the United States. (Tel. 202/485–9666.)

**Mid-Dec.–Jan. 1: Botanic Gardens' Poinsettia Show** bursts forth with more than 3,000 of the traditional holiday red, white, and pink flowers as well as a display of Christmas wreaths and trees. (U.S. Botanic Gardens, tel. 202/225–8333.)

**Mid-Dec.–Jan. 6: The Trees of Christmas** glow in all shapes and sizes at the Smithsonian's National Museum of American History. (Tel. 202/357–2627.)

**Mid–late Dec.: "Nutcracker Suite"** is performed by the Washington Ballet at Lisner Auditorium. Tickets are required. (Tel. 202/362–3606.)

**Mid–late Dec.:** *A Christmas Carol* returns year after year to historic Ford's Theatre. Tickets are required. (Tel. 202/347–4833.)

**Dec. 23–25: The Washington National Cathedral Christmas Celebration and Services** include Christmas carols and seasonal choral performances. (Tel. 202/537–6200.)

**Dec. 31: The New Year's Eve Celebration at the Old Post Office Pavilion,** the city's largest block party, features live entertainment. At midnight a giant U.S. Postal Service Love Stamp is lowered from the Pavilion's clock tower. (Tel. 202/387–8292.)

## What to Pack

What you pack depends largely on where you're headed. Washington is basically informal, although many restaurants require a jacket and tie. Theaters and nightclubs in the area range from the slightly dressy (John F. Kennedy Center) to extremely casual (Wolf Trap Farm Park). For sightseeing and casual dining, jeans and sneakers are acceptable just about anywhere. Summer is usually very hot and humid, so you'll want to have shorts and light shirts. Even in August, though, you might still want to have a shawl or light jacket for air-conditioned restaurants. Good walking shoes are a must since most of the city's interesting neighborhoods and sites are best explored on foot. The only really cold months, for which you'll need a heavy coat and snow boots, are January and February.

**Carry-on Luggage** New rules have been in effect since January 1, 1988 on U.S. airlines with regard to carry-on luggage. The model for the new rules was agreed to by the airlines in December 1987 and then circulated by the Air Transport Association, with the understanding that each airline would present its own version. Under the model, passengers on U.S. airlines are limited to two carry-on bags. For a bag you wish to store under the seat, the maximum dimensions are $9'' \times 14'' \times 22''$. For bags that can be hung in a closet or on a luggage rack, the maximum dimensions are $4'' \times 23'' \times 45''$. For bags you wish to store in an overhead bin, the maximum dimensions are $10'' \times 14'' \times 36''$. Any item that exceeds the specified dimensions may be rejected as a carry-on and taken as checked baggage. Keep in mind that an airline can adapt the rules to circumstances, so on an especially crowded flight don't be surprised if you are only allowed one carry-on bag.

In addition to the two carry-ons, you may bring aboard a handbag (pocketbook or purse); an overcoat or wrap; an umbrella; a camera; a reasonable amount of reading material; an infant bag; crutches, cane, braces, or other prosthetic device; and an infant/child safety seat.

Note that these regulations are for U.S. airlines only. Foreign airlines generally allow only one piece of carry-on luggage in tourist class, in addition to handbags and bags filled with duty-free goods. Passengers in first and business class are also allowed to carry on one garment bag. It is best to call your airline in advance to learn its rules regarding carry-on luggage.

**Checked Luggage** Luggage allowances vary slightly from airline to airline. Many carriers allow three checked pieces; some allow only two. Again, it is best to check before you go. In all cases, each piece of checked luggage may not weigh more than 70 pounds or be larger than 62 inches (length + width + height).

## Cash Machines

Virtually all U.S. banks now belong to a network of automatic teller machines (ATMs) that dispense cash 24 hours a day. There are eight major networks in the United States, the largest of which are Cirrus, owned by MasterCard, and Plus, affiliated with Visa. Some banks belong to more than one network. Each network has a toll-free number you can call to locate its machines in a given city. The Cirrus number is 800/424–7787; the Plus number is 800/843–7587. Note that these "cash cards" are not issued automatically; they must be requested at your bank branch.

Cards issued by Visa, American Express, and MasterCard can also be used in the ATMs, but the fees are usually higher than the fees on bank cards (and there is a daily interest charge on the loan). All three companies issue directories that list the national and international outlets that accept their cards. You can pick up a Visa or MasterCard directory at your local bank. For an American Express directory, call 800/CASH–NOW (this number can also be used for general inquiries). Contact your bank for information on fees and the amount of cash you can withdraw on any given day. Although each bank individually charges for taking money with the card, using your American Express, Visa, or MasterCard at an ATM can be cheaper than exchanging money in a bank because of variations in exchange rates.

## Traveling with Film

If your camera is new, shoot and develop a few rolls before leaving home. Pack some lens tissue and an extra battery for your built-in light meter. Invest about $10 in a skylight filter and screw it onto the front of your lens. It will protect the lens and also reduce haze.

Film doesn't like hot weather. If you're driving in summer, don't store film in your car's glove compartment or on the shelf under the rear window. Put it behind the front seat on the floor, on the side opposite the exhaust pipe.

On a plane trip, never pack unprocessed film in checked luggage; once your bags are X-rayed, you can say good-bye to your pictures. Always carry undeveloped film with you through security, and ask to have it inspected by hand. (It helps to isolate your film in a plastic bag, ready for quick inspection.) Inspectors at American airports are required by law to honor requests for hand inspection; abroad, you'll have to depend on the kindness of strangers.

The old airport scanning machines—still in use in some countries—use heavy doses of radiation that can turn a family portrait into an early-morning fog. The newer models—used in all U.S. airports—are safe for anything from five to 500 scans, depending on the speed of your film. The effects are cumulative; you can put the same roll of film through several scans without worry. After five scans, though, you're asking for trouble.

If your film gets fogged and you want an explanation, send it to the National Association of Photographic Manufacturers (600 Mamaroneck Ave., Harrison, NY 10528). They will try to determine what went wrong. The service is free.

## Traveling with Children

**Getting There** On domestic flights, children under 2 not occupying a seat travel free. Various discounts apply to children 2 to 12. Reserve a seat behind the bulkhead of the plane, which offers more leg room and can usually fit a bassinet (supplied by the airline). At the same time, inquire about special children's meals or snacks, offered by most airlines. (*See* "TWYCH's Airline Guide," in the February 1988 issue of *Family Travel Times* for a rundown of children's services furnished by 46 airlines; an update is planned for February 1990. *See* Publications, below, for ordering information.) Ask your airline in advance if you can bring aboard your child's car seat. (For the pamphlet "Child/Infant Safety Seats Acceptable for Use in Aircraft," write the Community and Consumer Liaison Division, APA–200, Federal Aviation Administration, Washington, DC 20591, tel. 202/267–3479.)

**Hotels** In addition to offering family discounts and special rates for children (for example, some large hotel chains do not charge anything extra for children under 12 if they stay in their parents' room), many hotels and resorts arrange for baby-sitting services and run a variety of special children's programs. If you are going to travel with your children, be sure to check with your travel agent for more information or ask a hotel representative about children's programs when you are making reservations.

**Baby-Sitting Services** Make your child-care arrangements with the hotel concierge or housekeeper.

**Publications** *Family Travel Times* is an 8- to 12-page newsletter published 10 times a year by TWYCH (Travel with Your Children, 80 8th Ave., New York, NY 10011, tel. 212/206–0688). The $35 subscription includes access to back issues and twice-weekly opportunities to call for specific information. Send $1 for a sample issue.

*Great Vacations with Your Kids,* by Dorothy Jordan (founder of TWYCH) and Marjorie Cohen, offers complete advice on planning a trip with children (toddlers to teens) and reports on special travel accommodations available to families (E.P. Dutton, 2 Park Ave., New York, NY 10016, tel. 212/725–1818; $11.95 paperback).

*Family Travel Guides* (Carousel Press, Box 6061, Albany, CA 94706, tel. 415/527–5849) is a catalog offering guidebooks, games, diaries, and magazine articles geared to traveling with children. To receive the catalog, send $1 for postage and handling.

*Kids and Teens in Flight* is a brochure developed by the Department of Transportation on children traveling alone. To order a free copy, tel. 202/366–2220.

*A Kid's Guide to Washington, D.C.* (Gulliver Books/Harcourt Brace Jovanovich, 111 Fifth Ave., New York, NY 10003; $6.95) includes games, photographs, maps, and a travel diary.

*Kidding Around Washington, D.C., A Young Person's Guide to the City* by Anne Pedersen (John Muir Publications, Box 613, Santa Fe, NM 87504; $9.95) highlights the sites in each neighborhood that are of most interest to children; it includes maps of each major sector of the city.

Home Exchange    See *Home Exchanging: A Complete Sourcebook for Travelers at Home or Abroad,* by James Dearing ($9.95 paperback, Globe Pequot Press, Box Q, Chester, CT 06412, tel. 800/243–0495, or in Connecticut, 800/962–0973).

## Hints for Disabled Travelers

Organizations    **The Information Center for Individuals with Disabilities** (Fort Point Place, 1st floor, 27–43 Wormwood St., Boston, MA 02217–1606, tel. 617/727–5540) offers useful problem-solving assistance, including lists of travel agents who specialize in tours for the disabled.

**Moss Rehabilitation Hospital Travel Information Service** (12th St. and Tabor Rd., Philadelphia, PA 19141, tel. 215/329–5715) provides information on tourist sights, transportation, and accommodations in destinations around the world. The fee is $5 for up to three destinations. Allow one month for delivery.

**Mobility International** (Box 3551, Eugene, OR 97403, tel. 503/343–1284) is a membership organization with a $20 annual fee offering information on accommodations and on organized study around the world.

**The National Park Service** provides a Golden Access Passport free of charge to those who are medically blind or have a permanent disability; the passport covers the entry fee for the holder and anyone accompanying the holder in the same private, noncommercial vehicle and allows the user a 50% discount on camping, boat launching, and parking. All charges except lodging are covered. Apply for the passport in person at any national recreation facility that charges an entrance fee; proof of disability is required. For additional information, write to the National Park Service (U.S. Dept. of Interior, 18th and C sts. NW, Washington, DC 20240).

**The Society for the Advancement of Travel for the Handicapped** (26 Court St., Penthouse Suite, Brooklyn, NY 11242, tel. 718/858–5483) offers access information. Annual membership is $40, $25 for senior travelers and students. If you are not a member, send $2 and a stamped, addressed envelope, for information on a specific country.

**Travel Industry and Disabled Exchange** (TIDE, 5435 Donna Ave., Tarzana, CA 91356, tel. 818/343–6339) is an industry-based organization with a $15-per-person annual membership fee. Members receive a quarterly newsletter and information on travel agencies and tours.

**Twin Peaks Press** (Box 129, Vancouver, WA 98666, tel. 206/694–2462 or 800/637–2256 for orders only) specializes in books for the disabled. *Travel for the Disabled* ($9.95) offers helpful hints as well as a comprehensive list of guidebooks and facilities geared to the disabled. *Directory of Travel Agencies for the Disabled* ($12.95) lists more than 350 agencies throughout the world. *Wheelchair Vagabond* ($9.95) helps independent travelers plan for extended trips in cars, vans, or campers. Twin

Peaks also offers a "Traveling Nurse's Network," which provides registered nurses trained in all medical areas to accompany and assist disabled travelers.

**Transportation**  **Greyhound/Trailways** (tel. 800/531–5332) will carry a disabled person and companion for the price of a single fare.

**Amtrak** (tel. 800/USA–RAIL) requests 72-hour notice to provide redcap service, special seats, or wheelchair assistance at stations that are equipped to provide this service. All handicapped and elderly passengers are entitled to a 25% discount on regular, nondiscounted coach fares. A special children's handicapped fare is also available and offers qualifying children age 2 to 11 a 25% discount on the already-discounted children's fare. Note that there are exceptions to these discounts on certain prescribed days on various routes. Always check first with Amtrak. For a free copy of "Access Amtrak," a guide to its services for elderly and handicapped travelers, write to Amtrak (National Railroad Corporation, 400 N. Capitol St. NW, Washington, DC 20001).

**Publications**  *Access America: An Atlas and Guide to the National Parks for Visitors with Disabilities* (Northern Cartographic, P.O. Box 133, Burlington, VT 05402, tel. 801/655–4321) contains detailed information about access for the 37 largest and most visited national parks in the United States. It costs $89.95 plus $5 shipping. Individuals and nonprofit organizations who order directly from the publishers save 25% ($67.45 plus $5 for shipping).

*Access to the World: A Travel Guide for the Handicapped,* by Louise Weiss, offers tips on travel and accessibility around the world. It is available from Henry Holt & Co. for $12.95 plus $2 shipping (tel. 800/247–3912; #0805 001417).

*Access Travel,* published in 1985 by the U.S. Office of Consumer Affairs, is a free brochure that lists design features, facilities, and services for the handicapped at 519 airport terminals in 62 countries. Order publication 570V by writing S. James, Consumer Information Center–K, Box 100, Pueblo, CO 81002.

*The Itinerary* (Box 1084, Bayonne, NJ 07002, tel. 201/858–3400) is a well-respected bimonthly travel magazine for the disabled. Call for a subscription ($10 for a year, $18 for two); it's not available in stores.

## Hints for Older Travelers

**Organizations**  **The American Association of Retired Persons** (AARP, 1990 K St. NW, Washington, DC 20049, tel. 202/872–4700) offers independent travelers a **Purchase Privilege Program,** which entitles members to discounts on hotels, airfare, car rentals, and sightseeing. The **AARP Travel Service** also arranges group tours in conjunction with two companies: Olson-Travelworld (100 N. Sepulvedo Blvd., El Segundo, CA 90245, tel. 800/227–7737) and RFD, Inc. (4401 W. 110th St., Overland Park, KS 66211, tel. 800/448–7010). AARP members must be at least 50 years old. Annual dues are $5 per person or per couple.

If you're planning to use an AARP or other senior-citizen identification card to obtain a reduced hotel rate, mention it at the time you make your reservation rather than when you check out. At restaurants show your card to the maitre d' before you're seated; discounts may be limited to certain set menus, days, or hours. Your AARP card will identify you as a retired person but will not ensure a discount in all hotels and restaurants. For a free list of hotels and restaurants that offer discounts, call or write the AARP and ask for the "Purchase Privilege" brochure or call the AARP Travel Service. When renting a car, remember that economy cars, priced at promotional rates, may cost less than the cars that are available with your ID card.

**Elderhostel** (80 Boylston St., Suite 400, Boston, MA 02116, tel. 617/426–7788) is an innovative program for people 60 or over (only one member of a traveling couple has to qualify). Participants live in dormitories on some 1,200 campuses around the world. Mornings are devoted to lectures and seminars, afternoons to sightseeing and field trips. The fee for a trip includes room, board, tuition (in the U.S. and Canada) and round-trip transportation (overseas). Special scholarships are available for those in the U.S. and Canada who qualify financially.

**The Golden Age Passport** is a free lifetime pass to all parks, monuments, and recreation areas run by the federal government. Permanent U.S. residents over 62 may pick up a pass in person at any national park that charges admission. The passport covers the entrance fee for the holder and anyone accompanying the holder in the same private (noncommercial) vehicle. It also provides a 50% discount on camping, boat launching, and parking (lodging is not included). Proof of age is necessary.

**Mature Outlook** (6001 N. Clarke St., Chicago, IL 60660, tel. 800/336–6330), a subsidiary of Sears, Roebuck, & Co., is a travel club for people over 50 years of age and offers a bimonthly newsletter and discounts at Holiday Inns. Annual membership is $9.95 per person or couple. Instant membership is available at participating Holiday Inns.

**National Council of Senior Citizens** (925 15th St. NW, Washington, DC 20005, tel. 202/347–8800) is a nonprofit advocacy group with some 4,000 local clubs across the country. Annual membership is $10 per person or $14 per couple. Members receive a monthly newspaper with travel information and an ID for reduced rates on hotels and car rentals.

**September Days Club** (tel. 800/241–5050) is run by the moderately priced Days Inns of America. The $12 annual membership fee for individuals or couples over 50 entitles them to reduced car-rental rates and reductions of 15 to 50% at 95% of the chain's more than 350 motels. Members also receive *Travel Holiday Magazine Quarterly*, which contains updated information and travel articles.

**Vantage Travel Service** (111 Cypress St., Brookline, MA 02146, tel. 800/322–6677) offers tours geared toward senior citizens. Nonsenior adult relatives and friends are welcome.

**Transportation** **Greyhound/Trailways** (tel. 800/531–5332) offers special fares for senior citizens; these fares are subject to date and destination restrictions.

**Amtrak** (*see* Hints for Disabled Travelers, above).

Publications   ***The Discount Guide for Travelers over 55,*** by Caroline and Walter Weintz, lists helpful addresses, package tours, reduced-rate car-rental agencies, and other useful information for travel in the United States and abroad. To order, send $7.95 to NAL/Cash Sales (Bergenfield Order Dept., 120 Woodbine St., Bergenfield, NJ 07021, tel. 800/526–0275).

***The Senior Citizens Guide to Budget Travel in the United States and Canada,*** by Paige Palmer, is available for $3.95 plus $1 for shipping from Pilot Books (103 Cooper St., Babylon, NY 11702, tel. 516/422–2225).

***Travel Tips for Senior Citizens*** (U.S. Dept. of State Publication 8970, revised Sept. 1987) is available for $1 from the Superintendent of Documents (U.S. Government Printing Office, Washington, DC 20402–9325, tel. 202/783–3238).

### Further Reading

Classic Washington novels include *Democracy*, by Henry Adams; *Advise and Consent*, by Allen Drury; and Gore Vidal's *Washington, D.C.*

Margaret Leach's *Reveille in Washington* recreates the city during the Civil War. In *All the President's Men*, Bob Woodward and Carl Bernstein detail the events of Watergate.

E.J. Applewhite comments on the architecture of the city in *Washington Itself.* Louis A. Halle's *Springtime in Washington* is the definitive look at the flora and fauna of the capital. In *Ear on Washington*, gossip columnist Diana McClellan recounts some of the town's juicier stories. *Literary Washington*, by David Cutler, explores past and contemporary writers who have lived in and written about the city. Famous quotes about the Federal City are compiled in *Washington: A Reader*, by Bill Adler, Sr.

Characters in Margaret Truman's mysteries have been found murdered everywhere from the Smithsonian to the Supreme Court.

# Arriving and Departing

### By Plane

Airports   Most national and international airlines as well as many regional and commuter carriers serve one or more of Washington's three airports. **National Airport,** in Virginia, 4 miles south of downtown Washington, is popular with politicians and their staffs. It is often cramped and crowded, but it's convenient to downtown (20 minutes by subway to the Metro Center stop). Many transcontinental and international flights arrive at **Dulles International Airport,** a modern facility 26 miles west of Washington. **Baltimore-Washington International (BWI) Airport** is in Maryland, about 25 miles northwest of Washington. All three airports are served by a variety of bus and limousine companies that make scheduled trips between airports and to downtown Washington.

Airlines   When buying your ticket, be sure to distinguish among nonstop flights (no changes, no stops), direct flights (no changes but one or more stops), and connecting flights (two or more planes, two or more stops).

National Airport is served by **American** (tel. 800/433–7300), **Continental** (tel. 800/525–0280), **Delta** (tel. 800/221–1212), **Eastern** (tel. 800/327–8376), **Midway** (tel. 800/621–5700), **Midwest** (tel. 800/452–2022), **Northwest** (tel. 800/225–2525), **Pan American** (tel. 800/442–5896), **Piedmont** (tel. 800/251–5720), **TWA** (tel. 800/221–2000), **United** (tel. 800/241–6522), and **USAir** (tel. 800/428–4322).

Major air carriers serving Dulles include **Aeroflot** (tel. 202/429–4922), **Air France** (tel. 800/237–2747), **All Nippon** (tel. 800/2FLY–ANA), **American** (tel. 800/433–7300), **British Airways** (tel. 800/247–9297), **Catskill Airways** (tel. 800/833–0196), **Continental** (tel. 800/525–0280), **Delta** (tel. 800/221–1212), **Lufthansa** (tel. 800/645–3880), **Northwest** (tel. 800/225–2525), **Pan American** (tel. 800/442–5896), **Saudi Arabian** (tel. 800/4SAUDIA), **TWA** (tel. 800/221–2000), **United** (tel. 800/241–6522), **USAir** (tel. 800/428–4322), and **Wings Airways** (tel. 800/648–WINGS).

Airlines that serve BWI include **Air Jamaica** (tel. 800/523–5585), **Allegheny Commuter** (tel. 800/428–4253), **America West** (tel. 800/247–5692), **American** (tel. 800/433–7300), **Business Express** (tel. 800/345–3400), **BWIA** (tel. 800/327–7401), **Continental** (tel. 800/525–0280), **Cumberland** (tel. 800/624–0070), **Delta** (tel. 800/221–1212), **Eastern** (tel. 800/327–8376), **Enterprise** (tel. 800/343–7300), **Henson/Jetstream** (tel. 800/368–5425), **Icelandair** (tel. 800/223–5500), **Mexicana** (tel. 800/531–7921), **Northwest** (tel. 800/225–2525), **PanAm Express** (tel. 800/223–1115), **Piedmont** (tel. 800/251–5720), **TWA** (tel. 800/221–2000), **United** (tel. 800/241–6522) and **USAir** (tel. 800/428–4322).

**Smoking** If cigarette smoke bothers you, request a seat far away from the smoking section. Remember, FAA regulations require U.S. airlines to find seats for all nonsmokers.

**Lost Luggage** Luggage loss is usually covered as part of a comprehensive travel insurance package that includes personal accident, trip cancellation, and sometimes default and bankruptcy insurance. Several companies offer comprehensive policies:

**Access America, Inc.** (a subsidiary of Blue Cross/Blue Shield; 600 3rd Ave., Box 807, New York, NY 10163, tel. 212/490–5345 or 800/284–8300).
**Carefree Travel Insurance** (Box 310, 120 Mineola Blvd., Mineola, NY 11501, tel. 516/294–0220 or 800/645–2424).
**Near Services** (1900 N. MacArthur Blvd., Suite 210, Oklahoma City, OK 73127, tel. 800/654–6700 or in Oklahoma City, 405/949–2500).
**Travel Guard International** (underwritten by Cygna; 1100 Centerpoint Dr., Stevens Point, WI 54481, tel. 715/345–0505 or 800/782–5151).

**Luggage Insurance** Airlines are responsible for lost or damaged property only up to $1,250 per passenger on domestic flights; and $9.07 per pound ($20 per kilo) for checked baggage on international flights, and up to $400 per passenger for unchecked baggage on international flights. If you're carrying valuables, either take them with you on the airplane or purchase additional insurance for lost luggage. Some airlines will issue additional insurance when you check in, but many do not. Rates are $1 for every $100 valuation, with a maximum of $400 valuation per passenger. Hand luggage is not included.

Insurance for lost, damaged, or stolen luggage is available through travel agents or directly through various insurance companies. Two companies that issue luggage insurance are **Tele-Trip** (3201 Farnam St., Omaha, NE 68131, tel. 800/228–9792), a subsidiary of Mutual of Omaha, and **The Travelers Insurance Co.** (Ticket and Travel Plans Dept., 1 Tower Sq., Hartford, CT 06183–5040, tel. 201/277–2318 or 800/243–3174). Tele-Trip, which operates sales booths at airports and also issues policies through travel agents, insures checked luggage for up to 180 days and for $500 to $3,000 valuation. For 1 to 3 days, the rate for a $500 valuation is $8.25; for 180 days, $100. The Travelers Insurance Company insures checked or hand luggage for $500 to $2,000 valuation per person, also for a maximum of 180 days. Rates for up to five days for $500 valuation are $10; for 180 days, $85. Both companies offer the same rates on domestic and international flights. Check the travel pages of your local newspaper for the names of other companies that insure luggage.

Before you go, itemize the contents of each bag in case you need to file an insurance claim. Be certain to put your home address on each piece of luggage, including carry-on bags. If your luggage is stolen and later recovered, the airline must deliver it to your home free of charge.

**Between the Airports and Downtown**
*By Metro*  If you are coming into Washington National Airport, don't have too much to carry, and are staying at a hotel near a subway stop, it makes sense to take the Metro downtown. You can walk to the station or catch the free airport shuttle that stops at each terminal and brings you to the National Airport station. The Metro ride downtown takes about 20 minutes and costs between 85 cents and $1.15, depending on the time of day.

*By Bus*  All of Washington's airports are served continuously by the buses of **Washington Flyer** (tel. 703/685–1400). The ride from National to downtown Washington costs $5 and takes 20 minutes; from Dulles it costs $12 and takes 45 minutes; from BWI, $12 and 50 minutes. An inter-airport express travels between Dulles and National. The 45-minute trips costs $12.

Some hotels provide van service to and from the airports; check with your hotel when making reservations or when you arrive.

*By Train*  Free shuttle buses take passengers to and from the train station at BWI airport. **Amtrak** and **MARC (Maryland Rail Commuter Service)** trains run between BWI and Washington's Union Station from around 6 AM to 11 PM. The cost for the 40-minute ride is $10 on an Amtrak train, $4.25 on a MARC train. (For MARC schedule information, call 800/325–RAIL.)

*By Taxi*  Expect to pay about $7 to get from National Airport to downtown; from Dulles, $35; from BWI, $40. Agree on a price with the driver before leaving the airport.

*By Limousine*  Call at least a day ahead and **Diplomat Limousine** (tel. 202/589–7620) will have a limousine waiting for you at the airport. The ride downtown from National costs $33. It costs $60 from Dulles and $90 from BWI. Sedans are slightly cheaper.

## By Car

If you are arriving by car note that I-95 skirts Washington as part of the Beltway, the six- to eight-lane highway that encircles the city. The eastern half of the Beltway is I-95, the western half is I-495. If coming from the south, take I-95 to I-395 and cross the 14th Street bridge to 14th Street in the District. From the north, stay on I-95 south before heading west on Route 50, the John Hanson Highway, which turns into New York Avenue.

I-66 approaches the city from the southwest, but there are weekday rush-hour restrictions. From 6:30 to 9 AM cars traveling eastbound inside the Beltway (I-495) must have at least three people in them. A similar high-occupancy vehicle (or "HOV") restriction applies westbound from 4 to 6:30 PM. If you're traveling at an off-peak hour, or have enough people in your car to satisfy the rules, you can get downtown by taking I-66 across the Theodore Roosevelt Bridge to Constitution Avenue. I-270 approaches Washington from the northwest before hitting 495. To get downtown take 495 east to Connecticut Avenue south, towards Chevy Chase.

The traffic lights in Washington sometimes stymie visitors. Most of the lights don't hang down over the middle of the streets but stand at the sides of intersections. Also keep in mind that radar detectors are illegal in Virginia and the District. Some final advice: A good map is invaluable for driving in Washington.

## Car Rentals

Ample public transportation and shuttle service from the airports to downtown make it relatively easy to get by in Washington without renting a car. Traffic is bad, and traffic rules can be confusing even to natives. If a rental car figures in your plans, however, there are plenty of companies to choose from. Most of the major car rental companies—including **Avis** (tel. 800/331–1212), **Budget** (tel. 800/527–0700), **Dollar** (tel. 800/421–6868), **Hertz** (tel. 800/654–3131), and **National** (tel. 800/328–4567)—have offices at the three airports and in the downtown hotel/business district.

## By Train

More than 50 trains a day arrive at Washington's newly restored **Union Station** on Capitol Hill (50 Massachusetts Ave. NE, tel. 202/484–7540 or 800/USA–RAIL). Washington is the last stop on Amtrak's Northeast Corridor line and is a major stop on most routes from the south and west. Metroliner trains travel between New York and Washington five times every weekday.

## By Bus

Washington is a major terminal for **Greyhound/Trailways Bus Lines** (1005 1st St. NE, tel. 202/289–5160). The company also has stations in nearby Silver Spring and Laurel, Maryland, and in Springfield, Virginia. Check with your local Greyhound/Trailways ticket office for prices and schedules.

# Staying in Washington

## Important Addresses and Numbers

**Tourist Information**

The **Washington Area Convention and Visitors Association** operates a tourist information center at 1455 Pennsylvania Avenue, NW (tel. 202/789–7000; tel. 202/789–8866 for recorded announcement of upcoming events). The **International Visitor Information Service** (733 15th St. NW, Suite 300, tel. 202/783–6540) answers foreigners' questions about Washington and has maps and brochures on area attractions in eight languages. Rangers from the National Park Service staff information-kiosks on the Mall, near the White House, next to the Vietnam Veterans Memorial, and at several other locations throughout the city. **Dial-A-Park** (tel. 202/485–PARK) is a recording of events at Park Service attractions in and around Washington. If you're planning on doing any sightseeing in Virginia, stop by the **Virginia Travel Center** (1629 K St. NW, tel. 202/659–5523).

**Emergencies**

Dial 911 for assistance. The hospital closest to downtown is **George Washington University Hospital** (901 23rd St. NW, tel 202/994–3211). The hospital closest to the Capitol and Union Station is **Capitol Hill Hospital** (700 Constitution Ave. NE, tel. 202/269–8769).

**Doctors and Dentists**

**Prologue** (tel. 202/DOCTORS) is a referral service that locates doctors, dentists, and urgent-care clinics in the greater Washington area. The Medical Society of the District of Columbia also runs a **Physicians Referral Service** (tel. 202/872–0003, Mon.–Fri., 9–4) that lists doctors within the District. The **DC Dental Society** (tel. 202/547–7615) operates a referral line during business hours.

**Late-night Pharmacies**

**Peoples Drug** operates two 24-hour pharmacies in the District. One is at 14th Street and Thomas Circle NW (tel. 202/628–0720), the other at 7 Dupont Circle NW (tel. 202/785–1466).

## Opening and Closing Times

**Banks** are generally open weekdays 9 to 3. On Friday many stay open until 5 or close at 2 and open again from 4 to 6. Very few banks in the city have lobby hours on Saturday.

**Museums** are generally open daily 10 to 5:30. Many private museums are closed on Monday. The Smithsonian sets special spring and summer hours annually for some of its museums (tel. 202/357–2700 for details).

**Stores** are generally open Monday to Saturday 10 to 7 (or 8). Some have extended hours on Thursday and many—especially those in shopping or tourist areas such as Georgetown—are open Sunday, anywhere from 10 to noon, closing at 5 or 6.

## Getting Around Washington

The city's streets are arranged, said Pierre L'Enfant, the man who designed them in 1791, "like a chessboard overlaid with a wagon wheel." Streets run north and south and east and west in a grid pattern; avenues—most named after states—run diagonally, connecting the various traffic circles scattered throughout the city. The District is divided into four sections: northwest, northeast, southwest, and southeast; the Capitol

Building serves as the center of the north/south and east/west axes. North Capitol and South Capitol streets divide the city into east and west; the Mall and East Capitol Street divide the city into north and south. Streets that run north to south are numbered; those that extend east to west are lettered from A to I and K to W, the letter J having been skipped. (Note that I Street is often written as "Eye Street.") After W, two-syllable alphabetical names are used for east/west streets (Adams, Belmont, Clifton, etc.), then three-syllable names (Albemarle, Brandywine, Chesapeake). After the three-syllable names to the north have been exhausted, the streets are named for trees (Aspen, Butternut, Cedar).

Make sure you have a destination's complete address, including the quadrant designation. There are four 4th and D Street intersections in Washington: one each in NW, NE, SW, and SE. Addresses in Washington are coded to the intersections they're closest to. For example, 1785 Massachusetts Ave. NW is between 17th and 18th Streets; 600 5th St. NW is at the corner of 5th and F, the sixth letter of the alphabet.

**By Subway** The **Washington Metropolitan Area Transit Authority** (WMATA) provides bus and subway service in the District and in the Maryland and Virginia suburbs. The **Metro,** opened in 1976, is one of the country's cleanest and safest subway systems. Trains run from 5:30 AM to midnight, Monday through Friday; 8 AM to midnight on Saturdays; 10 AM to midnight on Sundays. During the Monday to Friday rush hours (5:30–9:30 AM and 3–7 PM) trains come along every six minutes. At other times and on weekends and holidays trains run about every 12 to 15 minutes. The base fare is 85 cents; the actual price you pay depends on the time of day and the distance traveled. Children under five ride free when accompanied by a paying passenger, but there is a maximum of two children per paying adult.

The computerized **Farecard machines** in Metro stations can seem complicated. You'll need a pocketful of coins or crisp one- or five-dollar bills to feed into the machines; some stations also accept $10 bills. Ask a native for help if you're having trouble. Hang onto your paper Farecard—you'll need it to exit the station.

Some Washingtonians report that the Farecard's magnetic strip interferes with the strips on automatic teller and credit cards. Keep the cards separated in your pocket or wallet. You'll notice that some Farecards have advertisements on the back; others have a line with the words "Sign here" underneath. It's doubtful anyone in Washington has ever signed the back of a Farecard.

A $6 **Metro Family/Tourist Pass** entitles a family of four to one day of unlimited subway and bus travel any Saturday, Sunday, or holiday (except July 4). Passes are available at Metro Sales Outlets (including the Metro Center station) and at many hotels.

For general travel information, tel. 202/637–7000 or TTD 202/638–3780 seven days a week 6 AM to 11:30 PM; for consumer assistance, tel. 202/637–1328; for transit police, tel. 202/962–2121. A helpful brochure—"All About the Metro System"—is available by calling the travel information number or writing to: Office of Marketing, WMATA, 600 5th St. NW, Washington, DC 20001.

**By Bus** WMATA's red, white, and blue **Metrobuses** crisscross the city and nearby suburbs, with some routes running 24 hours a day. All bus rides within the District are 80 or 85 cents. Drivers accept exact change only.

Free transfers, good for two hours, are available on buses and in Metro stations. Bus-to-bus transfers are accepted at designated Metrobus transfer points. Rail-to-bus transfers must be picked up before boarding the train. There may be a transfer charge when boarding the bus. There are no bus-to-rail transfers.

**By Car** A car can be a drawback in Washington. Traffic is horrendous, especially at rush hours, and driving is often confusing, with many lanes and some entire streets changing direction suddenly at certain times of day. Parking is also an adventure; the police are quick to tow away or immobilize with a "boot" any vehicle parked illegally. Since the city's most popular sights are within a short walk of a Metro station anyway, it's best to leave your car at the hotel. Touring by car is a good idea only if you're considering visiting sites in suburban Maryland or Virginia.

Most of the outlying, suburban Metro stations have parking lots, though these fill quickly with city-bound commuters. If you plan to park in one of these lots, arrive early, armed with lots of quarters. Private parking lots downtown are expensive, charging as much as $4 an hour and up to $13 a day. There is free, three-hour parking around the Mall on Jefferson Drive and Madison Drive, though these spots always seem to be filled. You can park free—in some spots all day—in parking areas south of the Lincoln Memorial on Ohio Drive and West Basin Drive in West Potomac Park. There is also a huge new parking garage on Capitol Hill, behind Union Station. If you park by 9 AM you can stay until 7 PM for only $4.

If you find you've been towed from a city street, tel. 202/727–5000.

**By Taxi** Taxis in the District are not metered; they operate instead on a curious zone system. Even longtime Washingtonians will ask the cabdriver ahead of time how much the fare will be. The basic single rate for traveling within one zone is $2.65. There is an extra $1.25 charge each for additional passenger and a $1 surcharge during the 4 to 6:30 PM rush hour. Bulky suitcases larger than three cubic feet are charged at a higher rate. Two major companies serving the District are **Capitol Cab** (tel. 202/546–2400) and **Diamond Cab** (tel. 202/387–6200). Maryland and Virginia taxis are metered but cannot take passengers between points in Washington.

## Guided Tours

**Orientation Tours** Taking a narrated bus tour is a good way to get your bearings and make some decisions about what to see first. Both of the tour companies listed here allow you to get off and on as often as you like with no additional charge. If you want to conserve your energy for walking inside Washington's museums, art galleries, and other touring sights, rather than walking *between* them, a bus tour is the way to go.

**Tourmobile** (tel. 202/554–7950). Authorized by the National Park Service, Tourmobile buses ply a route that stops at 18 historic sites between the Capitol and Arlington Cemetery; the route includes the White House and the museums on the Mall. Tickets are $7.50 for adults, $3.75 for children age 3 to 11.

**Old Town Trolley Tours** (tel. 202/269–3020). Orange-and-green motorized trolleys take in the main downtown sights and also foray into Georgetown and the upper northwest, stopping at out-of-the-way attractions like the Washington Cathedral. Tickets are $11 for adults, $9 for students, senior citizens and active military, and free for children under 12 accompanied by a paid adult.

**Bus Tours**   **Gray Line Tours** (tel. 301/386–8300). A four-hour motorcoach tour of Washington, Embassy Row, and Arlington National Cemetery leaves Union Station at 9 AM and 2:30 PM (at 2 PM from November 1 to March 19); tours of Mount Vernon and Alexandria depart at 9 AM (adults $18, children $9). An all-day trip combining both tours leaves at 9 AM (adults $34, children $17).

**Special-Interest**   Special tours of government buildings—including the Ar-
**Tours**   chives, the Capitol, the FBI Building, the Supreme Court, and the White House—can be arranged through your representative's or senator's office. Only limited numbers of these so-called VIP tickets are available, so it's best to contact your representative up to six months in advance of your trip. With these special passes you won't have to wait in line as long as you would in the regular lines, and your tour will often take you through rooms not open to the public.

**Old Executive Office Building** (Pennsylvania Ave. and 17th St. NW, tel. 202/395–5895). Tours of this 1888 French Second Empire building, formerly the State, Navy, and War Building, are offered Saturday from 9 to noon. Inside you'll see the restored Victorian-style secretary of the navy's office (now used by the vice president), one of the building's two stained-glass rotundas, and the departmental libraries. Reservations are required.

**The Naval Observatory** (34th St. and Massachusetts Ave. NW, tel. 202/653–1543). Evening tours are given every Monday night, except on Federal holidays, to the first 100 people in line at the Observatory's front gate. The 90-minute tour starts at 7:30 standard time, 8:30 daylight-saving time. The selection of astronomical objects shown on the tour depends on the time of year, time of month, and sky conditions.

**St. John's Parish Georgetown House Tours** (3240 O St. NW, tel. 202/338–1796). For one weekend each April, owners of historic Georgetown houses open their doors to sightseers.

**State Department Diplomatic Reception Rooms** (23rd and C sts. NW, tel. 202/647–3241). These opulent 19th-century–style rooms installed on the top floor of the State Department are patterned after great halls in Europe and rooms found in Colonial American plantations. Filled with museum-quality furnishings—including a Philadelphia Highboy, Paul Revere bowl and the desk on which the Treaty of Paris was signed—these rooms are used 15 to 20 times a week to entertain foreign diplomats and heads of state. For a summer tour you may have to book up to three months in advance.

**Voice of America** (330 Independence Ave. SW, tel. 202/485–6231). The global radio network of the U.S. Information Agency, the VOA broadcasts in 43 languages. This 45-minute tour takes visitors past broadcast studios and the newsroom and explains VOA's purpose.

***The Washington Post*** (1150 15th St. NW, tel. 202/334–7969). Free 50-minute guided tours for ages 11 and up are run on Mondays and Thursdays from 10 to 3. You'll take in the news room, where the reporters work; the production room, where the paper is put together; the press room, where the paper is printed; and the mail room, where finished papers are stacked and bundled for shipment. The *Post* was one of the last major papers in the country to switch to cold type, and a display contrasts this computerized method of putting the paper together with the hot-type method used until 1980. Make reservations for this tour well in advance of your trip.

**Walking Tours**   **Black History National Recreation Trail.** Not a specific walking route but a group of sites within historic neighborhoods, this trail illustrates aspects of African-American history in Washington, from slavery days to the New Deal. A brochure outlining the trail is available from the National Park Service (P.O. Box 37127, Washington, DC 20013–7127, tel. 202/343–4747).

**Construction Watch and Site Seeing** (tel. 202/272–2448). The National Building Museum sponsors these architecturally oriented walking tours each spring and fall. On Construction Watch tours, architects and construction-project managers accompany visitors to buildings in various stages of completion and discuss the design and building process. Site Seeing tours are led by architectural historians and go to various Washington neighborhoods and well-known monuments, public buildings, and houses. Tickets average around $10. Call for schedule.

**Pacesetter Productions** (tel. 301/961–3529) has four self-guided walking tours on cassette. Two concentrate on Georgetown, one covers the Dupont Circle/Embassy Row area, and one the White House neighborhood. The 50-minute **"TapeWalks"** are available at bookstores and museum gift shops in Washington for $11.95 each.

**Smithsonian Resident Associate Program** (tel. 202/357–3030). Walking and bus tours of neighborhoods in Washington and communities outside the city are routinely offered by RAP. Many tours are themed and include sites that illustrate, for example, Art Deco influences, African-American architecture, or railroad history.

**Personal Guides**   **Guide Service of Washington** (tel. 202/628–2842). This company provides a licensed guide to accompany you in your car, van, or bus to show you the sights of the city, Mount Vernon, and Arlington. The cost for an English-speaking guide for a half-day tour is $72; $110 for a full day. Guides are available for tours in any of 20 languages.

**Other Tours**   **Goodwill Embassy Tour** (tel. 202/636–4225). Every second Saturday in May, a half dozen embassies in Washington open their doors as stops on a self-guided tour. The cost per ticket is about $25 and includes refreshments, a tour booklet, and free shuttle-bus transportation between embassies.

**Scandal Tours** (tel. 202/387–2253). This outrageous tour concentrates on Washington's seamier side with a 90-minute trip past such scandalous locales as Gary Hart's Capitol Hill town house; the Tidal Basin, where Congressman Wilbur Mills and stripper Fanne Fox took an unintended dip; the Old Executive Office Building, where Fawn Hall and Ollie North shredded documents together; and, of course, the Watergate. Costumed look-alikes ride on the bus and act out the scandals. Tours leave the Ritz Carlton Hotel on Saturday at 10, 12, 2, and 4:30; Sunday at 10, 12, 2, and 4. The cost is $20 per person. For $40, participants can attend a reception before the 4:30 Saturday tour. Reservations advised.

*Spirit of Washington* (Pier 4, 6th and Water sts. SW, tel. 202/554–8000 or 202/554–1542.) Moored at the heart of Washington's waterfront, this boat gives visitors a waterborne view of some of the area's attractions, including Old Town Alexandria, Washington National Airport, and Hains Point. Lunch cruises board Tuesday through Saturday at 11:30 AM; a Sunday brunch cruise sails at 1. Evening cruises board at 6:30 PM and include dinner and a floor show. A sister ship, the *Spirit of Mt. Vernon,* sails to George Washington's plantation home from mid-March to early October, Tuesday through Sunday. The four-hour trip embarks at 9 AM and 2 PM.

# 2 Portraits of Washington

# Life Inside the Beltway: The Folkways of Washington

*The longer you stay, you realize that sometimes you can catch more flies with honey than with vinegar.*

—Senator Strom Thurmond

*by Hedrick Smith*

*A Pulitzer Prize-winning reporter, Hedrick Smith was bureau chief and chief Washington correspondent of* The New York Times *for nearly a decade. Smith is the author of the international bestseller* The Russians *and is a frequent panelist on PBS's* Washington Week in Review.

Political Washington is a special community with a culture all its own, its own established rituals and folkways, its tokens of status and influence, its rules and conventions, its tribal rivalries and personal animosities. Its stage is large, but its habits are small-town. Members of Congress have Pickwickian enthusiasm for clubs, groups, and personal and regional networks to insure their survival and to advance their causes. They love the clubbiness of the member's dining rooms and such Capitol Hill watering holes as the Monocle or the Democratic Club. And downtown, politicians, lobbyists and journalists like to rub shoulders and swap stories at Duke Zeibert's, Mel Krupin's, or Joe and Mo's, where the movers and shakers have regular tables.

Political parties have a social impact; most politicians fraternize mainly with colleagues from within their own party. But when I first came to the city, I did not realize how personal relationships often cut across party and ideological lines, so that conservative lions and liberal leopards who roar at each other in congressional debates play tennis on the weekends or joke together in the Capitol cloakrooms. And yet, for all their backslapping gregariousness, politicians strike me as a lonely crowd, making very few deep friendships because almost every relationship is tainted by the calculus of power: How will this help me?

Above all, Washington is a state of mind. I'm not talking about the 3.5 million people who live in the Washington metropolitan area: the hospital administrators, shopkeepers, schoolteachers, and the people who inhabit the middle-class city of Washington and its Virginia and Maryland suburbs; rather, I'm referring to the hundred thousand or so whose life revolves around government, especially the few thousand at the peak who live and breathe politics. To the people of that world, this is the hub, the center, the focus of what Henry Adams once called "the action of primary forces." The conceit of this Washington is not all that different from the conceit of Paris or Moscow.

*From* The Power Game: How Washington Works *by Hedrick Smith. Copyright © 1988 by Hedrick Smith. Reprinted by permission of Random House, Inc.*

Example: The city and its suburbs are encircled by a sixty-four-mile freeway loop known as the beltway (U.S. 495). The political community of Washington talks as if that beltway formed a moat separating the capital from the country. "Inside the beltway," political Washington's favorite nickname for itself, is a metaphor for the core of government. Hardly a dinner or a meeting goes by without someone observing that the mood inside the beltway on Iran or a new Soviet-American summit or on protectionist measures is running ahead of the country, or that the president, any president, is in trouble inside the beltway but not "out there," with a wave of the hand toward the boondocks.

The distance between Washington and the rest of the country is partly a matter of language. Jargon is a vital element of the Washington game. Washington jargon is impenetrable and often deliberately so, to exclude all but the initiated.

For starters: Unless you're President Reagan, you can't be a major player in budget politics unless you know the difference between constant dollars and current dollars, between outlays and obligations, between the baseline and the outyears; you can't enter the arena of arms control without some grasp of launchers, throwweight, and RVs.* If you're an insider, you will have mastered such trivia as knowing that the shorthand for the Department of Housing and Urban Development is pronounced "HUD," but that the nickname for the Department of Transportation is pronounced "D-O-T" and never "dot." You will also know that bogeys are the spending targets the secretary of Defense gives the armed services and that beam-splitters are the nearly invisible TelePrompTers that flash the text of a speech to the president as he turns his head from side to side.

The split between capital and country also reflects a different awareness of how Washington really works. The veterans know that the important, knock-down, drag-out battles in Congress usually come on amendments to a piece of legislation, not on final passage of the bill. They understand that when some member rises on the floor of the House or Senate and says that a piece of legislation is a

---

*Constant dollars are economic figures adjusted for inflation; figures in current dollars are not adjusted. Outlays are actual government funds spent, but obligations are funds authorized for spending, perhaps in later years. The baseline is the cost of the current level of government services and programs, and the out-years are projections for future years. Launchers are bombers and missiles; throwweight is the overall payload a missile can heave aloft; and RVs are re-entry vehicles, or the nuclear warheads and decoys on a ballistics missile.*

"good bill" and that he wants "to offer a perfecting amendment," he is really getting ready to gut the legislation.
Sometimes an amendment is a complete substitute bill with
quite different impact and meaning, known in the trade as a
"killer amendment." That's the way the legislative game is
played.

In many other ways, political perceptions differ sharply inside the beltway and out in the country. For example . . .
New York State Congressman Jack Kemp has made a national splash with his tax issue, but political insiders regard
him as generally less influential with other House Republicans than Trent Lott of Mississippi, the House Republican
whip. "Lott swings plenty of votes," one Reagan White
House strategist confided to me. "You can't count on Kemp
to bring that many members with him." Over in the Senate,
Jesse Helms is the booming public voice of the New Right
but when it comes to working major issues with other Republicans, James McClure of Idaho, a quieter legislator, is
given more credit as the leader of Senate conservatives. In
1984, McClure, not Helms, was the conservatives' candi-
date for majority leader. In short, Kemp and Helms are the
national figures with mass appeal; Lott and McClure
are rated by their peers as more solid performers. The
most striking modern case of a politician who was
no great shakes as a congressman or senator but who
won a mass following—and the presidency—was Jack
Kennedy.

## A City of Cocker Spaniels

What really sets Washington apart, of course, is the heady
brew of power and prominence. Washington combines the
clout of the corporate boardroom and military command
with the glamour of Hollywood celebrities and Super Bowl
stars. That magnetism and the stakes of the battle are what
draw armies of politicians, lobbyists, lawyers, experts,
consultants, and journalists to Washington. It is a self-
selected group, ambitious and aggressive, marked by collective immodesty. Politicians love to be noticed, and they
take their notices very seriously, assuming their own importance and grasping for daily confirmation in the
attention of the press and television.

Many people treat the word *politician* as a synonym for hy-
pocrisy, but I believe most politicians come to Washington
largely motivated by a sense of public service, and usually
with a deeper interest in policy issues than is felt by people
back home. Most politicians really want to contribute to the
public weal, as protectors of their home districts or expo-
nents of some cause; their early motivation is the ideal of
better government. Most people who make a career of government could earn a good deal more money in other walks
of life. And they toss into the bargain the loss of personal
privacy for themselves and for their families. Not all politi-

cians are that self-sacrificing, but I believe a majority are; only a small minority seem charlatans. Their agendas differ greatly, but if one urge unites them all—and really makes Washington tick—it is the urge for that warm feeling of importance.

That ache for applause and recognition shows in the weighty tread of senators moving onto the floor and glancing upward for some sign of recognition from the galleries. It shows in the awkward jostling for position as a group of congressmen approach the television cameras and microphones outside a hearing room, or after a White House session with the president. I have marveled at it in the purgatorial patience of politicians with endless handshakes, speeches, receptions. I have sensed it, too, in the flattered eagerness of corporate executives arriving at a White House dinner in their limousines. And I have felt it in the smug satisfaction of a select group of columnists and commentators called to a special briefing from the president in the family theater of the White House. None of us is completely immune to that siren song of being made to feel important.

"Washington is really, when you come right down to it, a city of cocker spaniels," Elliott Richardson once remarked. Richardson, a Republican Brahmin from Boston, held four cabinet positions in the Nixon and Ford administrations and after a few years out of the limelight felt the ache for attention badly enough to make an unsuccessful try for the Senate.

"It's a city of people who are more interested in being petted and admired than in rendering the exercise of power," Richardson contended. "The very tendency of the cocker spaniel to want to be petted and loved can in turn mean that to be shunned and ignored is painful, and there is a tendency in Washington to turn to the people who are in the spotlight and holding positions of visibility at a given time."

In their collective vanity, the power players are willing to endure long hours of boredom to bathe in the roar of the crowd. Talking with me in his Senate study one rainy afternoon about the vanity of the political breed, Senator Charles McC. Mathias, the Maryland Republican, recalled an incident at an American Legion dinner in Washington years ago. As Mathias arrived, he saw two fellow Republican warhorses—Leverett Saltonstall of Massachusetts with his arm in a sling and Everett Dirksen hobbling on crutches.

"It was one of those many functions which you attend but where your absence might not even be noted," Mathias observed. "Saltonstall and Dirksen had valid excuses [to stay away], but they came anyway. And I thought: Is there never surcease from this demand and this compulsion to get out to these things? But of course, they would be put at the head table and introduced, and the spotlight would fall upon them, and the people from Massachusetts and Illinois would wave their napkins in the air when their names were mentioned, and the band would play their state anthems. It is all utterly meaningless, and yet those two wanted to be part of the act, and the applauders wanted the act, too."

Washington is a city mercurial in its moods, short in its attention span, and given to fetishes. Events flash and disappear like episodes in a soap opera, intensely important for a brief period and then quickly forgotten. Like a teenager, the political community lurches from one passion to the next, seized for a season by the Gramm-Rudman budget-balancing act, later consumed by a battle with Japan over trade sanctions, or gossiping madly over the millionaire antics of White House officials turned lobbyists.

But whatever the twist and turns, the themes are invariably political. People visiting from New York or Los Angeles complain that Washington is a guild town with just one industry and one preoccupation. New York has the intensely self-preoccupied worlds of Wall Street, Broadway, publishing, and advertising, and Chicago with its corporate headquarters, grain trade, steel industry, and distribution centers. Each city has variety, while Washington, in spite of its growing world of art, theaters, opera and symphony, has only one passion.

"It's a one-subject town," lamented Austin Ranney, a political scientist from California who spent a decade at the American Enterprise Institute in Washington. "I don't know how many dozens or hundreds of dinner parties I went to, largely as an outsider, an observer, and yet I almost never had a conversation about music, about novels, or very briefly about anything except the weather. It was always politics, politics, politics, of the insider variety."

## Congress: High School Networks

. . . In self-defense, politicians naturally band together in power networks, either within the executive branch, on Capitol Hill, or bridging the two. Obviously, the two main political parties are the basic networks of power. But the weak, loose structure of American political parties makes other networks essential. In Congress, individual members are far less creatures of party than are their counterparts in European legislatures, whether the British Parliament, the French National Assembly, or the Canadian House of Commons, where parties provide strong organizational spine. Despite a bit of a comeback in Congress in this decade, American parties are more amorphous than they have been earlier in our history. And so, members make up their own alliance games. . . .

The most natural networks are the product of generations, not the normal twenty-year generations but political generations based on when each new batch of politicians arrived in the city. California political scientist Nelson Polsby compares the Washington political community to a formation of geological strata, each new political generation layering on top of the preceeding ones, each providing identity and a network of connections to its members. It is an apt image. The sediment of old generations hardens because so many politicians remain in Washington. Today, there are networks of older Democrats from the Kennedy and Johnson years, Republicans from the Nixon and Ford administrations, Carter Democrats and more recently the new generation of Reaganite and New Right Republicans with their conservative caucuses, think tanks and political action committees.

These generational clusters are neighborhoods in the political city. Lasting alliances get forged in the crucible of political campaigns or service in the battles between one administration and its Congress. "You have a special connection with people who are alumni of the various political wars you have fought in," remarked Dennis Thomas, former legislative strategist in the Reagan White House. . . .

Many of the most potent networks are factions of the two parties. Senator Jesse Helms and his right-wing Republican colleagues use the Steering Committee as their network to push issues or pet nominees for top administration positions, or to block the legislative initiatives of moderate Republicans or Democrats. The Steering Committee, and other networks like it, are called prayer groups, so nicknamed because they are not official arms of the Senate, just as prayer groups are usually not official arms of the church. In the House, Republicans have political fraternities, such as The Chowder and Marching Society and S.O.S. (the initials are secret). But the rough policy counterpart to the Steering Committee among House Republicans is the Conservative Opportunity Society, formed by partisans of supply-side, tax-cutting economics and less government. Moderate Republicans join the Wednesday Club, which lunches on Wednesday.

House Democrats have their own splinter groups. The liberal wing of the House Democratic Caucus gravitates to the Democratic Study Group and the Arms Control Caucus. Conservative southern Democrats (who call themselves boll weevils because, like the cotton weevil, they bore from within the boll) have formed the Conservative Democratic Forum. The list of networking groups goes on—many of them crossing party lines: the black caucus, women's caucus, Hispanic caucus, automotive caucus, footwear caucus, space caucus, military-reform caucus, textile caucus, even the mushroom caucus.

But for most members of Congress, the most important initial networks are the freshmen classes—the legislators who arrive in Congress in the same year, especially if their first election came during a political high tide. Among Democrats, the biggest and most potent freshman class in recent years was the class of '74, the year when Watergate helped elect seventy-five new Democrats to the House. Among Republicans, the big years were the class of '78, when the pendulum began to swing back toward the GOP, bringing thirty-six new Republicans into the House, and the class of '80, when the Reagan sweep helped lift sixteen new Republicans into the Senate and fifty-two into the House.

Cutting across these freshmen-class layers are state and sectional ties. The big state delegations—California, New York, Texas, Pennsylvania, Illinois—marshall their troops for issues of local importance, whether military contracts or pet provisions in tax legislation. Significantly, whole state delegations, Republicans and Democrats, liberals and conservatives, work together for parochial interests. The big states demand, and usually get, a set share of seats on the most powerful committees that deal with spending and taxes: Appropriations and Ways and Means in the House; Appropriations and Finance in the Senate. Then, there are broader regional coalitions, the Northeast-Midwest Caucus, or the looser clustering of western and Sunbelt politicians.

The kind of regional splits that now divide Snowbelt (Midwest and Northeast) and Sunbelt (South and West) date back in American history to Jeffersonian times. Historian James Sterling Young has written that back then, members of Congress lived together for months in boarding houses arranged along sectional lines. Those "boarding house fraternities," as Young called them, enforced an iron social and political discipline that would be the envy of congressional leaders today. Sectional ties are still strong, but they lack the raw power of social ostracism used in the Jeffersonian era to whip members into line.

For many decades, congressional committees have been important hubs of power, focusing the work of their members. Farm-state senators and congressmen gravitate to the agriculture committees; Rocky Mountain politicians want to be on the interior committees that affect land use and environment; those from big cities head for labor and education; and so on. Sitting side by side on those committees, parceling out funds from the federal pork barrel, committee members form alliances.

The committees become the members' power bases for larger struggles with other power groups. Each committee forms the anchor of an "iron triangle": the committee members and their staffs, the government agencies which the committee oversees, and the interest groups and lobbyists interested in issues which the committee handles (banking, labor, health, etc.). Sometimes the legs of the triangle clash, but more often all three legs work things out to forge policy in their area and then combine forces to battle other special interest communities and their committees over slicing up the budget and setting priorities. The committees are the hubs of the political action.

The congressional networks evoke those in high school, as Barney Frank suggested. "Everybody's got the same networks—your class, the people you were elected with. That's like your high school class," Frank observed. "Then the people from your region, they're like the people whose neighborhood you live in. And then, the people whose committee you're on, they're like the other students you used to go to class with. Those are the three networks that everybody has. And you may be able to pick up some over and above that."

One of the most important informal networks that has developed is among younger House members who play sports or work out together in the House gym. Located in the subbasement of the Rayburn Office Building, the gym is a hideaway for members; they alone can use it. It is barred to their staffs, reporters, constituents, and most lobbyists (former members turned lobbyists can enter, but can do no serious lobbying on the premises). Senators have their own "baths." The House gym is not large; it has a sixty-foot pool, $28,000 in Nautilus equipment, a half-length basketball court which doubles for paddleball, as well as steam, massage, and locker rooms. Some members do little more than take a steam bath, shave, shower, and go back to work refreshed; others work out daily.

But many find that playing sports with political adversaries eases the wounds of political combat. "Ours is a very conflict-ridden profession," Frank remarked. "I vote against you. I think you're wrong. I mean, people in other professions are able to muffle that better. We are forced daily to conflict with each other. The gym promotes some stability, which is very important. But also, it's an information kind of thing. You get to know what people are like, what's important to them. You get information about what's going on with this, what's going on with that. It's that kind of chatter. And occasionally you will talk about some specific bill."

Frank, a Jewish bachelor in his late forties whose pudgy cheeks once bulged around horn-rimmed glasses, lost seventy pounds through strict dieting and weight lifting. Now, at two hundred pounds, he has shoulders like a New England Patriots tackle. He mixes with the other side: One of his weight-lifting partners is Vin Weber, a staunch Republican right-winger from Minnesota and from the far end of the ideological spectrum. That is typical of the gym. The regular pickup basketball games are bipartisan: plenty of hard-court razzing goes on, but serious partisanship is left off the court. "Republicans and Democrats play together," says Thomas Downey, a Long Island Democrat with a snappy jump shot. "It's a great way to release tension."

## Workaholics: The Lonely Crowd

From afar, politicians appear as disembodied villains or cardboard celebrities. The demands of televised image making for blow-dried breeziness and self-assured opinions on any subject under the sun often disguise their humanity and vulnerability. The common perception often misses the mark.

I have frequently run into the popular assumption that politicians work less hard and have an easier life than people in the private sector. My experience is the opposite: People coming into government from private life are shocked at the compulsive intensity and workaholic ethic of Washington, in Congress or high in the executive branch.

Not surprisingly, the White House is such a pressure cooker that after a year as cabinet secretary and aide to Reagan, Al Kingon, the former Wall Streeter and publisher of *Saturday Review* magazine, confessed to me that he had found the workload "overwhelming—beyond my wildest dreams." Normal days found him starting work at seven A.M. and ending late at night, with many a cold or canceled dinner. The late Malcolm Baldrige told me that he worked fifty-percent longer hours as secretary of Commerce than he did as chief executive officer of Scovill Manufacturing Company. As a corporate number one, he used to make speeches saying that any business leader who was working more than an eight-hour day wasn't delegating enough to subordinates. But in Washington, Baldrige said, "I found eight hours isn't enough—I need twelve. And I stopped making those speeches." People leaving high government positions say the pressure is less on the outside. David Gergen, former White House communications director, told me he found the pace less frantic as editor of *US News & World Report*.

For senators and members of Congress, the pressures are unrelenting. Days are a kaleidoscopic jumble: breakfasts with reporters, morning staff meetings, simultaneous committee hearings to juggle, back-to-back sessions with lobbyists and constituents, phone calls, briefings, constant buzzers interrupting office work to make quorum calls and votes on the run, afternoon speeches, evening meetings, receptions, fund-raisers, all crammed into four days so they can race home for a weekend gauntlet of campaigning. It's a rat race to beat the pell-mell existence of ambitious New York lawyers, Chicago stockbrokers, or independent Texas oilmen, and about as sterile personally. Part of this is necessity. Part of it is the high-powered, super-achiever,

Benjamin Franklin work ethic that drives the city: people proving their own importance.

"The problem with Washington is it's all an input town" was the shrewd comment of Chris Matthews, spokesman for former House Speaker Tip O'Neill. "You can't measure outputs. You measure input. This is a town where the GNP is government. And government is measured not by output but by how many hours you put in. Everybody says, 'I've been really busy this week. Are you busy? I've been busy. I must be busy.' And it's like busy-ness is a value in itself."

"A lot of us have that as part of our makeup," Senator David Durenburger, a thoughtful, introspective Minnesota Republican, acknowledged over dinner. "A lot of us have that need to be driven. You don't find many laid-back people in politics. What you really love is that whether you get up at six or eight in the morning, there's always too much to do.

"You are important if you are in demand. You work hard to prove how valuable you are. It's a volume-oriented kind of operation: the more hands you shake, the more letters you write, the more times you appear on TV, the more hearings you hold, the more valuable you are. Somehow quality is subsumed by quantity."

He quoted the advice of one senior senator at a prayer breakfast: "If you want to really keep on a fast track, always have more than two things to do for any space on your schedule. Have people telling you about all the other things you should do. Go into politics, because there's always too much to do. And in politics, you can justify workaholism. After all, it's important for the country."

The irony is that Ronald Reagan, with the most powerful, most demanding job of all, has made a mockery of workaholism. Quite deliberately, he worked a relatively short day, in his office from about nine to four, taking naps or going off horseback riding, and then attending some official dinner or tackling a bit of overnight reading, though sometimes it was left unread while he and Nancy watched television. Reagan really preferred oral briefings. National security advisers read him documents aloud, got his approval, and initialed them on his behalf. On Iran, for example, Reagan apparently never bothered to look at the critical decision paper of January 17, 1986, that formally authorized the arms-for-hostages deal.

When the press and other politicians nicked Reagan for being too hands-off and laid-back, Reagan poked fun at his lazy ways. At one press dinner, he joshed, "It's true that hard work never killed anybody, but I figure why take the chance at this late age." The audience roared at his admission.

Until the Iran-*contra* scandal broke, Reagan got away with his light routine partly because Jimmy Carter had slaved like an indentured servant and the public watched him sink in the morass of detail. Reagan's gentler pace made him look at ease with the presidency and with his power, and that was reassuring to the public. What's more, Reagan clearly has enjoyed the time-consuming ceremonial part of the job, and that enjoyment radiated self-confidence. For a long time, and during his first four years certainly, Reagan got away with going light on substance by delegating enormous authority to a superb staff.

What the public didn't notice, or didn't mind, was that Reagan did not have the driving curiosity that most presidents have about major issues or the way their administrations operate, both to educate themselves and to protect themselves from trouble. Reagan trusted others to keep him out of harm's way. But Reagan's second-term staff was not sharp enough, either in judgment or political skill, and Reagan's failure to control the staff got him into a mountain of trouble, climaxed by the Iran affair. Then his laid-back, hands-off style backfired badly.

For many other politicians and government officials, the intense type-A Washington life-style takes its toll in divorce and family tensions. Washington has one of the highest numbers of psychiatrists per capita in the country, about as many as New York, testimony that workaholism and the pressure-cooker atmosphere of Washington life are an occupational hazard. Washington's monochrome life-style also makes for grayness. Occasionally, of course, poets emerge in Congress (Senator William Cohen of Maine who wrote *The Baker's Nickel* and also coauthored a spy novel, *Double Man*, with Gary Hart), journalists put on amateur theatrical skits (the Gridiron Club), and everyone admires the cherry blossoms in springtime. People do get away for weekends on Chesapeake Bay or in the Blue Ridge Mountains. But there are not many real time-outs.

A few years ago, Blythe Babyak, a television journalist from New York who had a commuting marriage with Richard Holbrooke, a State Department policymaker, complained about the dessicated existence.

"Washington is a fifties kind of place," she observed in *Newsweek*, "a town whose inhabitants are relieved of the uncertainty about life's goals, those that provoke a deeper examination of our own lives and those of others. Washingtonians know what counts: getting ahead in a clearly defined bureaucratic context—running the country, running the world. That's what they think they are doing, and, indeed, that is what they do. Day and night. Breakfast meeting, lunch, and dinner—to the exclusion of life's trifles and its mysteries."

Weekday evenings bring no relief because political Washington treats social life as an extension of business. People are often booked three or four nights a week, sometimes to several events a night, and people relate to each other in terms of position and title. At dinners or other informal occasions, there are implicit quid pro quos. Journalists turn to officials and politicians for stories; the politicians trade for favorable mention. Lobbyists need politicians for legislation, and the politicians need the lobbyists for money and votes. Of course, there are times of levity and humor, but the underlying transactions of the political bazaar sap most occasions of serendipity.

"People will go to an embassy party if they think they might see someone they have missed during the day," wrote Sondra Gotlieb, the irreverent wife of the Canadian ambassador. "Powerful Jobs comes to parties to trade information with other Powerful Jobs they hadn't made contact with during the day."

## More Women, but Still a Man's Town

Over the past fifteen years, the power and responsibility of women has grown in the power game, though the feminist push has not changed the way the game is played. Politics has been a man's sport, and women have learned to play hardball.

Starting with the 1972 presidential campaign of George McGovern, women have become far more numerous, active, and visible in Washington—whether as a vice-presidential nominee, cabinet member, or Supreme Court justice, or as members of Congress, staffers, lobbyists, or journalists. The McGovern campaign, with its strong antiwar plank and its domestic themes of equality and social justice, fueled an explosion of feminist political activity and drew hundreds of able women into politics at the state and national level. The reforms that broke up the old power baronies in Congress opened up further opportunities.

In 1972, there were two women senators and thirteen women members of the House. By 1987, the figures were two senators and twenty-two House members. The inertia of past habits and the inertia of incumbency slow change. It takes years for the pipeline of qualified women candidates to develop at the grass-roots level. But at the state level, the tide of women is rising. In 1974, Ella Grasso of Connecticut became the first woman elected governor in modern times; now there are three. The numbers of women in state legislatures has tripled since 1973, to the point where women held fifteen percent of the seats nationwide in 1987.

The numbers tell only part of the story: On Capitol Hill, manners have changed dramatically since 1973, when Patricia Shroeder, as a freshman anti–Vietnam War Democrat from Colorado, had to endure unprintable sexist insults from F. Edward Hebert, the Armed Services Committee chairman. His high-handed tactics help cost him his chairmanship two years later. More recently, women have become sought after by party leaders. Both party caucuses in the House have women in at least one leadership position. The women who in 1977 formed a caucus on women's issues open to both men and women have become more assertive, but it took until 1985 for women members to get admitted to the House members' gym, which remained a male holdout.

"You have a different kind of women in Congress now than a couple of decades ago," observed Ann Lewis, former political director of the Democratic National Committee. "They are far less likely now to be widows carrying out the family legacy and far more likely to be pursuing careers of their own. Take someone like Barbara Mikulski, who has just won a Senate seat in Maryland. She is sought after by other Democrats as a fund-raiser for their campaigns."

The growth of women's political activism has spread into other fields: Congressional liaison for executive agencies, lobbying, public relations, journalism. Women lobbyists set up their own association in 1975 and now claim eight hundred members, the most prominent of whom are Anne Wexler and Nancy Reynolds, drawn from the Carter and Reagan White Houses and now with one of the best-known lobbying firms in town. Women journalists, barred from the National Press Club, flocked, in the 1970s, to the rival Washington Press Club, which gained several hundred members; the National Press Club agreed to a merger in 1985. Public relations has become such a promising field for women that Sheila Tate, former press secretary to Nancy Reagan and now a top public relations executive, told me that she worries that it may be turning into a "pink-collar ghetto for women."

"Washington is still a male-dominated city," Tate said, "because power is at the White House and on Capitol Hill. Those are earned offices. But one half of the staffers on the Hill are women. That's created a need for more women lobbyists. Women are better communicators than men."

. . . There are still policy and political arenas where men prevail almost totally, or only grudgingly let in women— among them defense, intelligence, arms control, the senior White House staff, and political campaign strategy. That point was politely but firmly impressed on me by Katharine Graham. As one of the most powerful women in the country, Kay Graham is no upstart feminist at seventy, but like many a forceful woman, she expects men to accept women more fully as equals.

"It's true there are a lot of women in good jobs," she said. "We have Nancy Kassebaum in the Senate and Elizabeth Dole in the cabinet." Then she paused and went on, both an edge and a sadness in her voice: "But I want to tell you, it's still a very male-chauvinist town, this town. And this has no impact on me anymore, but I think it's very hard on spouses who come down here from places where they've had jobs and they've mattered on their own. And they get to dinner and they absolutely are treated like somebody's wife. I mean people say, 'What does your husband think?'

"I just came back from an arms-control seminar up at the Wye Plantation," she went on, "and the administration people there were kind of applauding themselves on their press relations. I looked around the room and there wasn't a single woman there. There was *no* woman. I thought, this arms control is still a very male area."

. . . Washington is still a male town, and football is its game. I have friends who like to compare politics to poker, with its high-stakes betting, its bluffing and its uncertainty. Others think of it more as a horse race or a steeplechase.

More often, politicians turn for analogies to those quintessentially American pastimes, baseball and football. Barry Carter, a former national security aide and now a law professor at Georgetown University, sees baseball as the sports metaphor for politics: the confrontation of pitchers and batting stars balanced by the intricate choreography of fielding plays or hit-and-run situations. Perhaps, but any city that cannot sustain a major-league baseball team is not a baseball city at heart. The Washington Senators packed up in 1972 and moved to Minnesota.

Washington is a football city, and football is the right metaphor for its politics. Washington Redskins games are sellouts every year, in Super Bowl seasons or when the team is way down in the league. In fact, one of the most coveted perks in Washington is a good season ticket to the Redskins games or, better yet, an invitation to the private box of Jack Kent Cooke, the Redskins' owner. Football thrives as a link between the two cities of Washington: the solidly middle class, overwhelmingly black central city and the largely white, upper-middle-class political city which resides mostly in the bedroom suburbs of Maryland and Virginia. The Redskins provide the missing symbol for a community that sprawls from the District of Columbia into two states, lacking a single mayor or governor or any other unifying institution.

What's more, football fits the rhythm and soul of the power game. Political Washington is a city with a terribly short attention span, quick to shift from one political melodrama to another, more given to the game-of-the-week mentality than the quiet patience of a baseball season with 162 games. Moreover, the action of the power game more nearly mirrors football. Both are contact sports.

Consider the action: Baseball offers a neat linear focus, pitcher versus batter, the crack of the bat, a fielder nimbly gathering the small white globe against a field of green, the race between his throw and the batter streaking to first base. To be sure, a bases-loaded home run or the flying spikes of a stolen base offer high drama. But generally, baseball presents a more orderly test of skills than the jarring mêlée of line play on the gridiron or the crunch of ballcarrier and tacklers that evokes the brawling confusion and partisan wrangling in Congress or the bruising clashes between White House and Capitol Hill. In football, as in politics, the pass patterns are tricky; action everywhere at once.

Consider, too, the very rhythm of play: In baseball, a rally can erupt in any inning, a low-scoring tie game can stretch into extra innings with no time limit, or a game can simply peter out in the ninth. But in football, especially pro football, the length of the game is set and the script is usually predictable. As millions of television viewers can testify, you can skip a lot of the early action so long as you're glued to your set just before halftime and late in the fourth quarter. Then, the offense goes into its two-minute drill, with frantic time-outs, commercials, worried consultations between coach and quarterback, and the inevitable injuries, all building the suspense. In those final seconds, everything goes razzle-dazzle, and those moments determine whether the fans go home in delirium or dragging in despair.

That mirrors the pace of the Congress, slogging through inconclusive months of tedium on the budget, some dull midfield maneuvering on the MX missile, diverted by the distraction of a hostage crisis. With the onset of the summer recess, the tempo quickens, commencing the political razzle-dazzle. Both parties, both houses go into their two-minute drills. New budget and tax formulas emerge. Compromise is in the air. Then a slow period in August and early September, building up to the political equivalent of a frantic fourth quarter. In the melodramatic windup, the president threatens to shut down the government. From the sidelines comes the magic play. Somehow a deal is struck in the final seconds. Congress and the White House play right on the brink. Like football players, they gamble on winning in the final crunch and time their best plays for the deadline.

Government, of course, is a serious game about policy, but as the football metaphor suggests, a lot of it is for show, and the action is fairly well established, year after year. The repetitive gambits and maneuvers make it easier for us spectators to study the players and the playing fields, in order to understand the action better.

# The Federal Government: How Our System Works

*by Betty Ross*

*A longtime resident of the nation's capital, Betty Ross is the author of* A Museum Guide to Washington, D.C., *and* How to Beat the High Cost of Travel *and has contributed to numerous newspapers and magazines.*

New York may be the fashion capital of the United States and Los Angeles the center of entertainment, but government—and power—is the name of the game in Washington.

The federal government is a major employer, an important landlord, and a source of contracts, contacts, or conversation for Washingtonians. It is a patron of the arts and a provider for the needy. To some, pervasive government is what's wrong with Washington. To others—particularly the party in power—it's what's right.

The federal government occupies some of the choicest real estate in town, yet pays no taxes to the District of Columbia. On the other hand, although citizens of the District *do* pay taxes, they could not vote until some 20 years ago. This has changed; now they can help elect the president, but still they have only a nonvoting delegate in Congress.

In Washington, the "separation of powers" doctrine becomes more than just a phrase in the Constitution. A visit here gives you a chance to see the legislative, executive, and judicial branches of government in action, to see how the system of checks and balances works. As Boswell put it, you have an opportunity, "instead of thinking how things may be, to see them as they are."

### The Legislative Branch

In Pierre L'Enfant's eighteenth-century plan for the city of Washington, the U.S. Capitol and the White House were just far enough away from each other on Pennsylvania Avenue to emphasize the separation of powers between the legislative and executive branches. L'Enfant chose Jenkins Hill as the site for the Capitol; it is the focal point of an area now called Capitol Hill.

Guided tours of the Capitol leave from the Rotunda almost continuously from 9 AM to 3:30 PM daily throughout the year. The Senate side of the Capitol faces Constitution Avenue, while the House side can be approached from Independence Avenue.

Drop by the office of your senator or representative to pick up passes to the Visitors' Galleries. Without a pass, you are not permitted to watch the proceedings. There are two Senate office buildings at First and Constitution Avenue NE, named respectively, for former Senators Everett Dirksen and Richard Russell. A third, honoring Senator Philip A. Hart, opened in November 1982 at Second and Constitution NE.

The House office buildings, named for former Speakers Joseph Cannon, Nicholas Longworth, and Sam Rayburn, are located in that order along Independence Avenue between First Street, SE, and First Street, SW. It is generally agreed by residents and visitors alike that the Rayburn Building is the least attractive and, at $75 million, one of the most expensive structures in the city.

According to the Constitution, "the Congress shall assemble at least once in every year, and such meeting shall begin at noon on the 3rd day of January, unless they shall by law appoint a different day." In the years before air conditioning, Congress usually recessed during the summer and reconvened in the fall. Today, however, with Congressional calendars more crowded and air conditioning commonplace, sessions frequently last much longer. It is not unusual for the House and/or Senate to sit through the summer and well into the fall.

Congressional sessions usually begin at noon; committee meetings are generally held in the morning. Check the *Washington Post*'s "Today in Congress" listings to find out what is going on.

Don't be surprised to see only a handful of senators or members of Congress on the floor during a session. Much Congressional business dealing with constituent problems is done in committees or in offices. When a vote is taken during a session, bells are rung to summon absent members to the floor.

To save time, many senators and members of Congress make the brief trip between their offices and the Capitol on the Congressional subway. Visitors may ride, too. The Senate restaurant in the Capitol—famed for its bean soup—is open to the public at all times. Cafeterias in the Rayburn, Longworth, and Dirksen office buildings are also open to visitors. Watch the hours, however. From 11:30 AM to 1:15 PM, only members of Congress and their staffs are admitted.

There are two Senators from each state, who are elected for six-year terms at an annual salary of $89,500 each. The 435 members of the House serve for two years and also receive $89,500 per year.

## How a Bill Becomes Law

Legislation is a complicated, time-consuming process. Here, briefly, is the usual legislative procedure in the House of Representatives.
—A bill is introduced by a member, who places it in the "hopper," a box on the clerk's desk. It is numbered (H.R. . . . ), sent to the Government Printing Office, and made available the next morning in the House Document Room.

—It is referred to a committee.

—The committee reports on the bill, usually after holding a hearing, either before the full committee or before a subcommittee.

—The bill is placed on the House calendar.

—Any bill that involves the Treasury is considered by the House sitting as a Committee of the Whole. In that case, the Speaker appoints a chairman who presides and there is a period of general debate, followed by a reading for amendment, with speeches limited to five minutes.

—A bill is given a second reading and consideration in the House. (Bills considered in Committee of the Whole, however, receive a second reading in committee.) Amendments may be added after the second reading.

—It is given a third reading, which is by title only. The Speaker puts the question to a vote and it may be defeated at this stage by a negative vote.

—If it passes, however, it is sent to the Senate.

—The Senate considers the bill, usually after it has been referred to a committee and reported favorably by that committee.

—If the Senate rejects the House bill, it notifies the House. Otherwise, the bill is returned to the House from the Senate, with or without amendments.

—The House considers the Senate amendments.

—Differences between House and Senate versions of a bill are resolved by a joint House-Senate conference committee.

—The bill is printed in final form or "enrolled" on parchment paper.

—It is proofread by the enrolling clerk, who certifies its correctness.

—Once certified, the bill is signed, first by the Speaker of the House and then by the president of the Senate.

—It is sent to the president of the United States.

—The president approves or disapproves the bill, usually after referring it to the appropriate department for recommendations.

—If the president vetoes the bill, it is returned to the Congress. If it fails to pass by a two-thirds vote, no further action is taken.

—If the bill has either been approved by the president or passed over a veto, it is filed with the secretary of state and then becomes law.

Such a brief summary cannot possibly convey the intrigue, the drama, and the behind-the-scenes maneuvering by members, their staffs, and lobbyists involved in the legislative process. Often the stakes are high and the battles hard fought. If you are lucky, you may be able to watch an important debate or a newsworthy vote during your visit to Capitol Hill.

## The Executive Branch

The White House is at 1600 Pennsylvania Avenue NW, the most prestigious address in the country. However, its first occupant, Abigail Adams, was disappointed in the damp, drafty "President's Palace." She complained that it had "not a single apartment finished" and "not the least fence, yard, or other convenience without." On the other hand, Thomas Jefferson found the house "big enough for two emperors, one Pope, and the grand lama"—and still unfinished.

When Franklin Delano Roosevelt became president in 1932, the entire White House staff consisted of fewer than 50 people. Today, approximately 1,800 people work for the executive office of the president. They are crammed into offices in the east and west wings of the White House and in the ornate Executive Office Building (formerly the State, War and Navy Building), adjacent to the White House to the west on Pennsylvania Avenue.

The president's annual salary is $200,000; the vice president receives $115,000. They are elected for a four-year term. If the president dies or becomes incapacitated, the vice president is next in line of succession. He is followed, in order, by the speaker of the House of Representatives, the president pro tempore of the Senate, the secretaries of state, treasury, and defense, the attorney general, the postmaster general, and the secretaries of the interior, agriculture, commerce, labor, health and human services, housing and urban development, transportation, energy, and education.

## The Judicial Branch

Traditionally, the opening session of the Supreme Court, on the first Monday in October, marks the beginning of Washington's social season, and the quadrennial inaugural festivities add to the excitement. The inaugural week in January usually includes a star-studded gala, as well as receptions honoring the new president, vice president, and their wives.

The Supreme Court meets from October through June in a Corinthian-columned white-marble building at First and Maryland Avenue, N.E. Until 1935, the Justices used various rooms in the Capitol. For a while, in the nineteenth century, they met in taverns, boardinghouses, and at the home of the Clerk of the Court, Elias Boudinot Caldwell, at Second and A streets, S.E. You can see the Old Supreme Court Chamber on the ground floor of the Capitol.

Approximately 5,000 cases are submitted for appeal each year and the justices choose about 3 percent—roughly 160 cases in all—those which raise Constitutional questions or affect the life or liberty of citizens.

Justice Felix Frankfurter said, "The words of the Constitution are so unrestricted by their intrinsic meaning or by their history or by tradition or by prior decisions that they leave the individual Justice free, if indeed they do not compel him, to gather meaning not from reading the Constitution but from reading life."

In the courtroom, the nine black-robed justices are seated in high-backed black leather chairs in front of heavy red velvet draperies. Lawyers for each side present their oral arguments, with the justices often interjecting questions or comments. Generally, the court sits for two weeks and then recesses for two weeks to do research and write opinions.

They are on the bench Monday, Tuesday, and Wednesday from 10 AM to noon and from 1 to 3 PM from October through April and they usually hear about four cases a day. During this first part of the term, the justices meet privately every Wednesday afternoon and all day Friday to discuss the cases they have heard that week and to take a preliminary vote on decisions.

The chief justice assigns different members to write the opinions. If he is on the minority side in a particular case, however, the senior Justice in the majority assigns the opinion. Any Justice may write his or her own opinion, agreeing or disagreeing with the majority. During the remainder of the term, in May and June, the justices usually meet every Thursday to decide on releasing their opinions.

Monday is "Decision Day," probably the most interesting time to visit the Supreme Court. That is when the Justices announce their decisions and read their opinions.

Throughout the year, in the courtroom, staff members give a brief lecture about the court Monday through Friday, every half-hour from 9:30 AM to 4:30 PM. Lectures are not given on holidays or when the justices are on the bench hearing cases. In addition to exhibits about the Supreme Court and its justices, the court boasts one of the best government cafeterias in town—second only to those at the National Gallery of Art. It is open to the public.

Supreme Court justices are appointed by the president with the advice and consent of the Senate. They serve for life or, as the Constitution says, "during good behavior."

Associate justices receive $110,000 per year; the chief justice's salary is $115,000. After ten years of service, they may resign or retire with full pay.

Veteran court-watcher Anthony Lewis called the Supreme Court a "symbol of continuity, instrument of change," and added that "no more remarkable institution of government exists than the Supreme Court of the United States."

## Lobbyists

Virtually every special-interest group in the country, as well as a sprinkling of foreign governments, is represented by someone who "lobbies" for its cause in Washington. Lobbyists frequently conduct their business over luncheons, cocktails, and dinners, as well as on the golf courses or tennis courts of suburban country clubs. Power is the magnet that draws them to the nation's capital.

Lobbyists' backgrounds are as diverse as the causes they represent. They are usually lawyers, public relations executives, or former congressional staff members. Many were once members of Congress or high government officials from all over the U.S. who have developed "Potomac fever," that is, they do not return home but find being a Washington representative the ideal way to continue to influence public policy.

Sometimes, it appears that every group is well represented here except the average citizen. Under those circumstances, if you have a pet project, discuss it with your senator or member of Congress—he or she is your lobbyist. In doing so—like Washington's highly skilled and well-paid lobbyists—you would simply be exercising your First Amendment rights to express your beliefs and influence your government.

# 3 Exploring Washington

## Orientation

*by John F. Kelly*

*John F. Kelly is an editor for the Washington Post's Weekend section.*

The Byzantine workings of the Federal government; the nonsensical, sound-bite-ready oratory of the well-groomed politician; murky foreign policy pronouncements issued from Foggy Bottom; and $600 toilet seats ordered by the Pentagon cause many Americans to cast a skeptical eye on anything that happens "inside the Beltway." Washingtonians take it all in stride, though, reminding themselves that, after all, those responsible for political hijinks don't come *from* Washington, they come *to* Washington. Besides, such ribbing is a small price to pay for living in a city whose charms extend far beyond the bureaucratic. World-class museums and art galleries (nearly all of them free), tree-shaded and flower-filled parks and gardens, bars and restaurants that benefit from a large and creative immigrant community, and nightlife that seems to get better with every passing year are as much a part of Washington as floor debates or filibusters.

The location of the city that calls to mind politicking, back scratching, and delicate diplomacy is itself the result of a compromise. Tired of its nomadic existence after having set up shop in eight different locations, Congress voted in 1785 to establish a permanent "Federal town." Northern lawmakers wanted the capital on the Delaware River, in the north, southerners wanted it on the Potomac, in the south. A deal was struck when Virginia's Thomas Jefferson agreed to support the proposal that the Federal government assume the war debts of the colonies if New York's Alexander Hamilton and other northern legislators would agree to locate the capital on the banks of the Potomac. George Washington himself selected the exact site of the capital, a diamond-shaped, 100-square-mile plot that encompassed the confluence of the Potomac and Anacostia rivers, not far from the president's estate at Mount Vernon. To give the young city a bit of a head start, Washington included the already thriving tobacco ports of Alexandria, Virginia, and Georgetown, Maryland, in the District of Columbia.

Charles Pierre L'Enfant, a young French engineer who had fought in the Revolution, offered his services in creating a capital "magnificent enough to grace a great nation." His 1791 plan owes much to Versailles, with ceremonial circles and squares, a grid pattern of streets, and broad diagonal avenues. It was these grand streets that sparked the first debates over L'Enfant's design and its execution. The families that owned the estates and tobacco farms that would be transformed into Washington had agreed to sell the sites needed for public buildings at $66.66 an acre, with the understanding that profits could be made by selling the remaining land to those who wanted to be near the Federal government. They also agreed to turn over for free the land to be used for streets and highways. When they discovered that L'Enfant's streets were 100 feet wide and that one thoroughfare—the Mall—would be 400 feet across, they were horrified. Half the land on the site would be turned over to the government for free for roads.

L'Enfant won the battle of the roads but he couldn't control his obstinate ways and fought often with the three city commissioners Washington had appointed. When the nephew of one of the commissioners started to build a manor house where L'Enfant had planned a street, the Frenchman ordered it torn down.

The overzealous L'Enfant was fired and offered $2,500 and a lot near the White House in pay. He refused, thinking it poor compensation for the services he had performed. (A visionary who was a little too headstrong for his own good, L'Enfant spent his later years petitioning Congress with long, rambling missives demanding satisfaction. He died penniless in 1825.)

L'Enfant had written that his plan would "leave room for that aggrandizement and embellishment which the increase in the wealth of the nation will permit it to pursue at any period, however remote." At times it must have seemed remote indeed, for the town grew so slowly that when Charles Dickens visited Washington in 1842 what he saw were "spacious avenues that begin in nothing and lead nowhere; streets a mile long that only want houses, roads, and inhabitants; public buildings that need but a public to be complete and ornaments of great thoroughfares which need only great thoroughfares to ornament."

It took the Civil War—and every war thereafter—to energize the city, by attracting thousands of new residents and spurring building booms that extended the capital in all directions. Streets in the once-backward town were paved in the 1870s and the first streetcars ran in the 1880s. Memorials to famous Americans like Lincoln and Jefferson were built in the first decades of the 20th century, along with the massive Federal Triangle, a monument to thousands of less-famous government workers.

Despite the growth and despite the fact that blacks have always played an important role in the city's history (black mathematician Benjamin Banneker surveyed the land with Pierre L'Enfant in the 18th century), Washington today remains essentially segregated. Whites—who account for about 30% of the population—reside mostly in northwest Washington. Blacks live largely east of Rock Creek Park and south of the Anacostia River.

It's a city of other unfortunate contrasts: Citizens of the capital of the free world couldn't vote in a presidential election until 1964, weren't granted limited home rule until 1974, and are represented in Congress by a single nonvoting delegate. Homeless people sleep on steam grates next to multimillion-dollar government buildings, and a flourishing drug trade has earned Washington the dubious distinction of murder capital of the United States. Though it's little consolation to those affected, most crime is restricted to neighborhoods far from the areas visited by tourists.

Still, there's no denying that Washington, the world's first planned capital city, is also one of its most beautiful. And though the Federal government dominates the city psychologically as much as the Washington Monument dominates it physically, there are parts of the capital where you can leave politics behind. The tours that follow will take you through the monumental city, the governmental city, and the residential city. As you walk, look for evidence of L'Enfant's hand, still present despite growing pains and frequent deviations from his plan. His Washington was to be city of vistas—pleasant views that would shift and change from block to block, a marriage of geometry and art. It remains this way today. Like its main industry, politics, Washington's design is a constantly changing kaleidoscope that invites contemplation from all angles.

**Exploring Washington, D.C.** *(Boxes Refer to Detail Maps)*

Tour 9

Tour 7

Tour 6

Tour 3

Tour 8

Tour 10

Massachusetts Ave.

California St.

S St.

R St.

32nd St.

31st St.

Wisconsin Ave.

S St.

Decatur Pl.

Sheridan Circle

R St.

Q St.

P St.

28th St.
29th St.
30th St.
31st St.

27th St.

N St.

O St.

M St.

C&O Canal

Whitehurst Fwy.

Francis Scott Key Br.

I-66

ROSSLYN

NW

SW

Theodore Roosevelt Island

George Washington Memorial Pkwy.

Rock Creek

M St.

26th St.

25th St.
24th St.

L St.

Washington Circle

Pennsylvania Ave.

23rd St.
22nd St.

G St.

F St.

E St.

Virginia Ave.

Florida Ave.

S St.

Massachusetts Ave.

Q St.

22nd St.
21st St.
20th St.

O St.

N St.

M St.

New Hampshire Ave.

29

New Hampshire Ave.

L St.

K St.

19th St.

M

Dupont Circle

T St.

New Hampshire Ave.

Corcora

Church St.
P St.

N St.

17th St.

18th St.

Connecticut Ave.

M

D St.

C St.

17th St.

Constitution Ave.

50

Lincoln Memorial

Reflecting Pool

Independence Ave.

Kutz Br.

Arlington Memorial Br.

Columbia Island

Lady Bird Johnson Park

Ohio Dr.

West Potomac Park

W. Basin Dr.

Tidal Ba

Memorial Dr.

M

ARLINGTON NATIONAL CEMETERY

Potomac River

VIRGINIA

## Tour 1: The Mall

*Numbers in the margin correspond with points of interest on the Mall map.*

The Mall is the heart of nearly every visitor's trip to Washington. With nine diverse museums ringing the expanse of green, it's the closest thing the capital has to a theme park (unless you count the Federal government itself, which has uncharitably been called "Disneyland on the Potomac"). As at a theme park, you may have to stand in an occasional line, but unlike the amusements at Disneyland almost everything you'll see here is free.

Don't expect to see it all in one day, though. The holdings of the museums and art galleries of the Smithsonian Institution—the largest museum complex in the world—total more than 135 million objects. Only 1% are on public display at any one time, but that's still over a million different objects vying for your attention. If you can, devote at least two days to the Mall. Do the north side one day and the south the next. Or split your sightseeing on the Mall into museums the first day, art galleries the second. Of course, the Mall is more than just a front yard for all these museums. It's a picnicking park and a jogging path, an outdoor stage for festivals and fireworks, and America's town green.

The Mall is bounded on the north and south by Constitution and Independence avenues, and on the east and west by 4th and 14th streets. All of the Smithsonian museums lie within these boundaries. (Nearest Metro stop, Smithsonian or Archives).

**❶** The best place to start an exploration of the museums on the Mall is in front of the first one constructed, the **Smithsonian Institution Building.** British scientist and founder James Smithson had never visited America. Yet his will stipulated that, should his nephew, Henry James Hungerford, die without an heir, Smithson's entire fortune would go to the United States, "to found at Washington, under the name of the Smithsonian Institution, an establishment for the increase and diffusion of knowledge among men."

Smithson died in 1829, Hungerford in 1835, and in 1838 the United States received $515,169 worth of gold sovereigns. After eight years of Congressional debate over the propriety of accepting funds from a private citizen, the Smithsonian Institution was finally established in 1846. The red sandstone, Norman-style headquarters building on Jefferson Drive was completed in 1855 and originally housed all of the Smithsonian's operations, including the science and art collections, research laboratories, and living quarters for the Institution's secretary and his family. Known as "the Castle," the building was designed by James Renwick, the architect of St. Patrick's Cathedral in New York City. The statue in front of the Castle's entrance is not of Smithson but of Joseph Henry, the scientist who served as the Institution's first secretary. Smithson's body was brought to America in 1904 and is entombed in a small room to the left of the Castle's Mall entrance.

Today the Castle houses Smithsonian administrative offices and is home to the Woodrow Wilson International School for Scholars. To get your bearings or to get help deciding which

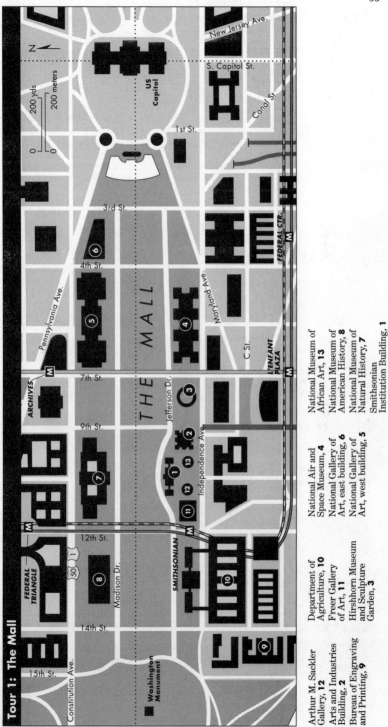

# Tour 1: The Mall

Arthur M. Sackler
Gallery, **12**
Arts and Industries
Building, **2**
Bureau of Engraving
and Printing, **9**

Department of
Agriculture, **10**
Freer Gallery
of Art, **11**
Hirshhorn Museum
and Sculpture
Garden, **3**

National Air and
Space Museum, **4**
National Gallery of
Art, east building, **6**
National Gallery of
Art, west building, **5**

National Museum of
African Art, **13**
National Museum of
American History, **8**
National Museum of
Natural History, **7**
Smithsonian
Institution Building, **1**

Mall attractions you want to devote your time to, visit the new **Smithsonian Information Center** in the Castle. An orientation film provides an overview of the various Smithsonian museums and monitors display information on the day's events. The Information Center opens at 9 AM, an hour before the other museums open, so you can plan your day on the Mall without wasting valuable sightseeing time. *1000 Jefferson Dr. SW, tel. 202/357–2700. Open daily 9–5:30.*

**2** This tour circles the Mall counterclockwise. Start by walking east on Jefferson Drive to the **Arts and Industries Building,** the second Smithsonian museum to be constructed. In 1876 Philadelphia hosted the United States International Exposition in honor of the nation's Centennial. After the festivities, scores of exhibitors donated their displays to the Federal government. In order to house the objects that had come its way, the Smithsonian commissioned this red-brick and sandstone building. Designed by Adolph Cluss, the building was originally called the United States National Museum, the name that is still engraved in stone above the doorway. It was finished in 1881, just in time for President James Garfield's inaugural ball.

The Arts and Industries Building housed a variety of artifacts that were eventually moved to other museums as the Smithsonian grew. It was restored to its original appearance and reopened during Bicentennial celebrations in 1976. Today the museum exhibits an extensive collection of American Victoriana; many of the objects on display—which include carriages, tools, printing presses, even a steam locomotive—are from the original Philadelphia Centennial. *900 Jefferson Dr. SW, tel. 202/357–2700. Open daily 10–5:30.*

In front of the Arts and Industries Building is a **carousel** that is popular with young and old alike. In warmer months it operates between 10 and 5:30 (75 cents a ride).

**3** The **Hirshhorn Museum** is the next building to the east on Jefferson Drive, and you would be hard pressed to find a piece of architecture that contrasts more with the gay Victoriana of the Arts and Industries Building. Dubbed "the Doughnut on the Mall," the reinforced-concrete building designed by Gordon Bunshaft is a fitting home for contemporary—and sometimes controversial—art. Opened in 1974, the museum manages a collection of 4,000 paintings and drawings and 2,000 sculptures donated by Joseph H. Hirshhorn, a Latvian-born immigrant who made his fortune in this country running uranium mines. American artists such as Eakins, Pollock, Rothko, and Stella are represented, as are modern European and Latin masters, including Francis Bacon, Fernando Botero, Magritte, Miró, and Victor Vasarely.

The Hirshhorn's impressive sculpture collection is arranged in the open spaces between the museum's concrete piers and across Jefferson Drive in the **Sculpture Garden**. The display in the Sculpture Garden includes the largest public American collection of works by Henry Moore, as well as works by Henri Daumier, Max Ernst, Alberto Giacometti, Pablo Picasso, and Man Ray. Auguste Rodin's *The Burghers of Calais* is a highlight. The largest piece in the Hirshhorn's collection is the 42-foot-high, 30-ton *Isis* by Mark di Suvero, which looks like a beached ship. Not surprisingly, the materials for this work were donated by the Institute of Scrap Iron and Steel, Inc. For those interested in wearable art, there is an assortment of contemporary jewelry and clothing in the museum's gift shop. *Independence Ave. at 7th St. NW, tel. 202/357–2700. Open daily 10–5:30. Extended spring/summer hours determined annually. Sculpture garden open daily 7:30–dusk.*

**❹** Cross 7th Street to get to the **National Air and Space Museum.** Opened in 1976, Air and Space is the most visited museum in the world, attracting 12 million people each year. (It's thought to be the single most-visited building on earth.) Twenty-three galleries tell the story of aviation, from man's earliest attempts at flight to his travels beyond our solar system. Suspended from the ceiling like plastic models in a child's room are dozens of aircraft, including the actual "Wright Flyer" that Wilbur Wright piloted over the sands of Kitty Hawk, North Carolina; Charles Lindbergh's "Spirit of St. Louis"; the X-1 rocket plane in which Chuck Yeager broke the sound barrier; and the X-15, the fastest plane ever built.

Other highlights include a walk-through model of the Skylab orbital workshop; the Voyager airplane that Dick Rutan and Jeana Yeager flew non-stop around the world; and the USS Enterprise model used in the "Star Trek" TV show. Visitors can also touch a piece of the moon: a 4-billion-year-old slice of rock collected by Apollo 17 astronauts. (Moon rock is one of the rarest substances on earth and, soon after the museum opened, a few zealous tourists tried to add the rock to their collections. The display is now wired with a motion alarm and watched by a uniformed guard.)

Don't let long lines deter you from seeing a show in the museum's **Langley Theater.** IMAX films shown on the five-story-high screen—including *The Dream is Alive, To Fly!, On the Wing, Flyers,* and *Living Planet*—usually feature swooping aerial scenes that will convince you you've left the ground. Buy your tickets ($2.25 for adults; $1.25 for children, students, and seniors) as soon as you arrive, then look around the museum. Upstairs, the **Albert Einstein Planetarium** projects images of celestial bodies on a domed ceiling. *Jefferson Dr. at Sixth St. SW, tel. 202/357–2700. Open daily 10–5:30.*

**Time Out**  Two restaurants opened in 1988 in the eastern end of the National Air and Space Museum. **The Wright Place** is a table-service restaurant; the **Flight Line** is a self-service cafeteria. They each have a large selection of foods, but at peak times lines can be long.

After touring the Air and Space Museum, walk east on Jefferson Drive toward the Capitol. What has been called the last open space left for a museum on the periphery of the Mall is bounded by 3rd and 4th streets and Independence Avenue and Jefferson Drive SW. There are tentative plans to build an American Indian museum on this spot.

To get to the museums on the north side of the Mall, walk north on 4th or 3rd Street. As you walk, look to the left for a good view of the Mall. Notice how the Castle projects slightly into the green rectangle. When it was built, in 1855, Pierre L'Enfant's plan for Washington had been all but forgotten. In this space west of the "Congress House," the Frenchman had envisioned a "Grand Avenue, 400 feet in breadth, and about a mile in length, bordered with gardens, ending in a slope from the houses on each side." In the middle of the 19th century, horticulturalist Andrew Jackson Downing took a stab at converting the Mall into a large, English-style garden, with carriageways curving through groves of trees and bushes. This was far from the "vast esplanade" L'Enfant had in mind, and by the dawn of the 20th century the Mall had become an eyesore. It was dotted with sheds and bisected by railroad tracks. There was even a railroad station at its eastern end.

In 1900 Senator James McMillan, chairman of the Committee on the District of Columbia, asked a distinguished group of architects and artists to study ways of improving Washington's park system. The McMillan Commission, which included architects Daniel Burnham and Charles McKim, landscape architect Frederick Law Olmsted, Jr., and sculptor Augustus Saint-Gaudens, didn't confine its recommendations just to parks; its 1902 report would shape the way the capital looked for decades. The Mall received much of the group's attention and is its most stunning accomplishment. L'Enfant's plan was rediscovered, the sheds, railroad tracks, and carriageways were removed, and Washington finally had the monumental core it had been denied for so long.

**5** Cross Madison Drive to get to the two buildings of the **National Gallery of Art,** one of the world's foremost collections of paintings, sculptures, and graphics. If you want to view the museum's holdings in (more or less) chronological order, it's best to start your exploration of this magnificent gallery in the **west building.** Opened in 1941, the domed building was a gift to the nation from financier Andrew Mellon. (The dome was one of architect John Russell Pope's favorite devices. He designed the domed Jefferson Memorial and, though it's difficult to see from outside, there's a dome on his National Archives, too.)

A wealthy banker and oilman, Andrew Mellon served as secretary of the treasury under three presidents and as ambassador to the United Kingdom. He first came to Washington in 1921, and lived for many years in a luxurious apartment near Dupont Circle, in a building that today houses the National Trust for Historic Preservation (*see* Tour 7: Dupont Circle). Mellon had long collected great works of art, acquiring them on his frequent trips to Europe. In 1931, when the Soviet government was short on cash and selling off many of its art treasures, Mellon stepped in and bought $6 million worth of Old Masters, including *The Alba Madonna* by Raphael and Botticelli's *Adoration of the Magi.* Mellon promised his collection to America in 1937, the year of his death. He also donated the funds for the construction of the huge gallery and resisted suggestions it be named after him.

For a glimpse of Andrew Mellon and other philanthropists who made the gallery possible, go to the ground floor **Founders Room,** near the Constitution Avenue entrance. There are comfortable chairs, a checkroom, and portraits of 10 of the museum's founding benefactors.

The west building's **Great Rotunda,** with its 16 marble columns surrounding a fountain topped with a statue of Mercury, sets the stage for the masterpieces on display in the more than 100 separate galleries. You'll probably want to wander the rooms at your own pace, taking in the wealth of art. A tape-recorded tour of the building's better-known holdings, narrated by National Gallery director J. Carter Brown, is available for a $3 rental fee at the ground floor sales area. If you'd rather explore on your own, get a map at one of the two information desks; one is just inside the Mall entrance (off of Madison Drive), the other is near the Constitution Avenue entrance on the ground floor.

The National Gallery's permanent collection includes works from the 13th to the 20th century. A comprehensive survey of Italian paintings and sculpture includes *The Adoration of the Magi* by Fra Angelico and Fra Filippo Lippi and *Ginevra de'Benci*, the only painting by da Vinci outside of Europe. Flemish and Dutch works, displayed in a series of attractive panelled rooms, include *Daniel in the Lions' Den*, by Rubens, and a self-portrait by Rembrandt. The Chester Dale Collection comprises works by Impressionist painters such as Degas, Monet, Renoir, and Mary Cassatt.

**❻** To get to the **National Gallery of Art's east building** you can take a moving walkway that travels below ground between the two buildings. But to appreciate I.M. Pei's impressive, angular east building, enter it from outside rather than from underground. Exit the west building through its eastern doors, and cross 4th Street. (As you cross, look to the north: Seeming to float above the Doric columns and pediment of the D.C. Superior Court is the green roof and red-brick pediment of the Pension Building, four blocks away.)

The east building opened in 1978 in response to the changing needs of the National Gallery. The awkward trapezoidal shape of the building site, which had been taken up by tennis courts and rose bushes planted during Lady Bird Johnson's spruce-up campaign, prompted Pei's dramatic approach: Two interlocking spaces shaped like triangles provide room for galleries, auditoriums, and administrative offices. While the east building's triangles contrast sharply with the symmetrical classical facade and gentle dome of the west building, both buildings are constructed of pink marble from the same Tennessee quarries. Despite its severe angularity, Pei's building is inviting. The axe-blade–like southwest corner has been polished smooth by thousands of hands irresistibly drawn to it.

Galleries in the east wing generally display modern art, though special exhibits are mounted periodically. An installation of 20th-century art will be on display through 1990, in honor of the building's 10th anniversary. Famous works by Picasso, Braques, Matisse, Mondrian, Magritte, Pollock, Rothko, Rauschenberg, Lichtenstein, and others make the exhibit a veritable "greatest hits" show. *Madison Dr. and 4th St. NW, tel. 202/737–4215. Open Mon.–Sat., 10–5; Sun. noon–9. Extended summer hours are determined annually.*

**Time Out** Two restaurants on the concourse level between the east and west buildings of the National Gallery offer bleary-eyed and foot-sore museum goers the chance to recharge. The **buffet** serves a wide variety of soups, sandwiches, salads, hot entrees, and desserts. The **Cascade Cafe** has a smaller selection, but customers enjoy the soothing effect of the gentle waterfall that splashes against the glass-covered wall.

Between 7th and 9th streets is the **National Sculpture Garden/Ice Rink.** In the winter skates are rented out for use on the circular rink. Ice cream and other refreshments are available at the green building during the summer.

**❼** The **National Museum of Natural History** houses the majority of the Smithsonian's collection of objects, a total of some 118 million specimens. It was constructed in 1910, and two wings were added in the '60s. It is a museum's museum, filled with bones, fossils, stuffed animals, and other natural delights. Exhibits also explore the exploits of humans, the world's most adaptive inhabitants.

The first-floor hall under the rotunda is dominated by a stuffed, eight-ton, 13-foot African bull elephant, one of the largest specimens ever found. (The tusks are fiberglass; the original ivory ones were apparently far too heavy for the stuffed elephant to support.) Off to the right (follow the elephant's tail) is the popular **Dinosaur Hall.** Fossilized skeletons on display range from a 90-foot-long diplodocus to a tiny thesalosaurus neglectus (a small dinosaur so named because its disconnected bones sat forgotten for years in a college drawer before being reassembled).

In the west wing are displays on birds, mammals, and sea life. Many of the preserved specimens are from the collection of animals bagged by Teddy Roosevelt on his trips to Africa. Not everything in the museum is dead, though. The sea-life display features a living coral reef, complete with fish, plants, and simulated waves. The halls north of the rotunda contain tools, clothing, and other artifacts from many cultures, including those of Native America and of Asia, the Pacific, and Africa. The Discovery Room, in the northwest corner, features elephant tusks, woolly-mammoth teeth, petrified wood, and hundreds of other natural-history objects that visitors can handle and examine.

The highlight of the second floor is the **mineral and gem collection.** Objects include the largest sapphire on public display in the country (the Logan Sapphire, 423 carats), the largest uncut diamond (the Oppenheimer Diamond, 253.7 carats), and, of course, the Hope diamond, a blue gem found in India and reputed to carry a curse (though Smithsonian guides are quick to pooh-pooh this notion). The amazing gem collection is second in value only to the crown jewels of Great Britain. Also on the second floor is the **Insect Zoo,** popular with children, less so with adults.

Kids also love "Uncle Beazley," a life-size fiberglass model of a triceratops (dinosaur) that sits on the Mall directly across from the museum. *Madison Dr. between 9th and 12th sts. NW, tel. 202/357–2700. Open daily 10–5:30. Extended summer hours determined annually.*

**❽** The **National Museum of American History**—the next building to the west, toward the Washington Monument—explores America's cultural, political, technical, and scientific past. It opened in 1964 as the National Museum of History and Technology and was renamed in 1980. The incredible diversity of artifacts here helps the Smithsonian live up to its nickname as "the Nation's attic." This is the museum that displayed Muhammed Ali's boxing gloves, the Fonz's leather jacket, and the Bunkers' living room furniture from "All in the Family." Visitors can wander for hours on the museum's three floors. The exhibits on the first floor emphasize the history of science and technology and include such items as farm machines, antique automobiles, early phonographs, and a 280-ton steam locomotive. The second floor is devoted to U.S. social and political history and features an exhibit on everyday American life just after the Revolution. The majority of the first ladies' gowns are being refurbished, but a few are on display on this floor. The third floor has installations on ceramics, philately, money, graphic arts, musical instruments, photography, and news reporting.

Be sure to check out Horatio Greenough's statue of the first president (by the west-wing escalators on the second floor). Commissioned by Congress in 1832, the statue was intended to grace the Capitol Rotunda. It was there for only a short while, however, since the toga-clad likeness proved shocking to legislators who grumbled that it looked as if the father of our country had just emerged from a bath. The statue was first banished to the east grounds of the Capitol, then given to the Smithsonian in 1908. *Madison Ave. between 12th and 14th sts. NW, tel. 202/357–2700. Open daily 10–5:30.*

To continue the loop of the Mall, head south on 14th Street. From here you'll be able to view the length of the Mall from its western end, this time seeing the Capitol from afar. Instead of turning east on Jefferson Drive, continue south on 14th Street. On the right you'll pass a turreted, castle-like structure called the **Auditor's Building.** Built in 1879, it was the first building dedicated exclusively to the work of printing America's money. In 1914 the money-making operation was moved one block **❾** south to the **Bureau of Engraving and Printing.** All the paper currency in the United States, as well as stamps, military certificates, and presidential invitations, is printed in this huge building. Despite the fact that there are no free samples, the 20-minute, self-guided tour of the Bureau—which takes visitors past presses that turn out some $40 million a day—is one of the city's most popular. *14th and C sts. SW, tel. 202/447–1391. Open Mon.–Fri. 9–2.*

Return up 14th Street and turn right onto Independence Avenue. Continuing down Independence Avenue back toward the **❿** Capitol, you'll walk between the two buildings of the **Department of Agriculture.** The older building on your left was started in 1905 and was the first building to be constructed by order of the McMillan Commission on the south side of the Mall. The cornices on the north side of this white-marble building feature depictions of forests and of grains, flowers, and fruits—some of the plants the department keeps an eye on. The newer building south of Independence Avenue, to your right, covers three city blocks (an example, perhaps, of big government).

The two complexes are joined by arches known as **"The Bridges of Sighs."** One is devoted to James Wilson, secretary of agriculture from 1897 to 1914; the other to Seaman A. Knapp, a distinguished warrior in the fight against the dreaded boll weevil.

**⓫** A few steps farther up Independence Avenue, across 12th Street, is the **Freer Gallery of Art,** a gift from Detroit industrialist Charles L. Freer, who retired in 1900 and devoted the rest of his life to collecting oriental treasures. The Freer opened in 1923, four years after its benefactor's death. Now in the middle of a three-year renovation, the Freer is scheduled to reopen in 1992. Its collection includes more than 26,000 works of art from the Far and Near East, including Oriental porcelains, Japanese screens, Chinese paintings and bronzes, and Egyptian gold pieces. Freer's close friend James McNeill Whistler introduced him to Oriental art, and the American painter is represented in the vast collection. On display in Gallery 12 is the "Peacock Room," a blue-and-gold dining room decorated with painted leather, wood, and canvas and designed by Whistler for a British shipping magnate. Freer paid $30,000 for the entire room and moved it from London to the United States in 1904.

Just beyond the Freer turn left off of Independence Avenue into the **Enid Haupt Memorial Garden.** This four-acre Victorian-style garden is built largely on the rooftops of the Smithsonian's two newest museums, the Arthur M. Sackler Gallery and the National Museum of African Art, both of which opened in 1987 and sit underground like inverted pyramids.

When Charles Freer endowed the gallery that bears his name, he insisted on a few conditions: objects in the collection could not be loaned out, nor could objects from outside the collections be put on display. Because of these restrictions it was necessary to build a second, complementary, Oriental art museum. **⑫** The result was the **Arthur M. Sackler Gallery.** A wealthy medical researcher and publisher who began collecting Asian art as a student, Sackler allowed Smithsonian curators to select 1,000 items from his ample collection and pledged $4 million toward the construction of the museum. The collection includes works from China, the Indian subcontinent, Persia, Thailand, and Indonesia. Articles in the permanent collection include Chinese ritual bronzes, jade ornaments from the third millenium BC, Persian manuscripts, and Indian paintings in gold, silver, lapis lazuli, and malachite. *1050 Independence Ave. SW, tel. 202/357–2700. Open daily 10–5:30.*

The other half of the Smithsonian's new underground museum complex is the **National Museum of African Art.** Founded in **⑬** 1964 as a private educational institution, the museum became part of the Smithsonian in 1979. (Before it was moved here in 1987, the collection was housed in a Capitol Hill townhouse that once belonged to ex-slave Frederick Douglass.) Dedicated to the collection, exhibition, and study of the traditional arts of sub-Saharan Africa, the museum displays artifacts representative of some 900 cultures. The permanent collection includes masks, carvings, textiles, and jewelry, all made from materials such as wood, fiber, bronze, ivory, and fired clay. Because many pieces of African art are made of organic materials, the museum also runs a conservation laboratory, where curators work to arrest the decay of the valuable collection. *950 Independence Ave. SW, tel. 202/357–2700. Open daily 10–5:30.*

You'll find the nearest Metro station, Smithsonian, on Jefferson Drive in front of the Freer Gallery.

## Tour 2: The Monuments

*Numbers in the margin correspond with points of interest on the Monuments map.*

Washington is a city of monuments. In the middle of traffic circles, on tiny slivers of park, and at street corners and intersections, statues, plaques, and simple blocks of marble honor the generals, politicians, poets, and statesmen who helped shape the nation. The monuments dedicated to the most famous Americans are west of the Mall on ground reclaimed from the marshy flats of the Potomac. This is also the location of Washington's cherry trees, gifts from Japan and focus of a festival each spring.

On this tour we'll walk clockwise among the monuments and through the cherry trees. This can be a leisurely, half-day walk, depending on the speed you travel and the time you spend at each spot. If it's an extremely hot day you may want to hop a Tourmobile bus and travel between the monuments in air-conditioned comfort.

❶ We'll start in front of the tallest of them all, the **Washington Monument** (nearest Metro stop, Smithsonian). Located at the western end of the Mall, the Washington Monument punctuates the capital like a huge exclamation point. Visible from nearly everywhere in the city, it serves as a landmark for visiting tourists and lost motorists alike.

Congress first authorized a monument to General Washington in 1783. In his 1791 plan for the city, Pierre L'Enfant selected a site (the point where a line drawn west from the Capitol crossed one drawn south from the White House), but it wasn't until 1833, after years of quibbling in Congress, that a private National Monument Society was formed to select a designer and to search for funds. Robert Mills's winning design called for a 600-foot-tall decorated obelisk rising from a circular colonnaded building. The building at the base was to be an American pantheon, adorned with statues of national heroes and a massive statue of Washington riding in a chariot pulled by snorting horses.

Because of the marshy conditions of L'Enfant's original site, the position of the monument was shifted to firmer ground 100 yards southwest. (If you walk a few steps north of the monument you can see the stone marker that denotes L'Enfant's original axis.) The cornerstone was laid in 1848 with the same Masonic trowel Washington himself had used to lay the Capitol's cornerstone 55 years earlier. The Monument Society continued to raise funds after construction was begun, soliciting subscriptions of one dollar from citizens across America. It also urged states, organizations, and foreign governments to contribute memorial stones for the construction. Problems arose in 1854, when members of the anti-Papist "Know Nothing" party stole a block donated by Pope Pius IX, smashed it, and dumped its shards into the Potomac. This action, a lack of funds, and the onset of the Civil War kept the monument at a quarter of its final height, open at the top, and vulnerable to the rain. A clearly visible ring about a third of the way up the obelisk testifies to this unfortunate stage of the monument's history: Although all of the marble in the obelisk came from the same Maryland quarry, that used for the second phase of construction came from a different stratum and is of a slightly different shade.

In 1876 Congress finally appropriated $200,000 to finish the monument, and the Army Corps of Engineers took over construction. Work was finally completed in December 1884, when the monument was topped with a 7½-pound piece of aluminum, then one of the most expensive metals in the world. Four years later the monument was opened to visitors, who rode to the top

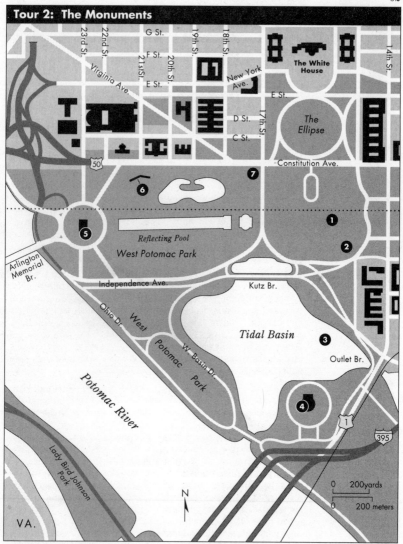

## Tour 2: The Monuments

Jefferson Memorial, **4**

Lincoln Memorial, **5**

Lock keeper's house, **7**

Sylvan Theater, **2**

Tidal Basin, **3**

Vietnam Veterans
Memorial and
Constitution
Gardens, **6**

Washington
Monument, **1**

in a steam-operated elevator. (Only men were allowed to take the 20-minute ride; it was thought too dangerous for women, who as a result had to walk up the stairs if they wanted to see the view.)

At 555 feet 5 inches, the Washington Monument is the world's tallest masonry structure. The view from the top takes in most of the District and parts of Maryland and Virginia. Visitors are no longer permitted to climb the 897 steps leading to the top. (Incidents of vandalism and a disturbing number of heart attacks on the steps convinced the Park Service that letting people walk up on their own wasn't such a good idea.) On Saturdays there are walk-down tours, with a Park Service guide describing the monument's construction and showing the 193 stone and metal plaques that adorn the inside.

There is usually a wait to take the minute-long elevator ride up the monument's shaft. The Park Service rangers standing at the head of the line are good at estimating how long you'll have to wait. Figure on a wait of approximately 10 to 15 minutes for each side of the monument that is lined with people. If the line goes all the way around the monument, you'll be in line anywhere from 40 minutes to an hour. *Constitution Ave. at 15th St. NW, tel. 202/426-6839. Open Apr.–Labor Day, daily 8 AM–midnight; Sept.–Mar., daily 9–5.*

After your ascent and descent, walk on the path that leads south from the monument. On your right you'll pass the open-air **Sylvan Theater,** scene of a variety of musical performances during the warmer months. Continue south and cross Independence Avenue at 15th Street. Just south of the red brick **Auditor's Building** (the first building constructed by the Federal government to print money) is the future site of the **United States Holocaust Memorial Museum,** scheduled for completion in 1992. Beyond that is the colonnaded **Bureau of Engraving and Printing.**

Carefully cross Maine Avenue at the light and walk down to the **Tidal Basin.** This placid pond was part of the Potomac until 1882, when portions of the river were filled in to improve navigation and create additional parkland, including that upon which the Jefferson Memorial was built. Paddleboats have been a fixture on the Tidal Basin for years. You can rent one at the boathouse on the east side of the basin, southwest of the Bureau of Engraving. *$5.50 an hour, $1.25 each additional quarter hour. Open daily 10–7.*

Continue down the path that skirts the Tidal Basin and cross the Outlet Bridge to get to the **Jefferson Memorial,** the southernmost of the major monuments in the District. Congress decided that Jefferson deserved a monument positioned as prominently as those in honor of Washington and Lincoln, and this spot directly south of the White House seemed ideal. Jefferson had always admired the Pantheon in Rome—the rotundas he designed for the University of Virginia and his own Monticello were inspired by the dome of the Pantheon—so architect John Russell Pope drew from the same source when he designed this memorial to our third president. Dedicated in 1943, it houses a statue of Jefferson. Its walls are lined with inscriptions based on his writings. One of the best views of the White House can be seen from the memorial's top steps. *Tidal Basin, south bank, tel. 202/426-6821. Open daily 8–midnight.*

After viewing the Jefferson Memorial, continue along the sidewalk that hugs the Tidal Basin. You'll see two grotesque sculpted heads on the sides of the **Inlet Bridge.** The inside walls of the bridge also sport two other interesting sculptures: bronze, human-headed fish that spout water from their mouths.

Once you cross the bridge, you have a choice: You can walk to the left, along the Potomac, or continue along the Tidal Basin to the right. The latter route is somewhat more scenic, especially when the cherry trees are in bloom. The first batch of these trees arrived from Japan in 1909. The trees were infected with insects and fungus, however, and the Department of Agriculture ordered them destroyed. A diplomatic crisis was averted when the United States politely asked the Japanese for another batch, and in 1912 Mrs. William Howard Taft planted the first tree. The second was planted by the wife of the Japanese ambassador.

The trees are now the centerpiece of Washington's Cherry Blossom Festival, held each spring. The festivities are kicked off by the lighting of a ceremonial Japanese lantern that rests on the north shore of the Tidal Basin, not far from where the first tree was planted. The once-simple celebration has grown over the years to include concerts, fashion shows, and a parade. Park Service experts try their best to predict exactly when the buds will pop. The trees are usually in bloom for about 10 to 12 days at the beginning of April. When winter refuses to release its grip, the parade and festival are held anyway, without the presence of blossoms, no matter how inclement the weather. And when the weather complies, and the blossoms are at their peak at the time of the festivities, Washington rejoices.

**West Potomac Park,** the green expanse to the west of the Tidal Basin, is a pleasant place to sit and rest for a while, to watch the paddleboats skim the surface of the Tidal Basin, and to feed the squirrels that usually approach looking for handouts. To get to our next stop, the Lincoln Memorial, walk northwest along West Basin Drive, then cut across to Ohio Drive. Cross Independence Avenue at the light; the traffic here can be dangerous.

As you walk north along Ohio Drive you'll pass a series of playing fields. Softball has become as competitive a sport as politics in Washington, and the battle to secure a field here or elsewhere in the city starts long before the season. Further along Ohio Drive, directly south of the Lincoln Memorial, is a granite sculpture honoring **John Ericsson,** builder of the ironclad *Monitor,* which took on the Confederate's *Merrimac* at Hampton Roads during the Civil War.

**❺** The **Lincoln Memorial** is considered by many to be the most inspiring monument in the city. It would be hard to imagine Washington without the Lincoln and Jefferson memorials, though they were both criticized when first built. The Jefferson Memorial was dubbed "Jefferson's muffin"; critics lambasted the design as outdated and too similar to that of the Lincoln Memorial. Some also complained that the Jefferson Memorial blocked the view of the Potomac from the White House. Detractors of the Lincoln Memorial thought it inappropriate that the humble Lincoln be honored with what amounts to a modified but nonetheless rather grandiose Greek temple. The white

Colorado-marble memorial was designed by Henry Bacon and completed in 1922. The 36 Doric columns represent the 36 states in the Union at the time of Lincoln's death; the names of the states appear on the frieze above the columns. Above the frieze are the names of the 48 states in the Union when the memorial was dedicated. (Alaska and Hawaii are noted by an inscription on the terrace leading up to the memorial.)

Daniel Chester French's somber statue of the seated president is in the center of the memorial and gazes out over the Reflecting Pool. While French's 19-foot-high sculpture looks as if it were cut from one huge block of stone, it actually comprises 28 interlocking pieces of Georgia marble. (The memorial's original design called for a 10-foot-high sculpture, but experiments with models revealed that a statue that size would be lost in the cavernous memorial.) Inscribed on the south wall is the Gettysburg Address, and on the north wall is Lincoln's second inaugural address. Above each inscription is a mural painted by Jules Guerin. On the south wall is an angel of truth freeing a slave; the unity of North and South are depicted on the opposite wall. The memorial served as a fitting backdrop for Martin Luther King's "I have a dream" speech in 1963.

Many visitors look only at the front and inside of the Lincoln Memorial, but there is much more to explore. On the lower level to the left is a display that chronicles the memorial's construction. There is also a set of windows that look onto the huge structure's foundation. Stalactites (hanging from above) and stalagmites (growing from below) have formed underneath the marble tribute to Lincoln. One of the most popular tours in Washington is of the bowels of the memorial. Also be sure to walk around the marble platform to the rear of the memorial. From there you'll have a clear view over the Arlington Memorial Bridge into Arlington National Cemetery. The Doric-columned Arlington House, once home of General Robert E. Lee, overlooks the cemetery. On a clear night you can see the eternal flame that burns over John F. Kennedy's grave.

Although visiting the area around the Lincoln Memorial during the day allows you to take in an impressive view of the Mall to the east, the best time to see the memorial itself is at night. Spotlights illuminate the outside, while inside, light and shadows play across Lincoln's gentle face. *West end of Mall, tel. 202/426–6895. Open daily 8 AM–midnight. "Caves" tour, tel. 202/426–6842 at least 6 weeks in advance.*

❻ Walk down the steps of the Lincoln Memorial and to the left to get to the **Vietnam Veterans Memorial** and **Constitution Gardens.** The Vietnam Veterans Memorial is another landmark that encourages introspection. The concept came from Jan Scruggs, a former infantry corporal who had served in Vietnam. The stark design of Maya Ying Lin, a 21-year-old Yale architecture student, was selected in a 1981 competition. Upon its completion in 1982, the memorial was decried by some veterans as a "black gash of shame." With the addition of Frederick Hart's statue of three soldiers and a flagpole just south of the Wall, most critics were won over.

The Wall is one of the most visited sites in Washington, its black granite panels reflecting the sky, the trees, and the faces of those looking for the names of friends or relatives who died in the war. The names of more than 58,000 Americans are etched on the face of the memorial in the order of their deaths. Directories at the entrance and exit to the Wall list the names in alphabetical order. For help in finding a specific name, ask a ranger at the blue-and-white hut near the entrance. Thousands of offerings are left at the Wall each year: letters, flowers, medals, uniforms, snapshots. The National Park Service collects these and stores them in a warehouse in Lanham, Maryland, where they are fast becoming another memorial. *Constitution Gardens, 23rd St. and Constitution Ave. NW, tel. 202/634–1568. Open 24 hours a day.*

Continue east through Constitution Gardens. Veterans groups often have tents set up near the Wall; some provide information on soldiers who remain missing in action, others are on call to help fellow veterans deal with the sometimes powerful emotions that come from visiting the Wall for the first time.

The area that is now Constitution Gardens was once covered with "temporary" buildings that the Navy put up during World War I and didn't take down until after World War II. Many ideas were proposed to develop this 50-acre site south of Constitution Avenue between 17th and 23rd streets. President Nixon is said to have favored a design resembling the Tivoli Gardens in Copenhagen. When the present gardens were finally finished in 1976, many Washingtonians thought them a little on the plain side.

**Time Out**  At the circular **snack bar** just west of the Constitution Gardens lake you can get hot dogs, potato chips, candy bars, soft drinks, and beer at prices lower than those charged by most street vendors.

Walk north to Constitution Avenue and head east. The stone
❼ **lock keeper's house** at the corner of Constitution Avenue and 17th Street is the only remaining monument to Washington's short, unsuccessful experiment with a canal. L'Enfant's design called for a canal to be dug from the Tiber—a branch of the Potomac that extended from where the Lincoln Memorial is now —across the city to the Capitol and then south to the Anacostia River. (L'Enfant even envisioned the president riding in a ceremonial barge from the White House to the Capitol.) The City Canal became more nuisance than convenience, and by the Civil War it was a foul-smelling cesspool that often overran its banks. The stone building at this corner was the home of the canal's lockkeeper until the 1870s, when the waterway was covered over with B Street, which was renamed Constitution Avenue in 1932.

The nearest Metro station is Federal Triangle, five blocks to the east on 12th Street.

## Tour 3: The White House

*Numbers in the margin correspond with points of interest on the White House Area map.*

In a city full of immediately recognizable images, perhaps none is more familiar than the White House. This is where the buck stops and where the nation turns in times of crisis. On this tour we'll visit the White House, then strike out into the surrounding streets to explore the president's neighborhood, which includes some of the oldest houses in the city.

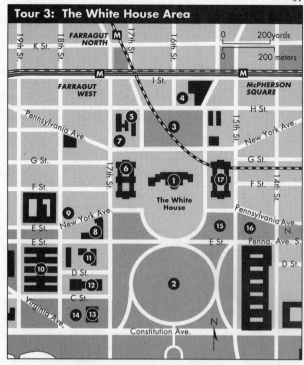

**Tour 3: The White House Area**

To reach the start of our tour, take the Metro to the McPherson Square station. We'll begin our exploration in front of 1600 Pennsylvania Avenue. Pierre L'Enfant called it the President's House; it was known formally as the Executive Mansion; and in 1902 Congress officially proclaimed it the **White House,** though, contrary to popular belief, it had been given that nickname even before it was painted to cover the fire damage it suffered during the War of 1812. Irishman James Hoban's plan, based on the Georgian design of Leinster Hall near Dublin and of other Irish country homes, was selected in a contest, in 1792. The building wasn't ready for its first occupant until 1800, so George Washington never lived here. Completed in 1829, it has undergone many structural changes since then: Thomas Jefferson, who had entered his own design in the contest under an assumed name, added terraces to the east and west wings. Andrew Jackson installed running water. James Garfield put in the first elevator. Between 1948 and 1952 Harry Truman had the entire structure gutted and restored, adding a second-story porch to the south portico. Each family that has called the White House home has left its imprint on the 132-room mansion. Most recently, George Bush installed a horseshoe pit.

Tuesday through Saturday morning, from 10 AM to noon, selected public rooms on the ground floor and first floor of the White House are open to visitors. Expect a long line, but the wait is worthwhile if you're interested in a firsthand look at what is perhaps the most important building in the city. During the summer, you'll need tickets to tour the mansion. The blue-and-green ticket booth is on the **Ellipse** just south of the White House and is open between 8 AM and noon, Tuesday through Saturday, dispensing free tickets on a first-come, first-served basis. (Tickets are often gone by 9 AM.) Your ticket will show the approximate time of your tour. There is seating on the Ellipse for those waiting to see the White House. Volunteer marching bands, drill teams, and other musical groups usually perform here, entertaining those who are stuck in line. If you write your representative or senator's office well in advance of your trip, you can receive special VIP passes for tours between 8 and 10 AM. On selected weekends in April and October, the White House is open for garden tours.

You'll enter the White House through the East Wing lobby on the ground floor, walking past the Jacqueline Kennedy Rose Garden. Your first stop is the large white-and-gold **East Room,** the site of presidential news conferences. In 1814 Dolley Madison saved the room's full-length portrait of George Washington from torch-carrying British soldiers by cutting it from its frame, rolling it up, and spiriting it out of the White House. (No fool she, Dolley also rescued her own portrait.) A later occupant, Teddy Roosevelt, allowed his children to ride their pet pony in the East Room.

The Federal-style **Green Room,** named for the moss-green watered silk that covers its walls, is used for informal receptions and "photo opportunities" with foreign heads of state. Notable furnishings in this room include a New England sofa that once belonged to Daniel Webster and portraits of Benjamin Franklin, John Quincy Adams, and Abigail Adams. The president and his guests are often shown on TV sitting in front of the Green Room's English Empire mantel, engaging in what are invariably described as "frank and cordial" discussions.

The elliptical **Blue Room,** the most formal space in the White House, is furnished with a gilded Empire-style settee and chairs that were ordered by James Monroe. (Monroe asked for plain wooden chairs, but the furniture manufacturer thought such unadorned furnishings too simple for the White House and took it upon himself to supply chairs more in keeping with their surroundings.) The White House Christmas tree is placed in this room each year. Another well-known elliptical room, the president's **Oval Office,** is in the semi-detached West Wing of the White House, along with other executive offices.

The **Red Room** is decorated as an American Empire–style parlor of the early 19th century, with furniture by the New York cabinetmaker Charles-Honoré Lannuier. You'll recognize the marble mantel as the twin of the mantel in the Green Room.

The **State Dining Room,** second in size only to the East Room, can seat 140 guests. The room is dominated by G.P.A. Healy's portrait of Abraham Lincoln, painted after the president's death. The stone mantel is inscribed with a quotation from one of John Adams's letters: "I pray heaven to bestow the best of blessings on this house and all that shall hereafter inhabit it. May none but honest and wise men ever rule under this roof." In Teddy Roosevelt's day a stuffed moose head hung over the mantel. *1600 Pennsylvania Ave. NW, tel. 202/456–7041. Open Tues.–Sat. 10 AM–noon.*

**❸ Lafayette Square,** bordered by Pennsylvania Avenue, Madison Place, H Street, and Jackson Place, is an intimate oasis in the midst of downtown Washington. With such an important resident living across the street, National Capital Park Service

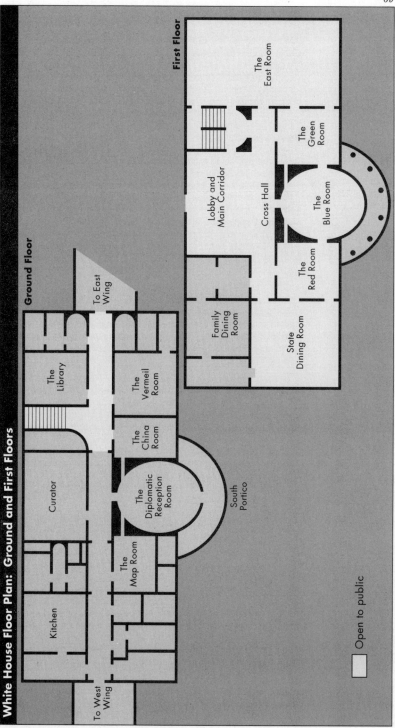

# White House Floor Plan: Ground and First Floors

## Ground Floor

To West Wing

Kitchen

Curator

The Library

To East Wing

The Map Room

The Diplomatic Reception Room

The China Room

The Vermeil Room

South Portico

## First Floor

Lobby and Main Corridor

Cross Hall

Family Dining Room

State Dining Room

The Red Room

The Blue Room

The Green Room

The East Room

Open to public

gardeners lavish extra attention on the square's trees and flower beds.

When George Washington proposed the location for the Executive Mansion, the only building north of Pennsylvania Avenue was the Pierce family farmhouse, which stood at the northeast corner of what is today Lafayette Square. An apple orchard and a family burial ground were the area's two other main features. During the construction of the White House, workers' huts and a brick kiln were set up, and soon private residences began popping up around the square (though sheep would continue to graze on it for years). L'Enfant's original plan for the city designated this area as part of "President's Park"; in essence it was the president's front yard, just as what is now the Ellipse was once his backyard. The egalitarian Thomas Jefferson, concerned that large, landscaped White House grounds would give the wrong impression in a democratic country, ordered that the area be turned into a public park. Soldiers camped in the square during the War of 1812 and the Civil War, turning it at both times into a muddy pit. Today, protesters set their placards up in Lafayette Square, jockeying for positions that face the White House. While the National Park Service can't restrict the protesters' freedom of speech, it does try to restrict the size of their signs.

Standing in the center of the park—and dominating the square —is a large **statue of Andrew Jackson.** Erected in 1853 and cast from bronze cannon that Jackson had captured during the War of 1812, this was the first equestrian statue made in America. (An exact duplicate faces St. Louis Cathedral in New Orleans' Jackson Square.)

Jackson's is the only statue of an American in the park. The other statues are of foreign-born soldiers who helped in America's fight for independence. In the southeast corner is the park's namesake, the **Marquis de Lafayette,** the young French nobleman who came to America to fight in the Revolution. When Lafayette returned to the United States in 1824 he was given a rousing welcome: He was wined and dined in the finest homes and showered with gifts of cash and land. (You can imagine how this must have made his countryman Pierre L'Enfant feel. The designer of the city Lafayette took by storm had by that time been forgotten.)

Head north on **Madison Place.** The colonnaded building across the street at the corner of Pennsylvania Avenue is an annex to the Treasury Department. The modern red-brick building at 717 Madison Place houses a variety of judicial offices. Its design—with the squared-off bay windows—is echoed in the taller building that rises behind it and is mirrored in the **New Executive Office Building** on the other side of Lafayette Square. Planners in the '20s recommended that the private homes on Lafayette Square, many built in the Federal period, be torn down and replaced with a collection of uniform neoclassical-style government buildings. A lack of funds kept the neighborhood intact, and in the '60s John and Jacqueline Kennedy worked to save the historic town houses.

The next house down, yellow with a second-story ironwork balcony, was built in 1828 by Benjamin Ogle Tayloe (son of the man who built Octagon House, described below). During the McKinley administration, Ohio Senator Marcus Hanna lived here, and the president's frequent visits earned it the nickname the "Little White House." Dolley Madison lived in the next-door Cutts-Madison House after her husband died. Both the Tayloe and Madison houses are now part of the Federal Judicial Center.

Continue down Madison Place. The next statue is that of **Thaddeus Kosciuszko,** the Polish general who fought alongside American colonists against the British. If you head east on H Street for half a block, you'll come to the **United States Government Bookstore** (1510 H St. NW, tel. 202/635–5075), the place to visit if you'd like to buy a few pounds of the millions of tons of paper the government churns out each year. Here is where you'll find a copy of the latest Federal budget or *The Surgeon General's Report on Nutrition and Health.*

**Time Out** Presidential advisor Bernard Baruch used to eat his lunch in Lafayette Park, and you can too. **Loeb's Restaurant** (around the corner at 15th and I Streets NW) is a New York-style deli that serves up salads and sandwiches to eat there or to go.

**4** On H Street is the golden-domed **St. John's Episcopal Church,** the so-called "Church of the Presidents." Every president since Madison has visited the church, and many worshipped here on a regular basis. Built in 1816, the church was the second building on the square. Benjamin Latrobe, who worked on both the Capitol and the White House, designed it in the form of a Greek cross, with a flat dome and a lantern cupola. The church has been altered somewhat since then; later additions include the Doric portico and the cupola tower. You can best sense the intent of Latrobe's design while standing inside under the saucer-shaped dome of the original building. Not far from the center of the church is pew 54, where visiting presidents are seated. The kneelers of many of the pews are embroidered with the presidential seal and the names of several chief executives. Brochures are available inside for those who would like to take a self-guided tour. *16th and H streets. NW, tel. 202/347–8766. Open Mon.–Sat. 8–4. Tours by appointment Sun. after 11 AM service.*

Just east of the church is the four-story **St. John's Parish House,** built in 1836 by Matthew St. Clair Clark, clerk of the House of Representatives. The house's most famous resident was Lord Alexander Baring Ashburton, the British Minister who lived here in 1842 while negotiating a dispute over the position of the U.S.-Canadian border. The house later served as the British legation.

Across 16th Street stands the **Hay-Adams Hotel,** one of the most opulent hostelries in the city and a favorite with Washington insiders and visiting celebrities. It takes its name from a double house, owned by Lincoln biographer John Hay and historian Henry Adams, that stood on this spot. Next to it is the **Chamber of Commerce of the United States,** its neoclassical facade typical of the type of building that might have surrounded Lafayette Park had JFK not intervened. The statue at the northwest corner of Lafayette Square is of **Baron von Steuben,** the Prussian general who drilled Colonial troops during the Revolution.

**5** The red-brick, Federal-style **Decatur House** on the corner of H Street and Jackson Place was the first private residence on

President's Park (the White House doesn't really count as *private*). Designed by Benjamin Latrobe, the house was built for naval hero Stephen Decatur and his wife Susan in 1819. Decatur had earned the affection of the nation in battles against the British and the Barbary pirates. Planning to start a political career, he used the prize money Congress awarded him to build this home near the White House. Tragically, only 14 months after he moved in, Decatur was killed in a duel with James Barron, a disgruntled former Navy officer who held Decatur responsible for his court-martial. Later occupants of the house included Henry Clay, Martin Van Buren, and the Beales, a prominent family from the West whose modifications of the building include a parquet floor showing the state seal of California. The house is now operated by the National Trust. The first floor is furnished as it was in Decatur's time. The second floor is furnished in the Victorian style favored by the Beale family, who owned it until 1956 (the Decatur House was thus the first and *last* private residence on Lafayette Square). The National Trust store around the corner (entrance on H Street) sells a variety of books, postcards, and gifts. *748 Jackson Place NW, tel. 202/842–0920. Open Tues.–Fri. 10–2; Sat. and Sun. 12–4. Admission: $3 adults, $1.50 seniors and students under 18, free to National Trust members. Tours on the hour and half hour.*

Head south on **Jackson Place.** Many of the row houses on this stretch date from the pre–Civil War or Victorian periods; even the more modern additions, though—such as those at 718 and 726—are designed in a style that blends with their more historic neighbors. **Count Rochambeau,** aide to General Lafayette, is honored with a statue at the park's southwest corner.

**❻** Directly across Pennsylvania Avenue, to the right of the White House, is the **Old Executive Office Building,** which has gone from being one of the most detested buildings in the city to one of the most beloved. It was built between 1871 and 1888 and originally housed the War, Navy, and State departments. Its architect, Alfred B. Mullett, patterned it after the Louvre, but detractors quickly criticized the busy French Empire design—with its mansard roof, tall chimneys, and 900 freestanding columns—as an inappropriate counterpoint to the Greek Revival Treasury Building that sits on the other side of the White House. Numerous plans to alter the facade foundered due to lack of money. The granite edifice may look like a wedding cake, but its high ceilings and spacious offices make it popular with occupants, who currently include the vice president, the Office of Management and Budget, the National Security Council, and other agencies of the executive branch. This building has played host to numerous historical events. It was here that Secretary of State Cordell Hull met with Japanese diplomats after the bombing of Pearl Harbor, and it was here that Oliver North and Fawn Hall shredded Iran-Contra documents.

The green canopy at 1651 Pennsylvania Avenue marks the entrance to **Blair House,** the residence used by heads of state visiting Washington. Harry S. Truman lived here from 1948 to 1952, while the White House was undergoing its much-needed renovation. A plaque on the fence honors White House policeman Leslie Coffelt, who died in 1950 when Puerto Rican separatists attempted to assassinate President Truman at this site.

Continue west on Pennsylvania Avenue. At the end of the block, with the motto "Dedicated to Art" engraved above the entrance, is the **Renwick Gallery.** The French Second Empire-style building was designed by Smithsonian Castle architect James Renwick in 1859 to house the art collection of Washington merchant and banker William Wilson Corcoran, founder of Riggs Bank. Corcoran was a Southern sympathizer who spent the duration of the Civil War in Europe. While he was away his unfinished building was pressed into service by the government. When the Corcoran finally opened in 1874 it was the first private art museum in the city. The gallery's Grand Salon at the top of the central stairway was furnished in an opulent Victorian style, with paintings hung in tiers, one atop the other. The Octagon Room, at the south end of the second floor, was built to display Hiram Powers's sculpture *The Greek Slave.* The statue—a nude woman with her wrists chained—was considered so shocking that separate viewing hours were established for men and women, and children under 16 were not allowed to see it at all. Corcoran's collection quickly outgrew the building and in 1897 was moved to a new gallery a few blocks south on 17th Street (described below). After a stint as the U.S. Court of Claims, this building was restored to its former glory, renamed after its architect, and opened as the Smithsonian's museum of American decorative arts in 1972. The collection covers a wide range of disciplines and styles; special exhibits have included such items as blown glass, Shaker furniture, and contemporary crafts. *Pennsylvania Ave. and 17th St. NW, tel. 202/357–2700. Open daily 10–5:30.*

Head south on 17th Street. You'll pass the **Winder Building** (604 17th St.), erected in 1848 as one of the first office blocks in the capital and used during the Civil War as the headquarters of the Union Army. Down another block on the right, at the corner of 17th Street and New York Avenue, is the **Corcoran Gallery of Art,** one of the few large museums in Washington outside the Smithsonian family. The Beaux Arts–style building, its copper roof green with age, was designed by Ernest Flagg and completed in 1897. The gallery's permanent collection numbers more than 11,000 works, including paintings by the first great American portraitists John Copley, Gilbert Stuart, and Rembrandt Peale. The Hudson River School is represented by such works as *Mount Corcoran* by Albert Bierstadt and Frederic Church's *Niagara.* There are also portraits by Sargent, Eakins, and Mary Cassatt. European artwork is included in the Walker Collection (late 19th- and early 20th-century paintings, including works by Gustave Courbet, Monet, Pissarro, and Renoir) and the Clark Collection (Dutch, Flemish, and French Romantic paintings, and works from the 18th-century Grand Salon of the Hotel d'Orsay in Paris). Also be sure to see Samuel Morse's *The Old House of Representatives* and Hiram Powers's *The Greek Slave,* which scandalized Victorian society. The adjacent Corcoran School is the only four-year art college in the Washington area. *17th St. and New York Ave. NW, tel. 202/638–1439 (recording), 202/638–3211. Open Tues.–Sat. 10–4:30, Thurs. 10–9. Closed Mon., Christmas, and New Year's Day.*

A block up New York Avenue, at the corner of 18th Street, is the **Octagon House,** built in 1801 for John Tayloe III, a wealthy Virginia plantation owner. Designed by William Thornton, the Octagon House actually has only six sides, not eight. Thornton chose the unusual shape to conform to the acute angle formed by L'Enfant's intersection of New York Avenue and 18th Street.

After the White House was burned in 1814 the Tayloes invited James and Dolley Madison to stay in the Octagon House. It was in a second-floor study that the Treaty of Ghent, ending the War of 1812, was signed. By the late 1800s the building was used as a rooming house. In this century the house served as the headquarters of the American Institute of Architects before the construction of AIA's rather unexceptional building behind it. In the '60s, Octagon House was restored to its former splendor, with detailed plaster molding around the ceilings, coal-burning stoves in the entryway, and the original 1799 Coade stone mantels (made using a now-lost method of casting crushed stone). Exhibits relating to architecture, decorative arts, and Washington history are mounted in the upstairs galies. *1799 New York Ave. NW, tel. 202/638–3105. Open Tues.–Fri. 10–4, Sat. and Sun. 1–4. Admission: $2 adults, $1.50 seniors, $1 children.*

**⑩** A block south on 18th Street is the **Department of the Interior** building, designed by Waddy B. Wood. At the time of its construction in 1937 it was the most modern federal building in the city and the first with escalators and central air-conditioning. While the outside of the building is somewhat plain, much of the interior is decorated with paintings that reflect the Interior Department's work. Hallways feature heroic oil paintings of dam construction, panning for gold, and cattle drives. You'll pass some of these if you visit the **Department of the Interior Museum** on the first floor. (You can enter the building at its E Street or C Street doors.) Soon after it opened in 1938, the museum became one of the most popular attractions in Washington; evening hours were maintained even during the Second World War. While some of the displays seem a bit dated —such as one that outlines "vital products derived from the range," including clock cords, emery cloth, hat sweatbands, and isinglass—this snapshot from the '30s is a welcome contrast to the high-tech, interactive video museums of today. Especially appealing are the meticulously created dioramas depicting various historical events and American locales, including a 1938 animated scene of Juneau, Alaska, complete with tiny train cars moving on a track. The Indian Craft Shop across the hall from the museum sells Native American pottery, dolls, carvings, jewelry, baskets, and books. It, too, has been part of the Department of the Interior since 1938. *C and E sts. between 18th and 19th sts. NW, tel. 202/343–2743. Open Mon.–Fri. 8–4.*

**⑪** Back on 17th Street (walk east on E Street) are the three buildings that house the headquarters of the **American Red Cross.** The main building, a neoclassical structure of blinding white marble built in 1917, commemorates the service and devotion of the women who cared for the wounded on both sides during the Civil War. The building's Georgian-style board of governors hall features three stained-glass windows designed by Louis Tiffany. *431 17th St. NW, tel. 202/737–8300. Open Mon.–Fri. 9–4.*

**⑫** A block south is **Memorial Continental Hall,** headquarters of the Daughters of the American Revolution. This Beaux-Arts building was the site each year of the D.A.R.'s congress until the larger Constitution Hall was built around the corner. An entrance on D Street leads to the **D.A.R. Museum.** Its 50,000-item collection includes fine examples of Colonial and Federal silver, china, porcelain, stoneware, earthenware, and glass. Thirty-three period rooms are decorated in styles representative of various U.S. states, ranging from an 1850 California adobe parlor to a New Hampshire attic filled with toys from the 18th and 19th centuries. *1776 D St. NW, tel. 202/879–3240. Open Mon.–Fri. 8:30–4, Sun. 1–5.*

Just across C Street to the south of Continental Hall is the **❸ House of the Americas,** the headquarters building of the Organization of American States. The interior of this building features a cool patio adorned with a pre-Columbian–style fountain and lush tropical plants. This tiny rain forest is a good place to rest when Washington's summer heat is at its most oppressive. The upstairs Hall of Flags and Heroes contains, as the name implies, busts of generals and statesmen from the various OAS member countries as well as each country's flag.

**❹** Behind the House of the Americas is the **Museum of Modern Art of Latin America,** with its entrance on 18th Street. The small gallery—the world's first devoted to art of this region—is in a building that formerly served as the residence for the secretary general of the OAS. *201 18th St. NW, tel. 202/789–6016. Open Tues.–Sat. 10–5.*

Next, head east on Constitution Avenue and take the first left, following the curving drive that encircles the Ellipse. The rather weather-beaten **gate house** at the corner of Constitution Avenue and 17th Street once stood on Capitol Hill. It was designed in 1828 by Charles Bulfinch, the first native-born American to serve as Architect of the Capitol, and was moved here in 1874 after the Capitol grounds were redesigned by Frederick Law Olmsted. A twin of the gatehouse stands at Constitution Avenue and 15th Street.

The **Ellipse** is bounded by Constitution Avenue, E Street, 15th Street, and 17th Street. From this vantage point you can see the Washington Monument and the Jefferson Memorial to the south and the red-tile roof of the Department of Commerce to the east, with the tower of the Old Post Office Building sticking up above it. To the north you have a good view of the back of the White House; the rounded portico and Harry Truman's second-story porch are clearly visible. The south lawn of the White House serves as a heliport for "Marine One," the president's helicopter. Each Monday after Easter the south lawn is also the scene of the White House Easter Egg Roll. The National Christmas Tree is set up each year in late November on the northern edge of the Ellipse and lighted by the president during a festive ceremony that marks the beginning of the year-end holiday season.

Across E Street to the northeast of the Ellipse, in a small park bounded by E Street, 15th Street, Treasury Place, and South **❺** Executive Place, stands the massive **William Tecumseh Sherman Monument.** Just north of this memorial is the southern facade of the Treasury Building, its entrance guarded by a **statue of Alexander Hamilton,** the department's first secretary.

**❻** Across 15th Street to the east is **Pershing Park,** a quiet, sunken garden that honors General "Blackjack" Pershing, commander of the American expeditionary force in World War I. Engravings on the stone walls recount pivotal campaigns from that war. Ice skaters glide on the square pool in the winter.

One block to the north is the venerable **Hotel Washington** (515 15th St.). Its lobby is narrow and unassuming, but the view from the rooftop Sky Top Lounge is one of the best in the city.

**17** To your left is the long side of the **Treasury Building,** the largest Greek Revival edifice in Washington. Pierre L'Enfant had intended for Pennsylvania Avenue to stretch in a straight, unbroken line from the White House to the Capitol. This plan was ruined by the construction of the Treasury building on this site just east of the White House. Designed by Robert Mills, the Treasury was constructed between 1836 and 1851.

Continue up 15th Street. The luxurious **Old Ebbitt Grill** (675 15th St. NW, tel. 202/347–4800) is a popular watering spot for journalists and television news correspondents.

The corner of 15th Street and Pennsylvania Avenue has been dubbed Washington's Wall Street. Adjacent to the imposing Treasury are brokerage firms and buildings belonging to Riggs Bank, American Security Bank, and Crestar Bank. American Security Bank likes to boast in its commercials that it's "Right on the money"—"the money" in this case being a $10 dollar bill. If you look at the back of one you'll see the Treasury Building and to its right the tiny American Security bank building. The Riggs Bank (next door) has an even more immodest advertising slogan: It calls itself "The most important bank in the most important city in the world." Washingtonians probably wouldn't argue about the second assertion.

The Metro stations nearest to the end of this tour are McPherson Square, two blocks north to 15th Street and a block to the west on I Street, and Metro Center, three blocks east on G Street.

---

**Tour 4: Capitol Hill**

*Numbers in the margin correspond with points of interest on the Capitol Hill map.*

The people who live and work on "the Hill" do so in the shadow of the edifice that lends the neighborhood its name: the gleaming white Capitol building. More than just the center of government, however, the Hill also includes charming residential blocks lined with Victorian row houses and a fine assortment of restaurants, bars, and shops. Capitol Hill's boundaries are disputed: It's bordered to the west, north, and south by the Capitol, Union Station, and I Street respectively. Some argue that Capitol Hill extends east to the Anacostia River, others that it ends at 11th Street near Lincoln Park. The neighborhood does in fact seem to grow as members of Capitol Hill's active historic-preservation movement restore more and more 19th-century houses.

**1** Start your exploration of the Hill inside the cavernous main hall of **Union Station,** which sits on Massachusetts Avenue north of the Capitol. In 1902 the McMillan Commission—charged with suggesting ways to improve the appearance of the city—recommended that the many train lines that sliced through the capital share one main depot. Union Station was opened in 1908 and was the first building completed under the Commission's

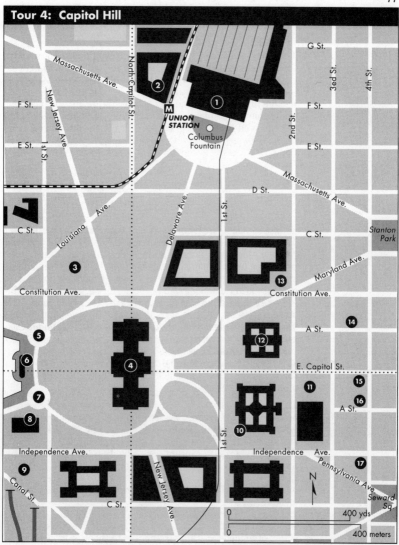

# Tour 4: Capitol Hill

Bartholdi Fountain, **9**
Capitol, **4**
Capitol Hill
Presbyterian
Church, **17**
City Post Office, **2**
Folger Shakespeare
Library, **11**

Frederick Douglass
Townhouse, **14**
Grant Memorial, **6**
James Garfield
Memorial, **7**
Library of
Congress, **10**
Peace Monument, **5**
Sewall-Belmont
House, **13**

South side of East
Capitol Street, **15**
Supreme Court
Building, **12**
Taft Memorial, **3**
326 A Street, **16**
Union Station, **1**
United States Botanic
Garden, **8**

plan. Chicago architect and commission member Daniel H.
Burnham patterned the station after the Roman Baths of
Diocletian.

For many visitors to Washington, the capital city is first seen
framed through the grand station's arched doorways. In its
heyday, during World War II, more than 200,000 people
swarmed through the station daily. By the '60s, however, the
decline in train travel had turned the station into an expensive
white-marble elephant. It was briefly, and unsuccessfully,
transformed into a visitors center for the Bicentennial; but by
1981 rain was pouring in through the neglected station's roof,
and passengers boarded trains at a ramshackle depot behind
the station.

The Union Station you see today is the result of a restoration
completed in 1988, an effort intended to be the beginning of a
revival of Washington's east end. It's hoped the shops, restaurants, and nine-screen movie theater in Union Station will
draw more than just train travelers to the Beaux Arts building.
The jewel of the structure remains its meticulously restored
main waiting room. With its 96-foot-high coffered ceiling gilded
with eight pounds of gold leaf, it is one of the city's great spaces
and is used for inaugural balls and other festive events. Forty-
six statues of Roman legionnaires, one for each state in the Union when the station was completed, ring the grand room. The
statues were the subject of controversy when the building was
first opened. Pennsylvania Railroad president Alexander Cassatt (brother of artist Mary) ordered sculptor Louis Saint-
Gaudens to alter the statues, convinced that the legionnaires'
skimpy outfits would scandalize female passengers. The sculptor obligingly added a shield to each figure, obscuring any
offending body parts.

The east hall, now filled with vendors, was once an expensive
restaurant. It is decorated with Pompeiian tracery and plaster
walls and columns painted to look like marble. At one time the
station also featured a secure presidential waiting room, now
the Adirondacks Restaurant. The private waiting room was by
no means a frivolous addition: Twenty years before Union Station was built, President Garfield was assassinated in the
public waiting room of the old Baltimore and Potomac terminal
on 6th Street.

---

**Time Out**     On Union Station's lower level you'll find more than 20 food
stalls, offering everything from pizza to sushi. A little less fre-
netic is the **American Cafe,** a Capitol Hill favorite, on the main
floor.

---

As you walk out Union Station's front doors, glance to the
right. At the end of a long succession of archways is the Wash-
**❷** ington **City Post Office,** also designed by Daniel Burnham and
completed in 1914. Nostalgic odes to the noble mail carrier are
inscribed on the exterior of the marble building; one of them
characterizes the mailman as "Messenger of sympathy and
love, servant of parted friends, consoler of the lonely, bond of
the scattered family, enlarger of the common life." While the
interior of the post office is now fitted with rather tacky veneer
counters, the modernization has left untouched the gray-green
marble columns in the east and west entryways and the decorative plaster ceilings in those two lobbies. Also attractive are the

bronze window screens from behind which postal employees once dispensed stamps.

Return to Union Station and walk to the plaza in front. At the center of the plaza is the **Columbus Memorial Fountain,** designed by Lorado Taft. A caped, steely-eyed Christopher Columbus stares into the distance, flanked by a hoary, bearded figure (the Old World) and an Indian brave (the New).

Head south from the fountain, away from Union Station, cross Massachusetts Avenue, and walk down Delaware Avenue. On the left you'll pass the **Russell Senate Office Building.** Note the delicate treatment below the second-story windows that resembles twisted lengths of fringed cloth. Completed in 1909, this was the first of the senate office buildings. Beyond it are the Dirksen and Hart office buildings. To the right, sticking up above the trees, is a memorial to **Robert A. Taft,** son of the 27th president and longtime Republican senator. The monolithic carillon is rather unattractive, resembling nothing so much as a huge room deodorizer.

❹ Cross Constitution Avenue and enter the **Capitol** grounds, landscaped in the late-19th century by Frederick Law Olmsted, Sr., who, along with Calvert Vaux, created New York City's Central Park. On these 68 acres you will find both the tamest squirrels in the city and the highest concentration of television news correspondents, jockeying for a good position in front of the Capitol for their "stand-ups." A few hundred feet northeast of the Capitol are two cast-iron car shelters, left over from the days when horse-drawn trolleys served the Hill. Olmsted's six pinkish, bronze-topped lamps directly east from the Capitol are a treat, too.

When planning the city, Pierre L'Enfant described the gentle rise on which the Capitol sits, known then as Jenkins Hill, as "a pedestal waiting for a monument." The design of this monument was the result of a competition held in 1792; the winner was William Thornton, a physician and amateur architect from the West Indies. With its central rotunda and dome, Thornton's Capitol is reminiscent of Rome's Pantheon, a similarity that must have delighted the Nation's founders, who felt the American government was based on the principles of the Republic of Rome.

The cornerstone was laid by George Washington in a Masonic ceremony on September 18, 1793, and in November 1800, both the Senate and the House of Representatives moved down from Philadelphia to occupy the first completed section of the Capitol: the boxlike portion between the central rotunda and today's north wing. (Subsequent efforts to find the cornerstone Washington laid have been unsuccessful, though when the east front was extended in the 1950s, workmen found a knee joint thought to be from a 500-pound ox that was roasted at the 1793 celebration.) By 1806 the House wing had been completed, just to the south of what is now the domed center, and a covered wooden walkway joined the two wings.

The Congress House grew slowly and suffered a grave setback on August 24, 1814, when British troops led by Sir George Cockburn marched on Washington and set fire to the Capitol and numerous other government buildings. (Cockburn reportedly stood on the House Speaker's chair and asked his men, "Shall this harbor of Yankee democracy be burned?" The ques-

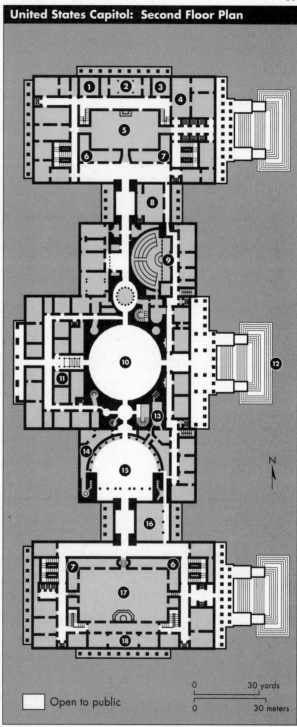

**United States Capitol: Second Floor Plan**

Ceremonial Office of the Vice President, **3**

Congresswomen's Suite, **13**

Democratic Cloakrooms, **6**

East Front, **12**

House Chamber, **17**

House Document Room, **14**

House Reception Room, **16**

Marble Room (Senators' Retiring Room), **2**

Old Senate Chamber, **9**

Prayer Room, **11**

President's Room, **1**

Senate Chamber, **5**

Senators' Conference Room, **8**

Senators' Reception Room, **4**

Statuary Hall, **15**

Representatives' Retiring Rooms, **18**

Republican Cloakrooms, **7**

Rotunda, **10**

N

0          30 yards

0          30 meters

Open to public

tion was rhetorical; the building was torched.) The wooden walkway was destroyed and the two wings gutted, but the walls were left standing after a violent rainstorm doused the flames. Fearful that Congress might leave Washington, residents raised money for a hastily built "Brick Capitol" that stood where the Supreme Court is today. Architect Benjamin Henry Latrobe supervised the rebuilding of the Capitol, adding such American touches as the corn-cob-and-tobacco-leaf capitals to columns in the east entrance to the Senate wing. He was followed by Boston-born Charles Bulfinch, and in 1826 the Capitol, its low wooden dome sheathed in copper, was finally finished.

North and south wings were added in the 1850s and '60s to accommodate a growing government trying to keep pace with a growing country. The elongated edifice extended farther north and south than Thornton had planned, and in 1855, to keep the scale correct, work began on a tall cast-iron dome. President Lincoln was criticized for continuing this expensive project while the country was in the throes of the bloody Civil War, but he called the construction "a sign we intend the Union shall go on." This twin-shelled dome, a marvel of 19th-century engineering, rises 285 feet above the ground and weighs 9 million pounds. It expands and contracts up to four inches a day, depending on the outside temperature. The figure on top of the dome, often mistaken for Pocahontas, is called *Freedom*. Sculptor Thomas Crawford had first planned for the 19-foot-tall bronze statue to wear the cloth liberty cap of a freed Roman slave, but southern lawmakers, led by Jefferson Davis, objected. An "American" headdress composed of a star-encircled helmet surmounted with an eagle's head and feathers was substituted. The statue has deteriorated badly over the years, and if it hasn't been removed on your visit to Washington it may soon be. There are plans to take it down for restoration.

The Capitol has continued to grow. In 1962 the east front was extended 34 feet, creating 100 additional offices. Preservationists have fought to keep the west front from being extended, since it is the last remaining section of the Capitol's original facade. A compromise was reached in 1983, when it was agreed that the facade's crumbling sandstone blocks would simply be replaced with stronger limestone.

Guided tours of the Capitol usually start beneath the dome in the Rotunda, but if there's a crowd you may have to wait in a line that forms at the top of the center steps on the east side. If you want to forgo the tour, which is brief but informative, you may look around on your own. Enter through one of the lower doors to the right or left of the main steps. Start your exploration under Constantino Brumidi's *Apotheosis of Washington*, the fresco in the center of the dome. Working as Michelangelo did in the Sistine Chapel, applying paint to wet plaster, Brumidi completed this fresco in 1865. The figures in the inner circle represent the 13 original states of the Union; those in the outer ring symbolize arts, sciences, and industry. The flat, sculpture-style frieze around the rim of the Rotunda depicting 400 years of American history was started by Brumidi. While painting Penn's treaty with the Indians, the 74-year-old artist slipped on the 58-foot-high scaffold and almost fell off. Brumidi managed to hang on until help arrived, but he died a few months later from shock brought on by the incident. The work was continued by another Italian, Filippo Costaggini, but the frieze wasn't finished until American Allyn Cox added the final touches in 1953.

Notice the Rotunda's eight immense oil paintings of scenes from American history. The four scenes from the Revolutionary War are by John Trumbull, who served alongside George Washington and painted the first president from life. Twenty-six people have lain in state in the Rotunda, including nine presidents, from Abraham Lincoln to Lyndon Baines Johnson. Underneath the Rotunda, above an empty crypt that was designed to hold the remains of George and Martha Washington, is an exhibit chronicling the construction of the Capitol.

South of the Rotunda is Statuary Hall, once the legislative chamber of the House of Representatives. The room has an interesting architectural feature that maddened early legislators: A slight whisper uttered on one side of the hall can be heard on the other. (Don't be disappointed if this parlor trick doesn't work when you're visiting the Capitol; sometimes the hall is just too noisy.) When the House moved out, Congress invited each state to send statues of two great deceased citizens for placement in the former chamber. Because the weight of the accumulated statues threatened to cave the floor in, some of the sculptures were dispersed to various other spots throughout the Capitol.

To the north, on the Senate side, you can visit the chamber once used by the Supreme Court as well as the splendid Old Senate Chamber, both of which have been restored. Also be sure to see the Brumidi Corridor on the ground floor of the senate wing. Frescoes and oil paintings of birds, plants, and American inventions adorn the walls and ceilings, and an intricate, Brumidi-designed bronze stairway leads to the second floor. The Italian artist also memorialized several American heroes, painting them inside trompe l'oeil frames. Trusting that America would continue to produce heroes long after he was gone, Brumidi left some frames empty. The most recent one to be filled, in 1987, honors the crew of the space shuttle Challenger.

If you want to watch some of the legislative action in the **House** or **Senate chambers** while you're on the Hill you'll have to get a gallery pass from the office of your representative or senator. (To find out where those offices are, ask any Capitol police officer, or dial 202/224–3121.) In the chambers you'll notice that Democrats sit to the right of the presiding officer, Republicans to the left—the opposite, it's often noted, of their political leanings. You may be disappointed by watching from the gallery. Most of the day-to-day business is conducted in the various legislative committees, many of which meet in the Congressional office buildings. The *Washington Post*'s daily "Today in Congress" lists when and where the committees are meeting. To get to a house or senate office building, go to the Capitol's basement and ride the miniature subway used by legislators. *East end of the Mall, tel. 202/224–3121. Open daily 9–4:30, 9–8 in summer.*

**Time Out**  A meal at a **Capitol cafeteria** may give you a glimpse of a well-known politician or two. A public dining room on the first floor, Senate-side, is open from 7:30 AM to 4:30 PM when Congress is in session, 7:30 to 3:30 at other times. A favorite with legislators is the Senate bean soup, made and served everyday since 1901 (no one is sure exactly why, though the menu, which you can take with you, outlines a few popular theories).

When you're finished exploring the inside of the Capitol, make your way to the **west side.** In 1981, Ronald Reagan broke with tradition and moved the presidential swearing-in ceremony to this side of the Capitol, which offers a dramatic view of the Mall and monuments below and can accommodate more guests than the east side, where all previous presidents were sworn in. Walk down the northernmost flight of steps and follow the red-and-black path that leads to Pennsylvania Avenue. The white-marble memorial in the center of the traffic circle in front of you **⑤** is the **Peace Monument,** which depicts America, grief-stricken over sailors lost at sea, weeping on the shoulder of History. Cross First Street carefully and walk to the left along the **Capi-** **⑥** **tol Reflecting Pool.** As you continue south you'll pass the **Grant Memorial.** At a length of 252 feet, it's the largest sculpture group in the city. The statue of Ulysses S. Grant on horseback is flanked by Union artillery and cavalry. Further south, in the intersection of First Street and Maryland Avenue SW, is the **⑦** **James Garfield Memorial.** The 20th president of the United States, Garfield was assassinated in 1881 after only a few months in office.

**⑧** Across Maryland Avenue is the **United States Botanic Garden,** a peaceful, plant-filled oasis between Capitol Hill and the Mall. The conservatory includes a cactus house, a fern house, and a subtropical house filled with orchids. Seasonal displays include blooming plants at Easter, chrysanthemums in the fall, and Christmas greens and poinsettias in December and January. Brochures just inside the doorway offer helpful gardening tips. *1st St. and Maryland Ave. SW, tel. 202/225–8333. Open Jun.– Aug. daily 9–9; Sept.–May daily 9–5.*

When you exit the Botanic Garden, walk away from the Capitol, take the first left along the pebbled sidewalk, and cross Independence Avenue. To the right is the **Hubert H. Humphrey Building,** home of the Department of Health and Human Services. The beige building gets a much-needed splash of color from *Shorepoints I,* the red abstract sculpture by James Rosati that sits in front of it.

Walk east on Independence Avenue. On the right, in a park **⑨** that is part of the Botanic Garden, you'll pass the **Bartholdi Fountain.** Frédéric-Auguste Bartholdi, sculptor of the more famous—and much larger—Statue of Liberty, created this de-lightful fountain for the Philadelphia Centennial Exhibition of 1876. With its aquatic monsters, sea nymphs, tritons, and lighted globes (once gas, now electric), the fountain represents the elements of water and light. The U.S. government pur-chased the fountain after the exhibition and placed it on the grounds of the old Botanic Garden on the Mall. It was moved to its present location in 1932.

Cross 1st Street SW and continue east on Independence Avenue past the **Rayburn, Longworth,** and **Cannon House office buildings.** At Independence Avenue and 1st Street SE is the **⑩** **Jefferson Building** of the **Library of Congress.** Like many build-ings in Washington that seem a bit overwrought (the Old Ex-ecutive Office Building is another example), the library was criticized when it was completed, in 1897. Some detractors felt its Italian-Renaissance design was a bit too florid. Congressmen were even heard to grumble that its dome competed with that of their Capitol.

Provisions for a library to serve members of Congress were originally made in 1800, when the government set aside $5,000 to purchase and house books that legislators might need to consult. This small collection was housed in the Capitol but was destroyed in 1814, when the British burned the city. Thomas Jefferson, then in retirement at Monticello, offered his personal library as a replacement, noting that "there is, in fact, no subject to which a Member of Congress may not have occasion to refer." Jefferson's collection of 6,487 books, for which Congress eventually paid him $23,950, laid the foundation for the great national library. (Sadly, another fire in 1851 wiped out two-thirds of Jefferson's books.) By the late 1800s it was clear the Capitol building could no longer contain the growing library, and the Jefferson Building was constructed. The **Adams Building,** on 2nd Street behind the Jefferson, was added in 1939. A third structure, the **James Madison Building,** was opened in 1980; it is just south of the Jefferson Building, between Independence Avenue and C Street.

The Library of Congress today holds some 87 million items, of which 27 million are books. Also part of the library is the Congressional Research Service, which, as the name implies, works on special projects for senators and representatives.

The Jefferson Building is in the midst of a seven-year renovation, and you may find parts of it closed. There is much to see on the outside, though. *The Court of Neptune,* Roland Hinton Perry's fountain at the base of the front steps, rivals some of Rome's best fountains. Perched above the library's entryway are busts of Dante, Goethe, Hawthorne, and other great writers. Keystone busts on the second-story windows represent 33 ethnic groups. Many of the decorations on the building symbolize the creative arts: You will see such items as drafting tools, manuscripts, and a multiplicity of artists' palettes carved in the main doorways.

Computer terminals have replaced card catalogs in the **Main Reading Room,** whose central disbursing desk is surrounded by mahogany reader's tables. The Great Hall, outside the Main Reading Room, is adorned with mosaics, cherubs, paintings, and a curving marble stairway. It's said the library's architects didn't plan to have so much artwork inside, but after having brought the building in under budget they decided to spend the balance on decorations. Sections of the library will be closed for renovations at various times throughout 1990. *1st St. and Independence Ave. SE, tel. 202/707–5458. Open Mon.–Fri. 8:30–9, Sat. 8:30–5, Sun. 1–5. Tours Mon.–Fri. 10–3.*

Walk north on 1st Street and turn right onto East Capitol Street. One block east, at the corner of 2nd Street, stands the **⓫ Folger Shakespeare Library.** The Folger Library's collection of works by and about Shakespeare and his times is second to none. The white-marble Art Deco building, designed by architect Paul Philippe Cret, is decorated with scenes from the Bard's plays. Inside is a reproduction of an inn-yard theater and a gallery, designed in the manner of an Elizabethan Great Hall, that hosts rotating exhibits from the library's collection. *201 E. Capitol St. SE, tel. 202/544–4600. Open Mon.–Sat. 10–4.*

Walk back down East Capitol Street and turn right onto 1st
Street. The stolid **Supreme Court Building** faces 1st Street
here. The justices arrived in Washington in 1800 along with the
rest of the government but were for years shunted around various rooms in the Capitol; for a while they even met in a tavern.
It wasn't until 1935 that the Court got its own building, this
white-marble temple with twin rows of Corinthian columns,
designed by Cass Gilbert. William Howard Taft, the only man
to serve as both president and chief justice, was instrumental
in getting the court a home of its own, though he died before it
was completed.

The Supreme Court convenes on the first Monday in October
and remains in session until it has heard all of its cases and
handed down all its decisions (usually the end of July). For two
weeks of each month (Monday through Wednesday), the justices hear oral arguments in the velvet-swathed court
chamber. Visitors who want to listen can choose from two lines.
One is a "three-to-five-minute" line, which shuttles visitors
through, giving them a quick impression of the court at work.
The other is for those who'd like to stay for the whole show. If
you choose the latter, it's best to be in line by 8:30 AM. The main
hall of the Supreme Court is lined with busts of former chief justices; the courtroom itself is decorated with allegorical friezes.
Perhaps the most interesting appurtenance in the imposing building, however, is a basketball court on one of the upper floors (it's
been called the highest court in the land). *1st and E. Capitol sts.
NE, tel. 202/479–3000. Open Mon.–Fri. 9–4:30.*

One block north of the Supreme Court, at the corner of
Constitution Avenue and 2nd Street, is the red-brick **Sewall-
Belmont House,** built in 1800 by Robert Sewall. Part of the
house dates to 1680, making it the oldest home on Capitol Hill.
From 1801 to 1813 Secretary of the Treasury Albert Gallatin
lived here. He finalized the details of the Louisiana Purchase in
his front-parlor office. The house became the only private residence burned in Washington during the British invasion of
1814, after a resident fired on advancing British troops from an
upper-story window. (It was, in fact, the only resistance the
British met. The rest of the country was disgusted at Washington's inability to defend itself.) The house is now the
headquarters of the National Woman's Party and features a
museum that chronicles the early days of the women's movement. The museum is filled with period furniture, and portraits
and busts of suffrage movement leaders such as Lucretia Mott,
Elizabeth Cady Stanton, and Alice Paul. *144 Constitution Ave.
NE, tel. 202/546–3989. Open Tues.–Fri. 10–3; Sat., Sun., and
most holidays 12–4.*

After seeing the Sewall-Belmont House, continue east on
Maryland Avenue, past the headquarters of the **Veterans of
Foreign Wars.** Only three blocks from the Capitol, the Hill's residential character asserts itself. At Stanton Square turn right
onto 4th Street NE, walk south two blocks, and then turn right
onto A Street. The gray house with the mansard roof at 316 A
Street is the **Frederick Douglass Townhouse.** The first Washington home of the famous abolitionist and writer, this
structure housed the Museum of African Art until 1987, when
the museum was moved to a new building on the Mall.

Walk back to 4th Street and down another block to East Capitol
Street, the border between the northeastern and southeastern

quadrants of the city. In the '50s there was a plan to construct government office buildings on both sides of East Capitol Street as far as Lincoln Park, seven blocks to the east. The neighborhood's active historic-preservation supporters suc-

⑮ cessfully fought the proposal. The houses on the **south side of East Capitol Street** are a representative sampling of homes on the Hill. The corner house, No. 329, has a striking tower with a bay window and stained-glass. Next door are two Victorian houses with iron trim below the second floor. A pre–Civil War, Greek-Revival frame house sits behind a trim garden at No. 317. The alley to the right of No. 317 also dates from the 19th century. The two parallel rows of bricks were intended for carriage wheels, while the stones in the center were trod by horses' hooves. If you walk through the alley you'll see a manhole cover halfway down on which you can barely make out the date "1895." You'll end up on A Street SE, in a quiet neighborhood behind the Library of Congress's Adams Building. To the

⑯ left, at **326 A Street,** is the stucco house that artist Constantino Brumidi lived in while he was working on the Capitol.

⑰ A block down 4th Street SE is the red-brick **Capitol Hill Presbyterian Church,** built in 1869. Before the congregation had a permanent home, it met in the Capitol building, which constituted a unification of church and state that would probably not be tolerated today.

**Time Out** **Duddington's** (319 Pennsylvania Ave. SE), named for a large estate laid out on this site in the 17th century, serves up burgers, subs, and pizza made with fresh dough. For dessert, sample the pastries and cookies at **Sherrill's Bakery** (233 Pennsylvania Ave. SE).

Turn right on Pennsylvania Avenue and head back toward the Capitol's familiar white dome. The south side of the street is lined with restaurants and bars frequented by those who live and work on the Hill.

You'll find the nearest Metro stop, Capitol South, on the corner of 1st and D streets SE.

### Tour 5: Old Downtown and Federal Triangle

*Numbers in the margin correspond with points of interest on the Old Downtown and Federal Triangle map.*

Just because Washington is a planned city doesn't mean the plan was executed flawlessly. Pierre L'Enfant's design has been alternately shelved and rediscovered several times in the last 200 years. Nowhere have the city's imperfections been more visible than on L'Enfant's grand thoroughfare, Pennsylvania Avenue. By the early '60s it had become a national disgrace, the dilapidated buildings that lined it home to pawn shops and cheap souvenir stores. While riding up Pennsylvania Avenue in his inaugural parade, a disgusted John F. Kennedy is said to have turned to an aide and said, "Fix it!" Washington's downtown—once within the diamond formed by Massachusetts, Louisiana, Pennsylvania, and New York avenues—had its problems, too, many as a result of the riots that rocked the capital in 1968. In their wake, many downtown businesses left the area and moved north of the White House.

In recent years developers have rediscovered "old downtown," and buildings are now being torn down or remodeled at an amazing pace. After several false starts Pennsylvania Avenue is shining once again. This tour explores the old downtown section of the city, then swings around to check the progress on the monumental street that links the Congress House—the Capitol—with the President's House.

**1** Start your exploration in front of the **Pension Building,** on F Street between 4th and 5th streets. (Nearest Metro stop, Judiciary Square.) The massive red-brick edifice was built between 1882 and 1887 to house workers who processed the pension claims of veterans and their survivors, an activity that intensified after the Civil War. The architect was U.S. Army Corps of Engineers General Montgomery C. Meigs, who took as his inspiration the Italian Renaissance–style Palazzo Farnese in Rome.

Before entering the building, walk down its F Street side. The terra-cotta frieze by Caspar Buberl between the first and second floors depicts soldiers marching and sailing in an endless procession around the building. The main images repeat themselves; but look for the slight differences Buberl added for variety. (There are three versions of the prow of the naval boat, for example, and in some panels one of the marching soldiers is smoking a pipe; in others, he's not.) Architect Meigs lost his oldest son in the Civil War, and, though the frieze depicts Union troops, he intended it as a memorial to all who were killed in the bloody war.

The open interior of the building is one of the city's great spaces and has been the site of inaugural balls for more than 100 years. (The first ball was for Grover Cleveland in 1885; because the building wasn't finished at the time, a temporary wooden roof and floor were erected.) The eight central columns rise to a height of 75 feet. Though they look like marble, each is made of 75,000 bricks, covered with plaster and painted to resemble Siena marble.

The Pension Building now houses the **National Building Museum,** devoted to architecture and the building arts. Recent temporary exhibits have explored the construction of the Statue of Liberty, the history of Washington's apartment buildings, and the Pension Building itself. In June 1990 the museum will unveil "Washington: Site, Symbol, and City," a permanent exhibit on the design of the capital. *F St. between 4th and 5th sts NW, tel. 202/272–2448. Open Mon.–Fri. 10–4; weekends and holidays 12–4; closed Thanksgiving, Christmas, and New Year's Day. Tours are offered Tues.–Fri. at 12:30, weekends and holidays at 1.*

**2** Across F Street from the Pension Building is **Judiciary Square.** Both city and federal courthouses are arranged around it. The **Old City Hall,** now a courthouse, stands two blocks to the south, on D Street between 4th and 5th streets. Head west on F Street. After you cross 5th Street, look back at the Pension Building. It's easier to see the interesting roof from this distance. The prison block–like structure north of the Pension Building houses the General Accounting Office.

Turn right on 6th Street and walk two blocks north. The Chinese characters on the street signs signal that you're entering Washington's compact **Chinatown,** bordered by G, E, 5th, and

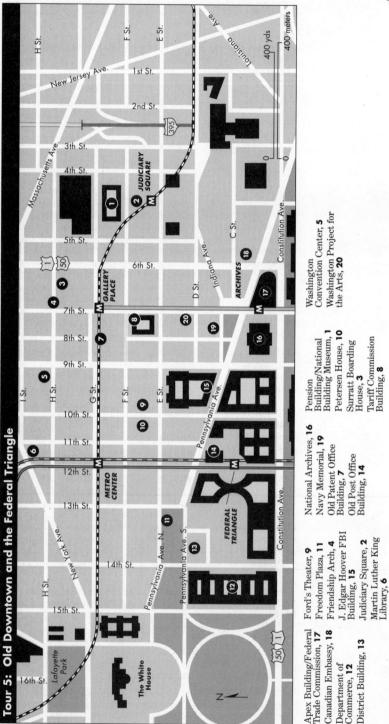

# Tour 5: Old Downtown and the Federal Triangle

88

400 yds
400 meters

Apex Building/Federal Trade Commission, **17**
Canadian Embassy, **18**
Department of Commerce, **12**
District Building, **13**
Ford's Theater, **9**
Freedom Plaza, **11**
Friendship Arch, **4**
J. Edgar Hoover FBI Building, **15**
Judiciary Square, **2**
Martin Luther King Library, **6**
National Archives, **16**
Navy Memorial, **19**
Old Patent Office Building, **7**
Old Post Office Building, **14**
Pension Building/National Building Museum, **1**
Petersen House, **10**
Surratt Boarding House, **3**
Tariff Commission Building, **8**
Washington Convention Center, **5**
Washington Project for the Arts, **20**

8th streets. The area is somewhat down-at-the-heels—you'll find boarded-up buildings and graffiti-covered walls—but this is the place to go for Chinese food in the District. Nearly every restaurant has a roast duck hanging in the window, and the shops here sell a wide variety of Chinese goods, from paperback books to traditional medicines.

**Time Out** If the smells of Chinese cooking have activated your taste buds, try the **Li Ho Food Restaurant** (501 H St. NW). Its servings are ample enough to once and for all vanquish the myth that Chinese food isn't filling.

❸ Turn left off 6th Street onto H Street. The **Surratt Boarding House,** where John Wilkes Booth and his co-conspirators plotted the assassination of Abraham Lincoln, is at 604 H St. NW. (It's now a Chinese restaurant called Go-Lo's.) The colorful and
❹ ornate 75-foot-wide **Friendship Arch** that spans H Street at 7th Street is a reminder of Washington's sister-city relationship with Beijing. The arch ruffled a few feathers among Taiwanese in the local Chinese community, who resented the presence of what they regarded as a communist monument. They have promised to build their own, noncommunist arch somewhere in Chinatown.

❺ To the west, at 9th and H streets, is the **Washington Convention Center.** Opened in 1983, the center pumped much-needed life into this part of downtown and spurred the development of nearby hotels and office buildings. The squat black building a
❻ block down, at 9th and G streets, is the **Martin Luther King Library,** designed by Mies van der Rohe. A mural on the first floor depicts events in the life of the civil rights activist.

Across the street, on the block bounded by F, G, 7th, and 9th
❼ streets, stands the **Old Patent Office Building,** which now houses two Smithsonian museums: the **National Portrait Gallery** on the south and the **National Museum of American Art** on the north. Construction on the south wing, which was designed by Washington Monument architect Robert Mills, started in 1836. When the huge Greek-Revival quadrangle was completed in 1867 it was the largest building in the country. Many of its rooms housed glass display cabinets filled with the models inventors were required to submit with their patent applications.

During the Civil War, the Patent Office, like many other buildings in the city, was turned into a hospital. Among those caring for the wounded here were Clara Barton and Walt Whitman. In the 1950s the building was threatened with demolition to make way for a parking lot, but the efforts of preservationists saved it. The Smithsonian opened it to the public in 1968.

The first floor of the National Museum of American Art holds displays of early-American art and art of the West, as well as a gallery of painted miniatures. Be sure to see *The Throne of the Third Heaven of the Nations' Millenium General Assembly*, by James Hampton. Discarded materials such as chairs, bottles, and light bulbs are sheathed in aluminum and gold foil in this strange and moving work of religious art. On the second floor are works by the American Impressionists, including John Henry Twachtman and Childe Hassam. There are also plaster models and marble sculptures by Hiram Powers, including the plaster cast of his famous work *The Greek Slave*. Also on this floor are massive landscapes by Albert Bierstadt and Thomas

Moran. The third floor is filled with modern art, including
works by Leon Kroll and Edward Hopper that were commissioned during the '30s by the federal government. The Lincoln
Gallery—site of the receiving line for Abraham Lincoln's 1865
inaugural ball—has been restored to its original appearance
and contains modern art by Jasper Johns, Robert Rauschenberg, Milton Avery, Kenneth Noland, and others. *8th and G
sts. NW, tel. 202/357–3095 or 2700. Open daily 10–5:30. Closed
Christmas.*

You can enter the National Portrait Gallery from any floor of
the National Museum of American Art or walk through the
courtyard between the two wings. The best place to start a cir-
cuit of the Portrait Gallery is on the restored third floor. Its
mezzanine level features a **Civil War exhibition,** with portraits,
photographs, and lithographs of such wartime personalities as
Julia Ward Howe, Frederick Douglass, Ulysses S. Grant, and
Robert E. Lee. There are also life casts of Abraham Lincoln's
hands and face. The gallery has been restored to its American
Victorian Renaissance–style splendor, complete with colorful
tile flooring and a stained-glass skylight. Highlights of the second floor include the **Hall of Presidents** (featuring a portrait or
sculpture of each chief executive) and the George Washington
"Lansdowne" portrait. *Time* magazine gave the museum its
collection of "Man of the Year" covers and many other photos
and paintings the magazine commissioned over the years. Parts
of this collection are periodically on display. *8th and F sts. NW,
tel. 202/357–2700. Open daily 10–5:30.*

**Time Out**  The **Patent Pending** restaurant, between the two museums,
serves an ample selection of salads, sandwiches, hot entrees,
and other treats. Tables and chairs in the large museum courtyard make sitting outside the thing to do when the weather is
pleasant.

If you leave the pair of museums in the Patent Office Building
by way of the National Portrait Gallery's F Street doors, you'll
come upon another of Washington's beautiful views. Directly
ahead, four blocks away in the Federal Triangle, is the **National
Archives** building. To the east is the green barrel-roof of **Union
Station,** and to the west you can see the **Treasury Department
Building.** Just across the F Street pedestrian mall and to the
❽ left is the **Tariff Commission Building,** designed by Robert
Mills and finished in 1866. When the Capitol was burned by the
British in 1814, Congress met temporarily in a hotel that stood
on this site. Another earlier building on the site housed the na-
tion's first public telegraph office, operated by Samuel F.B.
Morse.

The block of F Street between 9th and 10th streets has long
been a center of shopping in the District. It's dotted with cut-
rate electronics stores, pawn shops, and lingerie stores, and
the sidewalks are usually crowded with shoppers looking over
the wares of street vendors hawking everything from sweat-
shirts and sunglasses to perfumes and panty hose. Many residents fear that developers' new-found interest in old downtown
may threaten this lively part of the city.

❾ Turn left off F Street onto 10th Street. Halfway down the block
on the left is **Ford's Theater.** In 1861 Baltimore theater impresa-
rio John T. Ford leased the First Baptist Church building that

stood on this site and turned it into a successful music hall. The building burned down late in 1862, and Ford rebuilt it. The events of April 14, 1865, would shock the nation and close the theater. On that night, during a production of *Our American Cousin,* John Wilkes Booth entered the presidential box and assassinated Abraham Lincoln. The stricken president was carried across the street to the house of tailor William Petersen. Charles Augustus Leale, a 23-year-old doctor, attended to the president, whose injuries would have left him blind had he ever regained consciousness. To let Lincoln know that someone was nearby, Leale held his hand throughout the night. Lincoln

**⑩** died in the **Petersen House** the next morning. *516 10th St. NW, tel. 202/426–6830. Open daily 9–5.*

The federal government bought Ford's Theater in 1866 for $100,000 and converted it into office space. It was remodeled as a Lincoln museum in 1932 and was restored to its 1865 appearance in 1968. The basement museum—with artifacts such as Booth's pistol and the clothes Lincoln was wearing when he was shot—is undergoing a complete renovation and is scheduled to reopen with refurbished exhibits in April 1990. *511 10th St. NW, tel. 202/426–6927. Open daily 9–5. Theater closed when rehearsals or matinees are in progress (generally Thurs., Sat., Sun.); Lincoln Museum in basement remains open at these times.*

Continue south on 10th Street. On the left, at 10th and E streets, is the new **Hard Rock Cafe,** which opened in the fall of 1989 and is proof that Washington has finally arrived as an important world capital (if, that is, you equate importance with Hard Rock Cafe T-shirts). Turn right and continue along E Street. This unexceptional stretch contains some of Washington's more unimaginative office buildings but puts you in good position for a walk down the hypotenuse of Federal Triangle.

**⑪** **Freedom Plaza,** formerly Western Plaza, is bounded by 13th, 14th, and E streets and Pennsylvania Avenue. Its east end is dominated by a statue of General Casimir Pulaski, the Polish nobleman who led an American cavalry corps during the Revolutionary War and was mortally wounded in 1779 at the Siege of Savannah. He gazes over a plaza that is inlaid with a detail from L'Enfant's original 1791 plan for the Federal City. Bronze markers outline the President's Palace and the Congress House; the Mall is represented by a green lawn. Cut into the edges are quotations about the capital city, not all of them complimentary. To compare L'Enfant's vision with today's reality, stand in the middle of Pennsylvania Avenue and look west. L'Enfant had planned an unbroken vista from the Capitol to the White House, but the Treasury Building, constructed in 1842, ruined the view. Turning to the east you'll see the U.S. Capitol sitting on Jenkins Hill like an American Taj Mahal.

There's a lot to see and explore in the blocks near Freedom Plaza. The Beaux Arts **Willard Hotel** is on the corner of 14th Street and Pennsylvania Avenue. There was a Willard Hotel on this spot long before this ornate structure was built in 1901. The original Willard was the place to stay in Washington if you were rich or influential (or wanted to give that impression). Abraham Lincoln stayed there while waiting to move into the nearby White House. Julia Ward Howe stayed there during the Civil War and wrote *The Battle Hymn of the Republic* after gazing down from her window to see Union troops drilling on Pennsylvania Avenue. It's said the term "lobbyist" was coined to describe the favor seekers who would buttonhole President Ulysses S. Grant in the hotel's public rooms. The second Willard, with its mansard roof dotted with circular windows, was designed by Henry Hardenbergh, architect of New York's Plaza Hotel. Although it was just as opulent as the hotel it replaced, it fell on hard times after the second World War. In 1968 it closed, standing empty until 1986, when it reopened, amid much fanfare, after an ambitious restoration. The Willard's rebirth is one of the most visible successes of the Pennsylvania Avenue Development Corporation, the organization charged with reversing the decay of America's Main Street.

Just north of Federal Plaza, on F Street between 14th and 15th streets, are **The Shops,** a collection of upscale stores in the National Press Building. To the south is **Federal Triangle,** the mass of government buildings constructed from 1929 to 1938 between 15th Street, Pennsylvania Avenue, and Constitution Avenue. Before Federal Triangle was developed, government workers were scattered throughout the city, largely in rented offices. Looking for a place to consolidate this work force, city planners hit on the area south of Pennsylvania Avenue, then comprised of a notorious collection of rooming houses, taverns, tattoo parlors, and brothels known as "Murder Bay." A uniform classical architectural style, with Italianate red-tile roofs and interior plazas reminiscent of the Louvre, was chosen for the building project.

The base of Federal Triangle, and the first part completed, is **12** the **Department of Commerce** building, between 14th and 15th streets. When it opened in 1932 it was the world's largest government office building. In addition to the Commerce Department, the building houses the **National Aquarium.** Established in 1873, it's the oldest public aquarium in the United States. Displays feature tropical and freshwater fish, moray eels, frogs, turtles, piranhas, even sharks. A "touch tank" allows visitors to handle sea creatures such as crabs and oysters. *14th St. and Constitution Ave., tel. 202/377–2825. Open daily 9–5. Admission: $1.50 adults, 75 cents children and senior citizens. Sharks are fed Mon., Wed., and Sat. at 2; piranhas Tues., Thurs., and Sun. at 2.*

Federal Triangle's planners envisioned interior courts filled with plazas and parks, but the needs of the motor car foiled any such grand plans. The park that was planned for the spot of land across 14th Street from the Commerce Building is now an **13** immense parking lot. The Beaux Arts–classical **District Building,** at the corner of 14th and E streets, is the seat of the city's government. It was erected in 1908, and, though it didn't fit in with the original 1929 Federal Triangle plans, it survived.

This tour continues east on Pennsylvania Avenue, against the direction taken by newly inaugurated presidents on their way to the White House. Thomas Jefferson started the parade tradition in 1805 after taking the oath of office for his second term. He was accompanied by a few friends and a handful of congressmen. Four years later James Madison made things official by instituting a proper inaugural celebration. The flag holders on the lamp posts are clues that Pennsylvania Avenue remains the city's most important parade route. With the Capitol at one end and the White House at the other, the avenue symbolizes both the distance and the connection between these two branches of government.

Such symbolism may have been lost on early inhabitants of Washington. When Pennsylvania Avenue first opened in 1796, it was an ugly and dangerous bog. Attempts by Jefferson to beautify the road by planting poplar trees were only partially successful: Many were chopped down for firewood. In the mid-19th century, crossing the rutted thoroughfare was a dangerous proposition, and rainstorms often turned the street into a river. The avenue was finally paved with wooden blocks in 1871.

The **Bureau of Customs** stands on the southeast corner of Pennsylvania Avenue and 13th Street. Farther down, across 12th Street, is the Romanesque **Old Post Office Building.** When it was completed, in 1899, it was the largest government building in the District, the first with a clock tower, and the first with an electric power plant. Despite these innovations, it earned the sobriquet "old" after only 18 years, when a new District post office was constructed near Union Station. When urban planners in the '20s decided to impose a uniform design on Federal Triangle, the Old Post Office was slated for demolition (some critics said it stood out like an "old tooth"). First a lack of money during the Depression, then the intercession of preservationists, headed by Nancy Hanks of the National Endowment for the Arts, saved the fanciful granite building. Major renovation was begun in 1978, and in 1984 the public areas in the Old Post Office Pavilion—an assortment of shops and restaurants inside the airy central courtyard—were opened. In the last few years city boosters have tried to make the Old Post Office Washington's answer to Times Square. At midnight on New Year's Eve a giant, illuminated "LOVE" stamp drops from the clock tower, mimicking New York's more famous big apple.

Park Service rangers who work at the Old Post Office consider a trip to the observation deck in the **clock tower** to be one of Washington's best-kept secrets. While not as tall as the Washington Monument it offers nearly as impressive a view. Even better, it's usually not as crowded, the windows are bigger, and—unlike the monument's windows—they're open, allowing cool breezes to waft through. On the way down be sure to look at the Congress Bells, cast at the same British foundry that made the bells in London's Westminster Abbey. The bells are rung to honor the opening and closing of Congress and on other important occasions, such as when the Redskins win the Super Bowl. *Pennsylvania Ave. and 12th St. NW, tower tel. 202/523-5691, pavilion tel. 202/289-4224. Tower open daily mid-Apr.-mid-Sept. 8 **AM**-11 **PM**; mid-Sept.-mid-Apr. 10-5:45. Shops open Mon.-Sat. 10-8, Sun. noon-6.*

---

**Time Out** The lower level of the Post Office Pavilion is filled with fast-food restaurants. The waffle-cone ice cream confections available at **Scoops Homemade Cones** are especially refreshing on a hot, humid day.

---

Across Pennsylvania Avenue on the corner of 11th Street is the elaborately detailed, Beaux-Arts **Evening Star Building,** completed in 1899 and gutted in 1987 in preparation for its planned rebirth as a modern office building. The bureaus of out-of-town newspapers used to be housed in "Newspaper Row," a collection of buildings farther up the avenue, near 14th Street. Today, the **National Press Club building**—on 14th Street between E and F streets—is home to many news organizations.

As you cross 10th Street look to your left at the delightful trompe l'oeil mural on the side of the **Lincoln Building,** two blocks up on 10th Street. It looks as if there's a hole in the building. There's also a portrait of the building's namesake. Closer to Pennsylvania Avenue on 10th Street is an example of one of Washington's most strange and popular architectural conceits: a "façadamy." The multi-arched, red-brick facade of a 1909 building has been retained—like a bug stuck in amber—on the front of a massive shop-and-office block.

Continuing down Pennsylvania Avenue, the next big building on the right is the **Department of Justice.** Like the rest of Federal Triangle, it boasts some Art Deco features, including the cylindrical aluminum torche[g]res outside the doorways, adorned with bas-relief figures of bison, dolphins, and birds.

**⑮** Across from Justice is the **J. Edgar Hoover Federal Bureau of Investigation Building.** A hulking presence on the avenue, it was decried from birth as hideous. Even Hoover himself is said to have called it the "ugliest building I've ever seen." Opened in 1974, it hangs over 9th Street like a poured-concrete Big Brother. One thing is certain, it is secure. The tour of the building remains one of the most popular tourist activities in the city. Exhibits outline famous past cases and illustrate the Bureau's fight against organized crime, terrorism, bank robbery, espionage, and extortion. The tour ends with a live-ammo firearms demonstration. *10th St. and Pennsylvania Ave. NW (tour entrance on E St. NW), tel. 202/324–3447. Tours Mon.–Fri. 8:45–4:15. At peak times, there may be an hour wait for the tour.*

**⑯** The classical **National Archives** building is located at the corner of 9th Street and Pennsylvania Avenue. Designed by John Russell Pope, it breaks up the flowing lines of Federal Triangle. Beside it is a small park with a modest memorial to Franklin Roosevelt. The desk-sized piece of marble on the sliver of grass is exactly what the president asked for. The Archives building was erected in 1935 on the site of the old Center Market. This large block between 7th and 9th streets had been a center of commerce since the early 1800s, when barges plying the City Canal (which flowed where Constitution Avenue is now) were loaded and unloaded here. A vestige of this mercantile past lives on in the name given to the two semicircular developments across from the Archives—**Market Square.** City planners hope the residential development will enliven this stretch of Pennsylvania Avenue. Views from the windows of the apartments will certainly be majestic, and it's expected the rents will be equally impressive.

Turn right onto 9th Street and head to the Constitution Avenue side of the Archives. All the sculpture that adorns the building was carved on the site, including the two statues that flank the flight of steps facing the Mall, *Heritage* and *Guardianship*, by James Earle Fraser. Fraser also carved the scene on the pediment, which represents the transfer of historic documents to the recorder of the Archives. (Like nearly all pediment decorations in Washington, the scene is bristling with electric wires designed to thwart the advances of destructive pigeons.)

The Declaration of Independence, the Constitution, and the Bill of Rights are on display in the Rotunda of the Archives building, in a case made of bulletproof glass, illuminated with green light, and filled with helium gas (to protect the irreplaceable documents). At night and on Christmas—the only day the Archives are closed—the documents are lowered into a vault. *Constitution Ave. between 7th and 9th sts. NW, tel. 202/523-3000. Open daily 10–5:30.*

Continuing down Constitution Avenue you'll come to the tip of
**17** Federal Triangle. The **Apex Building,** completed in 1938, is the home of the **Federal Trade Commission.** The artwork that adorns this triangular building depicts various aspects of trade. Note the relief decorations representing *Agriculture* (the harvesting of grain, by Concetta Scaravaglione) and *Trade* (two men bartering over an ivory tusk, by Carl Schmitz) over the doorways on the Constitution Avenue side. Two heroic statues by Michael Lantz stand on each side of the rounded eastern portico and depict *Man Controlling Trade*—a muscular, shirtless workman wrestling with a wild horse. Just across 6th Street is a three-tiered fountain decorated with the signs of the zodiac; it is a memorial to Andrew Mellon, who as secretary of the treasury oversaw construction of the $125 million Federal Triangle. The impressive white-stone-and-glass building across Pennsylvania Avenue from Mellon's fountain is the new
**18** **Canadian Embassy.**

Backtrack a bit by circling the rounded end of the Federal Trade Commission building, crossing Pennsylvania Avenue, and heading west. Pioneering photographer **Matthew Brady** had his studio in the twin-towered building at 625 Pennsylvania Avenue. He's thought to have snapped some of his pictures of the city from the building's upper windows. For years after that it was better known as the home of Apex Liquors. Sears, Roebuck and Co. now owns the building, which serves as the huge retailer's Washington lobbying office.

There are a multitude of statues and monuments at this confluence of 7th Street and Pennsylvania and Indiana avenues, including memorials to the **Grand Army of the Republic** and
**19** **General Winfield Scott.** The **Navy Memorial,** a statue of a lone sailor staring out over a map of the world, stands across from the Archives and is framed by the new Market Square development. Less conventional is the **Temperance Fountain,** erected in the 19th century by a teetotaling physician named Cogswell. The doctor hoped that his fountain, which once dispensed ice-cold water, would lure people from the evils of alcohol.

The city is trying, with mixed results, to pump life into the neighborhoods north of Pennsylvania Avenue. **Seventh Street** has been designated an arts corridor, a gallery row of private art dealers. At one time, the street's cheap, older buildings were popular as artist's studios. Though the galleries remain, the development of Pennsylvania Avenue has forced the artists to find cheaper places to work.

**20** The **Washington Project for the Arts** has settled on Seventh Street, after several recent moves. WPA shows the challenging work of contemporary artists, many of them from the Washington area. The two floors of gallery space usually include displays of avant-garde media (photography and video) as well as visual art (paintings and sculpture). WPA's Bookworks sells an exhaustive selection of art books—both books about art and limited-edition books created by artists that are works of art themselves. *400 7th St. NW, (entrance on D St.), tel. 202/347–8304 or 4813. Open Tues.–Fri. 10–5, Sat. 11–5. Bookworks open Mon.–Fri. 11–6, Sat. 11–5.*

To reach public transportation, walk up 7th Street, then turn left on F Street and right on 9th to the Gallery Place Metro station. Or you can walk back down 7th to the National Archives station.

## Tour 6: Georgetown

*Numbers in the margin correspond with points of interest on the Georgetown map.*

Long before the District of Columbia was formed, Georgetown, Washington's oldest neighborhood, was a separate city that boasted a harbor full of ships and warehouses filled with tobacco. Washington has filled in around Georgetown over the years, but the former tobacco port retains an air of aloofness. Its narrow streets, which refuse to conform to Pierre L'Enfant's plan for the Federal City, make up the capital's wealthiest neighborhood and are the nucleus of its nightlife.

The area that would come to be known as George (after George II), then George Towne and, finally, Georgetown, was part of Maryland when it was settled in the early 1700s by Scottish immigrants, many of whom were attracted to the region's tolerant religious climate. Georgetown's position at the farthest point up the Potomac one could reach by boat made it an ideal transit-and-inspection point for farmers who grew tobacco in Maryland's interior. In 1789 the state granted the town a charter, but two years later Georgetown—along with Alexandria, its counterpart in Virginia—was included by George Washington in the Territory of Columbia, site of the new capital.

While Washington struggled, Georgetown thrived. Wealthy traders built their mansions on the hills overlooking the river; merchants and the working class lived in more modest homes closer to the water's edge. In 1810 a third of Georgetown's population was black—both freedmen and slaves. The Mt. Zion Church on 29th Street is the oldest black church in the city and was a stop on the Underground Railroad. Georgetown's rich history and success instilled in citizens of both colors feelings of superiority that many feel linger today. (When Georgetowners thought the dismal capital was dragging them down, they asked to be given back to Maryland, the way Alexandria was given back to Virginia in 1845). Tobacco eventually became a less important commodity, and Georgetown became a milling center, using water power from the Potomac. When the Chesapeake & Ohio Canal was completed in 1850, the city intensified its milling operations and became the eastern end of a waterway that stretched 184 miles to the west. The canal took up some of the slack when Georgetown's harbor began to fill with silt and the port lost business to Alexandria and Baltimore, but the canal never became the success it was meant to be.

In the years that followed, Georgetown was a far cry from the fashionable spot it is today. Clustered near the water were a foundry, a fishmarket, paper and cotton mills, and a power station for the city's streetcar system, all of which made Georgetown a smelly industrial district. It still had its Georgian, Federal, and Victorian homes, though, and when the New Deal and World War II brought a flood of newcomers to Washington, Georgetown's tree-shaded streets and handsome brick houses were rediscovered. Pushed out in the process were Georgetown's blacks, most of whom rented the houses they lived in.

Today Georgetown's zoning laws are among the city's strictest, and its historic preservationists are among the most vocal. Part of what the activists want protection from is the crush of people who descend on their community every night. This is Washington's center for restaurants, bars, nightclubs, and trendy boutiques. On M Street and Wisconsin Avenue, visitors can indulge just about any taste and take home almost any up-market souvenir. Harder to find is a parking place. The lack of a Metro station in Georgetown—due, some say, to residents' desires to keep out the riff-raff—means you'll have to take a bus or walk to this part of Washington. It is a leisurely stroll from either the Foggy Bottom or Dupont Circle Metro stops.

Georgetown owes some of its charm and separate growth to geography. This town-unto-itself is separated from Washington to the east by Rock Creek. On the south it's bordered by the Potomac, on the west by Georgetown University. How far north does Georgetown reach? Probably not much farther than the large estates and parks above R Street, though developers and real estate agents would be happy to take Georgetown right up to the Canadian border if it would increase the value of property along the way.

**①** Start your exploration of Georgetown in front of the **Old Stone House** (M Street between 30th and 31st streets), thought to be Washington's only surviving pre-Revolutionary building. Built in 1764 by a cabinetmaker named Christopher Layman, this fieldstone house was used both as a residence and a place of business by a succession of occupants. Five of the house's rooms are furnished with the sort of sturdy beds, spinning wheels, and simple tables associated with middle-class Colonial America. The National Park Service maintains the house and its lovely gardens in the rear, which are planted with fruit trees and seasonal blooms. Costumed guides answer questions about the house and its history. *3051 M St. NW, tel. 202/426–6851. Open Wed.–Sat. 9:30–5.*

**②** Around the corner, at 1221 31st Street, is the old Renaissance Revival–style **Customs House.** Built in 1858 to serve the port of Georgetown, it's been transformed into the Georgetown branch of the U.S. Postal Service, and there's really no reason to go inside unless you want to buy stamps or mail postcards.

Go back to M Street and cross over to Thomas Jefferson Street (between 30th and 31st streets). For most of its history, Georgetown was a working city, and the original names of its streets—Water Street, The Keys, Fishing Lane—bear witness to the importance of the harbor. The area south of M Street (originally called Bridge Street because of the bridge that spanned Rock Creek to the east) was inhabited by tradesmen, laborers, and merchants. Their homes were modest and close to Georgetown's industrial heart. The two-story brick

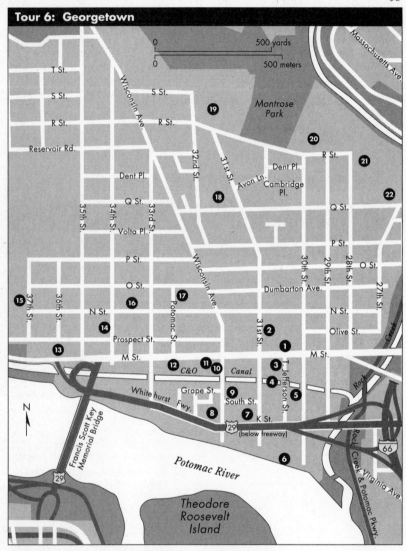

# Tour 6: Georgetown

Chesapeake & Ohio Canal, **4**

Cox's Row, **16**

Customs House, **2**

Dodge Warehouse, **8**

Dumbarton House, **22**

Dumbarton Oaks, **19**

Evermay, **21**

*Exorcist* steps, **13**

Foundry Mall, **5**

Georgetown Park, **11**

Georgetown University, **15**

Grace Episcopal Church, **9**

Halcyon House, **14**

Markethouse, **12**

Masonic lodge, **3**

Oak Hill Cemetery, **20**

Old Stone House, **1**

St. John's Church, **17**

Suter's Tavern, **7**

Tudor Place, **18**

Vigilant Firehouse, **10**

Washington Harbour, **6**

building at **1083 Thomas Jefferson Street** was built around 1865 as a stable for the horses and hearses of a nearby undertaker and cabinetmaker. The wide doors on the right let the horses in, while the hoist beam above the right-most window was used to lift hay and wood to the second floor. Three fine brick Federal houses stand south of the Georgetown Dutch Inn, at 1069, 1067, and 1063 Thomas Jefferson Street. The last has attractive flat lintels with keystones and a rounded keystone arch above the doorway. Across the street, at No. 1058, is a two-story

**❸** brick structure built around 1810 as a **Masonic lodge.** It features interesting detailing, including a pointed facade and recessed central arch, proof of the Masons' traditional attachment to the building arts.

As you walk south on Thomas Jefferson Street, you'll pass over
**❹** the **Chesapeake & Ohio Canal,** the waterway that kept Georgetown open to shipping after its harbor had filled with silt. George Washington was one of the first to advance the idea of a canal linking the Potomac with the Ohio River across the Appalachians. Work started on the C & O Canal in 1828, and when it opened in 1850, its 74 locks linked Georgetown with Cumberland, Maryland, 184 miles to the northwest (still short of its intended destination). Lumber, coal, iron, wheat, and flour moved up and down the canal, but it was never as successful as its planners had hoped it would be. Many of the bridges spanning the canal in Georgetown were too low to allow anything other than fully loaded barges to pass underneath, and competition from the Baltimore & Ohio Railroad eventually spelled an end to profitability. Today the canal is a part of the National Park system, and walkers follow the towpath once used by mules while canoers paddle the canal's calm waters. Between April and October you can go on a leisurely, mule-drawn trip aboard *The Georgetown* canal barge. Tickets are available
**❺** across the canal, in the **Foundry Mall** (1055 Thomas Jefferson St, NW, tel. 202/472–4376). The mall gets its name from an old foundry that overlooked the canal at 30th Street. Around the turn of the century it was turned into a veterinary hospital that cared for mules working on the canal. Today it's a restaurant.

**❻** Continue south, across K Street, and into **Washington Harbour,** a glittering, postmodern riverfront development that includes restaurants, offices, and apartments, and upscale shops. The plazas around its large central fountain and gardens are dotted with the eerily realistic sculptures of J. Seward Johnson, Jr. From the edge of Washington Harbour you can see the Watergate complex and Kennedy Center to the east.

**Time Out** If the breeze off the river has given you an appetite, stop at **Artie's Harbour Deli Cafe** for a sandwich. For dessert, select from the **Café Rosé's** waistline-threatening selection of authentic Viennese pastries. Both are in the Washington Harbour complex.

Georgetown's **K Street** is lined with the offices of architects, ad agencies, and public relations companies. In many of these offices you can hear the rumble of cars on the Whitehurst Freeway, the elevated road above K Street that leads to the Francis Scott Key Memorial Bridge. Though you'll probably have to peer through a vine-covered fence to see it, at the cor-
**❼** ner of 31st and K streets is a plaque commemorating **Suter's Tavern.** In March 1791, in the one-story hostelry that once

stood on this spot, George Washington met with the men who owned the tobacco farms and swampy marshes to the east of Georgetown and convinced them to sell their land to the government so work could begin construction of the District of Columbia.

At the foot of Wisconsin Avenue is another legacy from the area's mercantile past. The last three buildings on the west side were built around 1830 by trader and merchant **Francis Dodge.** Note the heavy stone foundation of the southernmost **warehouse,** its star-end braces and the broken hoist in the gable end. According to an 1838 newspaper ad, Georgetown shoppers could visit Dodge's grocery to buy such items as "Porto Rico Sugar, Marseilles soft-shelled Almonds and Havanna Segars."

Halfway up Wisconsin Avenue, on the other side of the street, stands the Gothic Revival **Grace Episcopal Church.** In the mid- to- late-19th century this church served the boatmen and workers from the nearby C & O Canal. At the time this was one of the poorest sections of Georgetown. (There are no "poor" sections in Georgetown anymore.)

Walking farther up Wisconsin Avenue you'll again cross the C & O Canal, this time via the only bridge that remains from the 19th century. On the north side is a simple granite obelisk honoring the men who built the waterway. A memorial of a more poignant sort can be found at the 1840 **Vigilant Firehouse,** north of the canal at 1066 Wisconsin Avenue. A plaque set in the wall reads: "Bush, the Old Fire Dog, died of Poison, July 5th, 1869, R.I.P."

The intersection of Wisconsin Avenue and M Street is the heart of boisterous Georgetown. This spot—under the gleaming, golden dome of Riggs Bank on the northeast corner—is mobbed every weekend and at special occasions such as Halloween and when the Redskins win the Super Bowl.

Turning left on M Street you'll come to the entrance to **Georgetown Park** (3222 M St, NW), a multilevel shopping extravaganza that answers the question "If the Victorians had invented shopping malls, what would they look like?" Such high-ticket stores as FAO Schwarz, Liberty of London, Polo/Ralph Lauren, and Godiva Chocolates can be found within this artful, skylit mass of polished brass, tile flooring, and potted plants. If you've always looked down your nose at mall architecture, Georgetown Park might win you over.

---

**Time Out** **Pizzeria Uno** (3211 M St.) has brought Chicago-style pizza to the heart of Georgetown. The deep-dish pies take a while to cook, but the wait is worth it. Those in a hurry may want to order the "personal-sized" pizza with soup or a salad: It's ready in five minutes and costs less than $5.

---

A stroll up either M Street or Wisconsin Avenue will take you past a dizzying array of merchandise, from expensive bicycling accessories to ropes of gold, from antique jewelry and furniture to the latest fashions in clothes and records. Walking west on M Street you'll come to the 1865 **Markethouse,** a brick market stall across from Potomac Street. There's been a market on this site since 1795, but the restored Markethouse sits empty, waiting for the right developer to breathe life into it.

M Street to the west leads to the **Key Bridge** into Rosslyn, Virginia. A house owned by Francis Scott Key, author of the national anthem, was demolished in 1947 to make way for the bridge that would bear his name. A nonprofit organization has been formed to build a memorial park on the small triangle of clear ground near the bridge.

The heights of Georgetown to the north above N Street contrast with the busy jumble of the old waterfront. To reach the higher ground you can walk up M Street past the old brick streetcar barn at No. 3600 (now a block of offices), turn right, and climb the **75 steps** that figured prominently in the eerie climax of the movie *The Exorcist.* If you would prefer a less-demanding climb, walk up 34th Street instead.

**Halcyon House,** at the corner of 34th and Prospect streets, was built in 1783 by Benjamin Stoddert, first secretary of the Navy. The object of many subsequent additions and renovations, the house is now a concatenation of architectural styles. Prospect Street gets its name from the fine views it affords of the waterfront and the river below.

The sounds of traffic diminish the farther north one walks from the bustle of M Street. To the west is **Georgetown University,** the oldest Jesuit school in the country. It was founded in 1789 by John Carroll, first American bishop and first archbishop of Baltimore. About 12,000 students attend Georgetown, known now as much for its perennially successful basketball team as for its fine programs in law, medicine, and the liberal arts. When seen from the Potomac or from Washington's high ground, the Gothic spires of Georgetown's older buildings give the university an almost medieval look.

Architecture buffs, especially those interested in Federal and Victorian houses, enjoy wandering along the red-brick sidewalks of upper Georgetown. Many of the homes here are larger and more luxurious than their waterfront counterparts, having been built by the harbor's wealthier citizens. Georgetown is today the home of Washington's elite, and the average house in upper Georgetown has two signs on it: a brass plaque notifying passersby of the building's historic interest and a window decal that warns burglars of its state-of-the-art alarm system. To get a representative taste of the houses in the area, continue north for a block on 34th Street and turn right onto N Street. The group of five Federal houses between 3339 and 3327 N Street are known collectively as **Cox's Row,** after John Cox, a former mayor of Georgetown, who built them in 1817.

The flat-fronted, red-brick Federal house at **3307 N Street** was the home of then-Senator John F. Kennedy and his family before the White House beckoned. Turn left onto Potomac and walk a block up to O Street. O Street still has two leftovers from an earlier age: cobblestones and streetcar tracks. Residents are proud of the cobblestones, and you'll notice that even the concrete patches have been scored to resemble the paving stones. **St. John's Church** (3240 O St. NW, tel. 202/338–1796) was built in 1809 and is attributed to Dr. William Thornton, architect of the Capitol. Later alterations have left it looking more Victorian than Federal. At the corner of the churchyard is a memorial to Colonel Ninian Beall, the Scotsman who received the original patent for the land that would become Georgetown.

Georgetown's largest estates sit farther north, commanding fine views of Rock Creek to the east and of the old tobacco town spread out near the river below. Depending on your mood, you can walk north either on Wisconsin Avenue (the bustling commercial route) or a block east, on 31st Street (a quieter residential street). If you choose Wisconsin Avenue you'll walk past more of Georgetown's trendy and traditional shops, including **Commander Salamander** (*see* Men's and Women's Clothing in Chapter 4) and the **Little Caledonia Shop** (*see* Crafts and Gifts in Chapter 4). Strolling 31st Street will give you a chance to admire more of the city's finest houses.

Whichever way you go, make your way to Q Street between 31st and 32nd streets. Through the trees to the north, at the **⑱** top of a sloping lawn, you'll see the neoclassical **Tudor Place**, designed by Capitol architect William Thornton and completed in 1816. The house was built for Thomas Peter, son of Georgetown's first mayor, and his wife Martha Custis, Martha Washington's granddaughter. It was because of this connection to the president's family that Tudor Place came to house many items from Mount Vernon. The yellow stucco house is interesting for its architecture—especially the dramatic, two-story domed portico on the south side—but its familial heritage is even more remarkable: Tudor Place stayed in the same family for 178 years, until 1983, when Armistead Peter III died. Before his death, Peter established a foundation to restore the house and open it to the public. On a house tour you'll see chairs that belonged to George Washington, Francis Scott Key's desk, and spurs of members of the Peter family who were killed in the Civil War (although the house was in Washington, the family was true to its Virginia roots and fought for Dixie). The grounds contain many specimens planted in the early-19th century. *1644 31st St. NW, tel. 202/965–0400. Tours Tues.–Sat. 10, 11:30, 1, and 2:30. Admission: $5. Reservations required.*

**⑲ Dumbarton Oaks**—not to be confused with the nearby Dumbarton House—is on 32nd Street, north of R Street. Career diplomat Robert Woods Bliss and his wife, Mildred, heiress to the Fletcher's Castoria fortune, bought the property in 1920 and set about taming the sprawling grounds and removing 19th-century additions that had marred the Federal lines of the 1801 mansion. In 1940 the Blisses conveyed the estate to Harvard University, which maintains the world-renowned collections of Byzantine and pre-Columbian art. The Byzantine museum includes secular and religious items, with beautiful examples of metalwork, enameling, ivory carving, and manuscript illumination. Pre-Columbian works—artifacts and textiles from Mexico and Central and South America—are arranged in an enclosed glass pavilion designed by Philip Johnson. Events at Dumbarton Oaks have not been confined to the study of dead cultures. In 1944 representatives of the United States, Great Britain, China, and the Soviet Union met in the music room here to lay the groundwork for the United Nations.

Anyone with even a mild interest in flowers, shrubs, trees—anything that grows out of the ground—will enjoy a visit to Dumbarton Oaks' 10 acres of formal gardens, one of the loveliest spots in all of Washington (enter via R Street). Designed by noted landscape architect Beatrix Farrand, the gardens incorporate elements of traditional English, Italian, and French styles. A full-time crew of a dozen gardeners toils to maintain the stunning collection of terraces, geometric gardens, tree-shaded brick walks, fountains, arbors, and pools. *Art collections: 1703 32nd St. NW, tel. 202/338–8278 (recorded information) or 202/342–3200. Open Tues.–Sun. 2–5. Gardens: 31st and R streets NW. Open Apr. 1–Oct. 31, daily 2 –6. Admission: $2 adults, $1 senior citizens and children, senior citizens free on Wed.; Nov. 1–Mar. 31, daily 2–5. Admission: free. Both gardens and collections are closed on national holidays and Christmas eve.*

Three other sylvan retreats lie north of R Street in upper Georgetown. Originally part of the Bliss estate, **Dumbarton Oaks Park** sprawls to the north and west. **Montrose Park** lies to the east of the estate. Further east is **Oak Hill Cemetery,** its funerary obelisks, crosses, and gravestones spread out like an amphitheater of the dead on a hill overlooking Rock Creek. Near the entrance is an 1850 Gothic-style chapel designed by Smithsonian Castle architect James Renwick. Across from the chapel is the resting place of actor, playwright, and diplomat John H. Payne, who is remembered today primarily for his song "Home Sweet Home." A few hundred feet to the north is the circular tomb of William Corcoran, founder of the Corcoran Gallery of Art. *30th and R sts. NW. Open Mon.–Fri. 9–4:30.*

Walking south on 28th Street you'll pass **Evermay** (1623 28th St. NW). The Georgian manor house, built around 1800 by real estate speculator Samuel Davidson, is almost hidden by its black-and-gold gates and high brick wall. Davidson wanted it that way. He sometimes took out advertisements in newspapers warning sightseers to avoid his estate "as they would a den of devils or rattlesnakes." The mansion is in private hands, but its grounds are often opened for garden tours.

A few steps east of 28th Street on Q Street is **Dumbarton House,** the headquarters of the National Society of the Colonial Dames of America. Its symmetry and the two distinctive bow wings on the north side make Dumbarton a distinctive example of Federal architecture. The man who built the house, Joseph Nourse, was registrar of the U.S. Treasury. Other well-known Americans have spent time at the house, including Dolley Madison, who is said to have stopped here when fleeing Washington in 1814. One hundred years later, the house was moved 50 feet up the hill, when Q Street was cut through to the Dumbarton Bridge.

Eight rooms inside Dumbarton House have been restored to their Colonial splendor and are decorated with period furnishings such as mahogany American Chippendale chairs, hallmark silver, Persian rugs, and a breakfront cabinet filled with rare books. Notable items include a 1789 Charles Willson Peale portrait of Benjamin Stoddert's children (with an early view of Georgetown harbor in the background), Martha Washington's traveling cloak, and a British redcoat's red coat. The docents are extremely knowledgeable and delight in explaining the intricate and sometimes confusing relationships between many of Colonial America's most famous families. *2715 Q St. NW, tel. 202/337–2288. Open Mon.–Sat. 9–12:30.*

**Tour 7: Dupont Circle**

*Numbers in the margin correspond with points of interest on the Dupont Circle map.*

Three of Washington's main thoroughfares intersect at Dupont Circle: Connecticut, New Hampshire, and Massachusetts avenues. With a handsome small park and a splashing fountain in the center, Dupont Circle is more than a deserted island around which traffic flows, making it an exception among Washington circles. The activity on the circle spills over into the surrounding streets, one of the liveliest, most vibrant neighborhoods in Washington.

Development near Dupont Circle started during the post–Civil War boom of the 1870s. As the city increased in stature, the nation's wealthy and influential citizens began building their mansions near the Circle. The area underwent a different kind of transformation in the middle of this century, when the middle and upper classes deserted Washington for the suburbs, and in the '60s the circle became the starting point for marches sponsored by various counterculture groups. Today the neighborhood is once again fashionable, and its many restaurants, off-beat shops, and specialty bookstores lend it a distinctive, cosmopolitan air.

❶ Start your exploration in **Dupont Circle** itself (Metro stop, Dupont Circle). Originally known as Pacific Circle, this hub was the westernmost circle in Pierre L'Enfant's original design for the Federal City. The name was changed in 1884, when Congress authorized construction of a bronze statue honoring Civil War hero Admiral Samuel F. Dupont. The statue fell into disrepair, and Dupont's family—who had never liked it anyway—replaced it in 1921 with the fountain you see today. The marble fountain, with its allegorical figures Sea, Stars, and Wind, was created by Daniel Chester French, the sculptor of Lincoln's statue in the Lincoln Memorial.

As you look around the circumference of the circle, you'll be able to see the special constraints within which architects in Washington must work. Since a half dozen streets converge on Dupont Circle, the buildings around it are, for the most part, wedge-shaped and set on oddly shaped plots of land like massive slices of pie.

Only two of the great houses that stood on the circle in the 19th century remain today. The Renaissance-style house at **15 Dupont Circle**, next to New Hampshire Avenue, was built in 1903 for Robert W. Patterson, publisher of the *Washington Times–Herald*. Patterson's daughter, Cissy, who succeeded him as publisher of the paper, was known for hosting parties that attracted such notables as William Randolph Hearst, Douglas MacArthur, and J. Edgar Hoover. In 1927, while Cissy was living in New York City and the White House was being refurbished, Calvin Coolidge and his family stayed in this Dupont Circle home. The Coolidges received American flyer Charles Lindbergh here; some of the most famous photographs of Lindy were taken as he stood on the house's balcony and smiled down at the crowds below. After Patterson's death the house was bought by the Washington Club. The **Sulgrave Club**, at the corner of Massachusetts Avenue, was also once a private home and is now likewise a club. Neither is open to the public.

105

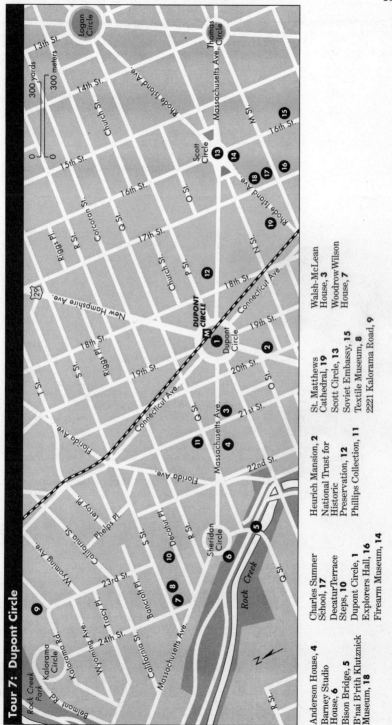

## Tour 7: Dupont Circle

300 yards
300 meters

Anderson House, **4**
Barney Studio
House, **6**
Bison Bridge, **5**
B'nai B'rith Klutznick
Museum, **18**

Charles Sumner
School, **17**
Decatur Terrace
Steps, **10**
Dupont Circle, **1**
Explorers Hall, **16**
Firearm Museum, **14**

Heurich Mansion, **2**
National Trust for
Historic
Preservation, **12**
Phillips Collection, **11**

St. Matthews
Cathedral, **19**
Scott Circle, **13**
Soviet Embassy, **15**
Textile Museum, **8**
2221 Kalorama Road, **9**

Walsh-McLean
House, **3**
Woodrow Wilson
House, **7**

Cross the traffic circle carefully and head south on New Hampshire Avenue. A block down on the left is the impressive **②** **Heurich Mansion,** whose dark sandstone walls and stolid countenance provide quite a contrast to the two gay houses on the circle. This severe, Romanesque Revival mansion was the home of Christian Heurich, a German orphan who made his fortune in this country in the beer business. Heurich's brewery was located in Foggy Bottom, where the Kennedy Center stands today. Brewing was a dangerous business in the 19th century, and fires had more than once reduced Heurich's beer factory to ashes. Perhaps because of this he insisted that his home, completed in 1894, be fireproof. Although 17 fireplaces were installed—some with onyx facings, one with the bronze image of a lion staring out from the back—not a single one ever held a fire.

After Heurich's widow died, in 1955, the house was turned over to the Historical Society of Washington, DC. Today it serves as the group's headquarters and houses its voluminous archives. All the furnishings in the house were owned and used by the Heurichs. The interior of the house is an eclectic Victorian treasure trove filled with plaster detailing, carved wooden doors, and painted ceilings. The downstairs breakfast room, where Heurich, his wife, and their three children ate most of their meals, is decorated like a rathskeller and is adorned with such German sayings as "A good drink makes old people young."

Heurich must have taken the German proverbs seriously. He drank his beer every day, had three wives (not all at once), and lived to be 102. (Heurich's grandson Gary recently started brewing the family beer in Pittsburgh. He ships it to Washington and vows to build someday another Heurich brewery there.) Docents who give tours of the impressive house are adept at answering questions about other Washington landmarks, too. *1307 Connecticut Ave. NW, tel. 202/785–2068. Open Wed.–Sat. noon–4. Admission: $2 adults, $1 seniors, students free.*

**Time Out** Behind the Heurich Mansion, on **Sunderland Place,** is a simple Victorian garden that is open to the public. It's the perfect place to rest your feet and eat your lunch. You can get hot dogs from the **street vendors** near Dupont Circle or sandwiches at the **Coffee Shop Carryout,** two blocks south at 1800 N Street.

Cross New Hampshire Avenue and turn left on O Street. The row houses on this block are a little less impressive than Heurich's castle, but they still fetch prices that start above $300,000. Many of the larger homes have been divided into apartments or condos.

Turn north on 21st Street and cross P Street. This area has a high concentration of restaurants and bars and is crowded and boisterous at night. It also serves as an informal crossroads for Washington's gay community. (There are several gay night spots farther up P Street.) At the corner of Massachusetts Avenue and 21st Street is the opulent **Walsh-McLean House.** Tom McLean was an Irishman who made a fortune with a Colorado gold mine and came to Washington to show his wealth. Washington was the perfect place to establish a presence for America's late–19th-century nouveau riche. It was easier to enter "society" in the nation's planned capital than in New York or Philadelphia, and wealthy industrialists and lucky entrepreneurs flocked to the city on the Potomac. Walsh announced his arrival with this 60-room mansion. His daughter, Evalyn Walsh-McLean, the last private owner of the Hope diamond (now in the Smithsonian's Museum of Natural History) was one of the city's leading hostesses. Today the house is used as an embassy by the Indonesian government. The **Jockey Club** restaurant in the red-brick Ritz-Carlton Hotel across the street was a favorite lunching spot of former first lady Nancy Reagan.

Head west on Massachusetts Avenue. The palatial home at No. 2118 is a mystery even to many longtime Washingtonians, who **4** assume it's just another embassy. **Anderson House** is not an embassy, though it does have a link to the diplomatic world. Larz Anderson was a diplomat whose career included postings to Japan and Belgium. Anderson and his heiress wife, Isabel, toured the world, picking up objects that struck their fancy. They filled their residence, which was constructed in 1905, with the booty of their travels, including choir stalls from an Italian Renaissance church, Flemish tapestries, and a large—if spotty—collection of oriental art. All this remains in the house, for visitors to see.

In accordance with Anderson's wishes, the building also serves as the headquarters of the **Society of the Cincinnati.** The oldest patriotic organization in the country, the society was formed in 1783 by a group of officers who had served with George Washington during the Revolutionary War. The group took the name Cincinnati from Cincinnatus, a distinguished Roman who, circa 500 BC, led an army against Rome's enemies and later quelled civil disturbances in the city. After each instance he returned to the simple life on his farm. The story impressed the American officers, who saw in it a mirror of their own situation: They too would leave the battlefields behind to get on with the business of forging a new nation. (One such member went on to name the city in Ohio.)

The society's membership requirements are even stricter than those of the Daughters of the American Revolution. Only those who had served to the end of the Revolutionary War as officers in a "Line" regiment (as distinguished from a militia or state regiment) were eligible for membership when the society was founded. Membership was passed—and continues to pass—to the eldest son, according to the rule of primogeniture. It's not surprising that many of the displays in the society's museum focus on the Colonial period and the Revolutionary War. One room—painted in a marvelous trompe l'oeil style that deceives visitors into thinking the walls are covered with sculpture—is filled with military miniatures from the United States and France. (Because of the important role France played in defeating the British, French officers were invited to join the society. Pierre L'Enfant, "Artist of the Revolution" and planner of Washington, designed the society's eagle medallion.)

The house is often used by the federal government to entertain visiting dignitaries. Amid the glitz, glamor, beauty, and patriotic spectacle of the mansion are two delightful painted panels in the solarium that depict the Andersons' favorite motor-car sightseeing routes around Washington. *2118 Massachusetts Ave. NW, tel. 202/785–0540. Open Tues.–Sat. 1–4.*

Head west on Q Street, past a row of expensive town houses, to
**5** the **Bison Bridge.** Tour guides at the Smithsonian's Museum of
Natural History are quick to remind visitors that America never had buffalo; the big animals that roamed the plains were
bison. Though many maps and guidebooks call this the Buffalo
Bridge, the four bronze statues by A. Phimister Proctor are of
bison. Officially called the **Dumbarton Bridge,** the structure
stretches across Rock Creek Park into Georgetown. Its sides
are decorated with busts of Native Americans, the work of architect Glenn Brown, who, along with his son Bedford,
designed the bridge in 1914. The best way to see the busts is to
walk the footpath along Rock Creek or to lean over the green
railings beside the bison and peer through the trees.

Walking north on 23rd Street you'll pass between two more embassies, those of Turkey and Romania, both of which sit on
**Sheridan Circle** and are topped with antennae as big as trampo-
lines used to send messages back to the homeland.

**6** The Mediterranean-style **Barney Studio House** at 2306 Massachusetts Avenue was the second home constructed on Sheridan
Circle. Alice Pike Barney was a Cincinnati heiress who early on
developed a love of art, artists, and the bohemian life-style.
Having toured the capitals of Europe, she felt Washington
paled in comparison. This was her assessment of Washington
culture at the turn of the century: "What is capital life after all?
Small talk and lots to eat, an infinite series of teas and dinners.
Art? There is none." Her own home eventually became a salon,
a meeting place for Washington's cultural elite. It also served
as her studio (Barney was an artist as well as an art lover). The
renovated home contains paintings by Barney and her friends,
as well as a collection of furniture, rugs, and other antiques.
*2306 Massachusetts Ave. NW, tel. 202/357-3111. Tours by ap-
pointment only; Wed. and Thurs. at 11 and 1 and second and
fourth Sun. of each month at 1.*

Although the entire Dupont Circle area is dotted with embassies, the stretch of Massachusetts Avenue northwest of Sheridan Circle is known as Embassy Row proper. The area is rife
with delegations from foreign countries, and a stroll down the
street will provide you with an opportunity to test your knowledge of the world's flags.

The **Cameroon Embassy** is housed in the mansion at 2349 Massachusetts Avenue. This fanciful castle, with its conical tower,
bronze weathervane, and intricate detailing around the windows and balconies, is the westernmost of the Beaux Arts–
style mansions built along Massachusetts Avenue in the late
19th and early 20th centuries.

Turn right on S Street. The statue on the left commemorates
Irish patriot **Robert Emmet;** it was dedicated in 1966 to mark
the 50th anniversary of Irish independence. A small reproduc-
**7** tion can be found in the **Woodrow Wilson House,** a few hundred
feet down S Street. Wilson is the only president who stayed in
Washington after leaving the White House. (He's also the only
president buried in the city, inside the Washington Cathedral.)
He and his second wife, Edith Bolling Wilson, retired in 1920 to
this Georgian Revival house designed by Washington architect
Waddy B. Wood. (Wood also designed the Department of the
Interior building on C Street.) The house had been built in 1915
for a carpet magnate, and on the first and third floors you can

still see the half-snaps that run along the edges of the floors to hold down the long-gone wall-to-wall carpeting.

President Wilson suffered a stroke toward the end of his second term, in 1919, and he lived out the last few years of his life on this quiet street. Edith made sure he was comfortable; she had a bed constructed that was the same dimensions as the large Lincoln bed Wilson had slept in in the White House. She also had the house's trunk lift electrified so the partially paralyzed president could move from floor to floor. When the streetcars stopped running in 1962 the elevator stopped working. It had received its electricity directly from the streetcar line.

After Edith died, in 1961, the house, along with its contents, was bequeathed to the National Trust for Historic Preservation. On view inside are such items as a Gobelins tapestry, a baseball signed by King George V, and the shell casing from the first shot fired by U.S. forces in World War I. The house also contains memorabilia related to the history of the short-lived League of Nations, including the colorful flag Wilson hoped would be adopted by that organization. *2340 S St. NW, tel. 202/387-4062. Open Mar.–Dec., Tues.–Sat. 10–4, Sun. 12–4; Feb., Sat. and Sun. 12–4. Closed Thanksgiving, Christmas, and all Jan. Admission: $3.50 adults, $2 senior citizens and students.*

**8** Just next door, in a house that was also designed by Waddy Wood, is the **Textile Museum.** Founder George Hewitt Myers purchased his first Oriental rug for his dorm room at Yale and subsequently collected more than 12,000 textiles and 1,400 carpets. An heir to the Bristol-Myers fortune, Myers and his wife lived two houses down from Wilson, at 2310 S Street, in a home designed by John Russell Pope, architect of the National Archives and Jefferson Memorial. Myers bought the house next door, at No. 2320, and opened his museum to the public in 1925. Rotating exhibits are taken from a permanent collection that includes Coptic textiles, Kashmir embroidery, Turkman tribal rugs, and pre-Columbian textiles from Central and South America. *2320 S St. NW, tel. 202/667-0441. Open Tues.–Sat. 10–5, Sun. 1–5. Closed Mon. and major holidays. Highlight tours: Sept.–May, Tues.–Wed. 1:30; Sun. 2. Suggested donation: $3 adults, 50 cents children.*

S Street is an informal dividing line between the Dupont Circle area to the south and the exclusive **Kalorama** neighborhood to the north. The name for this peaceful, tree-filled enclave—Greek for "beautiful view"—was contributed by politician and writer Joel Barlow, who bought the large tract in 1807. Kalorama is filled with embassies and luxurious homes. Walk north on 23rd Street until it dead-ends at the Tudor mansion at **9** **2221 Kalorama Road.** This imposing house was built in 1911 for mining millionaire W.W. Lawrence, but since 1936 it has been the residence of the French ambassador. For a taste of the beautiful view that so captivated Barlow, walk west on Kalorama Road, then turn right on Kalorama Circle. At the bottom of the circle you can look down over Rock Creek Park, the finger of green that pokes into northwest Washington.

Walk back down 23rd Street, head east on S Street, and turn right onto 22nd Street. Don't be put off by the "Dead End" sign; that's meant for cars, not pedestrians. You can then use **10** the **Decatur Terrace Steps**—built in 1911–12 by the Office of

Public Buildings and Grounds—to descend from S Street to Decatur Place.

Walk down 22nd Street and turn left on R Street. Here are more of the gracious town homes that are enjoying a second life as embassies. Many private art galleries—selling the work of local, national, and international artists—have sprung up on R Street between 22nd Street and Connecticut Avenue.

⑪ Washington has many museums that are the legacy of one great patron, but the **Phillips Collection,** at 21st and Q streets, is among the most beloved. In 1918 Duncan Phillips, grandson of a founder of the Jones and Laughlin Steel Company, started to collect art for a museum that would stand as a memorial to his father and brother, who had died within 13 months of each other. Three years later what was first called the Phillips Memorial Gallery opened in two rooms of this Georgian-Revival home near Dupont Circle. It was the first permanent museum of modern art in the country.

Not interested in a painting's market value or its faddishness, Phillips searched for works that impressed him as outstanding products of a particular artist's unique vision. Holdings include works by Braque, Cézanne, Klee, Matisse, John Henry Twachtman, and the largest museum collection in the country of the work of Pierre Bonnard. The exhibits change regularly. The collection's best-known paintings include Renoir's *Luncheon of the Boating Party*, *Repentant Peter*s by both Goya *and* El Greco, *A Bowl of Plums* by 18th-century artist Jean-Baptiste Siméon Chardin, Degas's *Dancers at the Bar*, Van Gogh's *Entrance to the Public Garden at Arles* and Cézanne's self-portrait, the painting Phillips said he would save first if his gallery caught fire. During the '20s, Phillips and his wife, Marjorie, started to support American Modernists such as John Marin, Georgia O'Keeffe, and Arthur Dove.

The Phillips is a comfortable museum. Works of a favorite artist are often grouped together in "exhibition units," and unlike most other galleries (where uniformed guards appear uninterested in the masterpieces around them) the Phillips employs students of art, many of whom are artists themselves, to sit by the paintings and answer visitors' questions.

The Phillips family moved out of the house in 1930. An annex was added in 1960 and renovated in 1989 to add 50% more exhibit space. *1600–1612 21st St. NW, tel. 202/387–2151. Open Tues.–Sat. 10–5, Sun. 2–7. Admission by donation.*

After visiting the Phillips, walk east on Q Street and turn south on Connecticut Avenue.

---

**Time Out** Connecticut Avenue above and below Dupont Circle is chockablock with restaurants that will satisfy any craving. Two favorites are the **Chesapeake Bagel Bakery** (1636 Connecticut Ave.), a low-key lunchroom that features a wide variety of bagel sandwiches, and **Cafe Splendide** (1521 Connecticut Ave., no credit cards), a cozy spot that serves soups, salads, German-style entrees, and bread and pastries baked on the premises.

---

⑫ Walk east on Massachusetts Avenue. The **National Trust for Historic Preservation** sits at the corner of 18th Street and Massachusetts Avenue in, naturally, a building that has been historically preserved. The building once housed some of the most luxurious apartments in the city. The Beaux Arts–style McCormick Apartments, designed by Jules H. de Sibour, were built in 1917 and contained only six apartments, one on each floor, each with 11,000 square feet of space. Some of Washington's most prominent citizens lived here, including hostess Perle Mesta and Andrew Mellon, secretary of the treasury under three presidents, whose top-floor flat contained many of the paintings that would later go to the National Gallery of Art. During World War II the building was converted to office space, and in 1977 it was bought by the National Trust. The building is closed to the public, but a quick peek at the circular lobby will give you an idea of the lavish world its one-time residents inhabited.

Continue down Massachusetts Avenue. You'll pass more embassies, including those of East Germany and Chile. (The mansion at 1746 Massachusetts Avenue, with the Louis XV facade, was the Canadian chancery until 1989, when the Canadians moved into their dramatic new embassy on Pennsylvania Avenue.) On the left is the **Brookings Institution,** one of dozens of think tanks in Washington that offer their partisan and nonpartisan advice to whoever is in power or whoever would like to be.

🔞 **Scott Circle** is at the center of the intersections of Massachusetts and Rhode Island Avenues and 16th Street. The equestrian statue of **General Winfield Scott** was cast from cannon captured in the Mexican War. Across the circle is an interesting memorial to **S.C.F. Hahnemann.** His statue sits in a recessed wall, his head surrounded by a mosaic of colorful tiles. (Who, you ask, was S.C.F. Hahnemann? He was the founder of the homeopathic school of medicine. Washington is a city of monuments, not all of them to people whose names are household words.) On the west side of the circle there is a statue of fiery orator **Daniel Webster.** If you walk to the south side of Scott Circle and look down 16th Street you'll get a view of the columns of the White House, framed by the buildings along 16th Street.

The headquarters of the National Rifle Association is also near the circle. There are dozens of guns on display in the NRA's 🔞 **Firearm Museum,** from muzzle-loading flintlocks used in the Revolutionary War to high-tech pistols used by Olympic shooting teams. Also on display are weapons that once belonged to presidents, such as Teddy Roosevelt's .32 caliber Browning pistol and a Winchester rifle used by Dwight Eisenhower. *1600 Rhode Island Ave. NW, tel. 202/828–6194. Open daily 10–4. Closed Christmas, New Years Day, Easter, and Thanksgiving.*

One block south on 16th Street stands the **Jefferson Hotel.** Designed by Jules H. de Sibour, the man responsible for the McCormick, it too started out as apartments but was converted to a hotel in the '50s. It has a reputation for luxury and discretion and is a favorite temporary home for White House cabinet members awaiting confirmation. Further down 16th Street, on 🔞 the left, you can see the hammer and sickle flying from the **Soviet Embassy.** (The Soviets have constructed a new, more modern embassy on a hill near the Washington Cathedral, but until problems with the microphone-infested American embassy in Moscow are straightened out, the State Department won't let them move in.)

Turn right onto M Street. On the southwest corner of 16th and M streets sits the headquarters of the **National Geographic Society.** Founded in 1888, the society is best known for its yellow-bordered magazine, found in family rooms and attics across the country. The society has sponsored numerous expeditions throughout its 100-year history, including those of Admirals Peary and Byrd and Captain Jacques Cousteau. **Explorers Hall,** entered from 17th Street, is the magazine come to life. Recently renovated, Explorers Hall invites visitors to learn about the world in a decidedly interactive way. You can experience everything from a minitornado to video "touch-screens" that explain various geographic concepts and then quiz you on what you've learned. The most dramatic events take place in Earth Station One, a 72-seat amphitheater that sends the audience on a journey around the world. The centerpiece is a hand-painted globe, 11 feet in diameter, that floats and spins on a cushion of air, showing off different features of the planet. Less high-tech, but no less popular, is Henry, a live blue-and-gold macaw that has been a fixture in Explorers Hall since 1964. *17th and M sts., tel. 202/857-7588. Open Mon.–Sat. and holidays 9–5, Sun. 10–5.*

Across M Street is the **Charles Sumner School,** built in 1872 for the education of black children in the city. It takes its name from the Massachusetts senator who delivered a blistering attack against slavery in 1856 and was savagely caned as a result by a congressman from South Carolina. The building was designed by Adolph Cluss, who created the Arts and Industries Building on the Mall. It is typical of the District's Victorian-era public schools. Beautifully restored in 1986, the school serves mainly as a conference center, though it hosts changing art exhibits and houses a permanent collection of memorabilia relating to the city's public school system. *1201 17th St. NW, tel. 202/727-3419. Often closed for conferences; call ahead for opening hours.*

Further up 17th Street, at the corner of Rhode Island Avenue, is the **B'nai B'rith Klutznick Museum,** devoted to the history of the Jewish people. The museum's permanent exhibits span 20 centuries and highlight Jewish festivals and the rituals employed to mark the various stages of life. A wide variety of Jewish decorative art, adorning such items as spice boxes and Torah wrappers, is on display. *1640 Rhode Island Ave. NW, tel. 202/857-6583. Open Sun.–Fri. 10–5. Closed Sat., legal holidays, and Jewish holidays.*

Half a block west on Rhode Island Avenue, across from a memorial to nuns who served as nurses during the Civil War, is **St. Matthews Cathedral,** the seat of Washington's Catholic archbishop. John F. Kennedy frequently worshiped in this Renaissance-style church, and in 1963 his funeral mass was held within its richly decorated walls. Set in the floor, directly in front of the main altar, is a memorial to the slain president: "Here rested the remains of President Kennedy at the requiem mass November 25, 1963, before their removal to Arlington where they lie in expectation of a heavenly resurrection." *1725 Rhode Island Ave. NW, tel. 202/347-3215. Open weekdays 6:30 AM–6:15 PM; Sat. 7:30 AM–6:30 PM; Sun. 6:30AM–7:30 PM. Tours Sun. 2:30–4:30.*

You are now equidistant from two Metro stations. Dupont Circle is two blocks north on Connecticut Avenue, and Farragut North is one block south.

## Tour 8: Foggy Bottom

*Numbers in the margin correspond with points of interest on the Foggy Bottom map.*

The Foggy Bottom area of Washington—roughly bordered by the Potomac, Rock Creek, Pennsylvania Avenue, and 20th Street—has three main claims to fame: the State Department, the Kennedy Center, and George Washington University. In 1763 a German immigrant named Jacob Funk purchased this land, and a community called Funkstown sprang up on the Potomac. This nickname is only slightly less amusing than the present one, an appellation that owes its derivation to the wharves, breweries, lime kilns, and glassworks that were built near the water. Smoke from these factories combined with the swampy air of the low-lying ground to produce a permanent fog along the waterfront.

The smoke-belching factories ensured work for the hundreds of German and Irish immigrants that settled in Foggy Bottom in the 19th century. By the '30s, however, industry was on the way out, and Foggy Bottom had become a poor, predominantly black part of Washington. The opening of the State Department headquarters in 1947 reawakened middle-class interest in the neighborhood's modest row houses. Many of them are now gone, and Foggy Bottom today suffers from a split personality, and tiny, one-room-wide row houses sit next to large, mixed-use developments.

Start your exploration near the Foggy Bottom Metro station on 23rd Street near I Street. The campus of **George Washington University** is to the east and south. GWU was founded in 1821 as the Columbian College in the District of Columbia. It was moved to Foggy Bottom in 1912, and in addition to modern university buildings now occupies many 19th-century residences.

**1** A block and a half south, at 728 23rd Street, is **St. Mary's Church,** designed by Smithsonian Castle architect James Renwick and built in 1887 for a black congregation.

**2** Walk west on I Street, crossing 24th Street and New Hampshire Avenue. Here are some of the modest, unadorned **houses** once occupied by Foggy Bottom's factory workers. Turn left on 25th Street. A collection of charming houses on the east side of the street (Nos. 813 to 803) sits between two residences with fanciful arched facades.

**3** Bear to the right around the traffic circle. Across Virginia Avenue is the **Watergate,** possibly the world's most notorious apartment/office complex, famous for the events that took place here on June 17, 1972. As Nixon aides E. Howard Hunt, Jr., and G. Gordon Liddy sat in the Howard Johnson Motor Lodge across the street, five men were caught trying to bug the headquarters of the Democratic National Committee on the sixth floor of 2600 Virginia Avenue. There's a doctor's office on the floor today. The name Watergate comes from the name of the monumental flight of steps leading up from the Potomac behind the Lincoln Memorial.

**4** Walk south on New Hampshire Avenue, past the Saudi Arabian Embassy, to the **John F. Kennedy Center for the Performing Arts.** The opening of the Kennedy Center in 1971 established Washington as a cultural city to be reckoned with. Concerts,

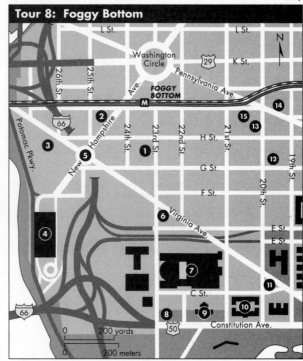

**Tour 8: Foggy Bottom**

ballets, opera, musicals, and drama are presented in the center's four theaters, and movies are screened almost every night in the theater of the American Film Institute.

The idea for a national cultural center had been proposed by President Eisenhower in 1958. John F. Kennedy had also strongly supported the idea, and after his assassination it was decided to dedicate the center to him as a living memorial. The Kennedy Center is an immense building. The Grand Foyer, lighted by 18 one-ton crystal chandeliers, is 630 feet long. (Even at this size it is mobbed at intermission.) Many of the center's furnishings were donated by foreign countries: The Matisse tapestries outside the Opera House came from France, the bronze sculptures on the plaza are from Germany, and the 3,700 tons of Carrara marble for the interior and exterior of the building were a gift from Italy. In the center of the foyer is a seven-foot-high bronze bust of Kennedy by sculptor Robert Berks. You can get one of the better views of the city from the center's rooftop terrace: To the north are Georgetown and the Washington Cathedral; to the west Theodore Roosevelt Island and Rosslyn, Virginia; and to the south the Jefferson and Lincoln memorials. *New Hampshire Ave. and Rock Creek Pkwy. NW, tel. 202/467–4600. Open Mon.–Sat. 10–9, Sun. and holidays noon–9. Tours Mon.–Sat. 10–1.*

**Time Out**   There are three restaurants on the top floor of the Kennedy Center. The **Roof Terrace Restaurant** is the most expensive, with a lunch menu that offers open-faced sandwiches and salads. The **Encore Cafeteria** has soups, chili, salads, and hot entrees starting at under $5. The **Curtain Call Cafe** is open before performances, Tuesday to Saturday.

Walk back up New Hampshire Avenue; then turn right on G Street, right on Virginia Avenue (follow the outstretched arm ❺ of the statue of **Benito Juárez**), and right on 23rd Street. The ❻ **Pan American Health Organization,** American headquarters of the World Health Organization, is in the curved building at 23rd Street and Virginia Avenue. Two blocks down is the massive **Department of State** building. Across C Street is the U.S. ❼ **Naval Medical Command.** In an early sketch of Washington, Thomas Jefferson placed the Capitol atop this hill. One of the federal government's earliest scientific installations was a naval observatory built here in 1844. By the 1880s, however, Foggy Bottom's smoke and haze forced officials to move the observatory to higher ground, in northwest Washington.

Continue down C Street and turn left onto Constitution Avenue. On the south side of Constitution are the Lincoln and ❽ Vietnam Veterans memorials (*see* Tour 2). The **American Pharmaceutical Association** building is on the corner of Constitution Avenue and C Street. This white-marble building was designed by John Russell Pope and completed in 1934. The APA is one of more than 3,000 trade and professional associations (as obscure as the Cast Iron Soil Pipe Institute and as well known as the National Association of Broadcasters) that have chosen Washington for their headquarters, eager to represent their members' interests before the government.

❾ One block east is the **National Academy of Sciences.** Inscribed in Greek under the cornice is a quotation from Aristotle on the value of science. To the left is Robert Berks's strangely gentle **sculpture of Albert Einstein,** done in the same lumpy mashed-potato style as the artist's bust of JFK in the Kennedy Center.

❿ The **Federal Reserve Building** (designed by Folger Library architect Paul Cret) is on Constitution Avenue between 21st and 20th streets. The imposing marble edifice, its bronze entryway topped by a massive eagle, seems to say, "Your money's safe with us." Even so, there isn't any money here. Fort Knox and New York's Federal Reserve Bank hold most of the Federal Reserve System's gold.

⓫ Turn left on 20th Street. The fountain one block up in **Robert Owen Park** is perfect for cooling hot and tired feet. Crossing Virginia Avenue and continuing north on 20th Street will take you back onto the campus of George Washington University. ⓬ Foggy Bottom's immigrant past is apparent in the **United Methodist Church** at 20th and G streets. Built in 1891 for blue-collar Germans in the neighborhood, the church still conducts ⓭ services in German. The former **Union Methodist Church,** a block and a half to the north, no longer has services in any language: The Mediterranean-style church now houses radio and TV studios for GWU's Communications Department.

Walk a half block north to Pennsylvania Avenue. To the right— near No. 1901—are the only two survivors of a string of 18th-⓮ century row houses known as the **Seven Buildings.** One of the five that have been demolished had served as President Madison's executive mansion after the British burned the White House in 1814. The two survivors are now dwarfed by the taller office block behind them.

A similar fate befell a row of residences further west on Pennsylvania Avenue between 20th and 21st streets. These Victorian houses have been hollowed out and refurbished and **⑮** serve as the entryway for a modern glass office building at **2000 Pennsylvania Avenue.** The backs of the buildings are under the sloping roof of the new development, preserved as if in an urban terrarium.

**Time Out**  Two of the transformed buildings now house good American-style restaurants that serve hearty fare such as steaks, sandwiches, oysters, and beer. **Wolensky's** and the **Devon Bar and Grill** cater to both a college crowd from nearby George Washington University and businesspeople from surrounding offices.

To get to the Foggy Bottom Metro station, walk three blocks west on I Street.

### Tour 9: Cleveland Park and the National Zoo

*Numbers in the margin correspond with points of interest on the Cleveland Park and the National Zoo map.*

Cleveland Park, a tree-shaded neighborhood in northwest Washington, owes its name to one-time summer resident Grover Cleveland and its development to the streetcar line that was laid along Connecticut Avenue in the 1890s. President Cleveland and his wife, Frances Folson, escaped the heat of downtown Washington in 1886 by establishing a summer White House on Newark Street between 35th and 36th streets. Many prominent Washingtonians followed suit. When the streetcar came through in 1892, construction in the area snowballed. Developer John Sherman hired local architects to design houses and provided amenities such as a fire station and a streetcar-waiting lodge to entice home buyers out of the city and into "rural" Cleveland Park. Today the neighborhood's attractive houses and suburban character are popular with Washington professionals.

Start your exploration at the Cleveland Park Metro station at Connecticut Avenue and Ordway Street NW. The small, some-**❶** what derelict, colonial-style **Park and Shop** on the east side of Connecticut Avenue has the distinction of being the first shopping center with off-street parking in the city. Built in 1930, it was at the time one of only a handful of shopping centers on the East Coast to offer this convenience. Off-street parking was then a rather revolutionary notion, and business and architectural publications of the day followed the center's progress with interest. A 1930 industry magazine explained, "Customers can leave their cars here without fear of violating traffic regulations," while the *Washington Post* gushed that the development was "modern to the nth degree." Fearing that a larger complex may obliterate the center, the active Cleveland Park Historical Society has been trying for years to have the Park and Shop designated a historic landmark.

**❷**  Half a block to the south is the **Cineplex Odeon Uptown** (3426 Connecticut Ave. NW, tel. 202/966–5400), a marvelous vintage-1936, Art-Deco movie house. Although many other big-screen theaters in the city have been chopped up and transformed into "multiplexes," the Uptown still has a single huge

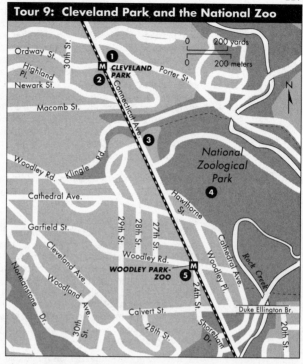

screen and an inviting balcony. The **Calliope Bookshop** next door (3424 Connecticut Ave. NW, tel. 202/364–0111) does a brisk business selling to uptown patrons waiting for the next show. It has a fine selection of literary fiction, poetry, philosophy, and art.

Continue south on Connecticut Avenue. You'll cross over a finger of Rock Creek Park via a span decorated with eight Art-Deco bridge lights. Beyond the bridge on the left is the city's finest Art-Deco apartment house, the **Kennedy-Warren** (3133 Connecticut Ave. NW). Opened in 1931, it features such period detailing as decorative aluminum panels and a streamlined entryway, stone griffins under the pyramidal copper roof, and stylized carved eagles flanking the driveways. Perhaps in keeping with its elegant architecture, the Kennedy-Warren is one of the last apartment buildings in town to still have a doorman (not to mention weekend dancing in its Aztec art deco–style ballroom).

On the same side of Connecticut Avenue is the **National Zoological Park,** part of the Smithsonian Institution and one of the foremost zoos in the world. Created by an Act of Congress in 1889, the 160-acre zoo was designed by landscape architect Frederick Law Olmsted, the man who designed the U.S. Capitol grounds. (Before the zoo opened in 1890, live animals used as taxidermists' models had been kept on the Mall.) The zoo's most famous residents are Hsing-Hsing and Ling-Ling, gifts from China in 1972 and the only giant pandas in the United States. After a string of unsuccessful pregnancies, it seems unlikely the two will ever produce offspring. The zoo has had success with numerous other species, however, including red pandas, Pere David's deer, golden lion tamarins, and pygmy hippopotamuses. The only Kimodo dragons in the country are at the National Zoo. Innovative compounds show many animals in naturalistic settings, including the Great Flight Cage, a walk-in aviary in which birds fly unrestricted. Giant crabs, octopuses, cuttlefish, and worms are displayed in an invertebrate exhibit. Zoolab, Birdlab, and Herplab all feature activities that teach young visitors about biology. Zoo officials recently outlined an ambitious plan to replace traditional animal displays with environments that combine animal species, living plants, museum specimens, and art. *3000 Connecticut Ave. NW, tel. 202/673–4717. Open daily except Christmas, May 1–Sept. 15: grounds 8 AM–8:30 PM, animal buildings 9–6. Sept. 16–Apr. 30: grounds 8–6, animal buildings 9–4:30. Admission: free. Limited paid parking is available.*

The stretch of Connecticut Avenue south of the zoo is bordered by more venerable apartment buildings. Passing Cathedral Avenue (the first cross-street south of the zoo) you enter a part of town known as **Woodley Park.** Like Cleveland Park to the north, Woodley Park grew as the streetcar advanced into this part of Washington. In 1800 Philip Barton Key, uncle of Francis Scott Key, built Woodley, a Georgian mansion on Cathedral Avenue between 29th and 31st streets. The white stucco mansion was the summer home of four presidents: Van Buren, Tyler, Buchanan, and Cleveland. It is now owned by the private Maret School.

At the corner of Connecticut Avenue and Woodley Road is the cross-shaped **Wardman Tower.** The Georgian-style tower was built by developer Harry Wardman in 1928 as a luxury apartment building to accompany a now-demolished luxury hotel he had built nearby 10 years earlier. Washingtonians called the project "Wardman's Folly," convinced no one would want to stay in a hotel so far from the city. The Wardman Tower was famous for its well-known residents, who included Dwight D. Eisenhower, Herbert Hoover, Clare Booth Luce, Dean Rusk, Earl Warren, and Caspar Weinberger. It is now part of the Sheraton Washington Hotel (*see* Upper Connecticut Avenue in Chapter 7).

Wardman's success spurred the development of the neighborhood's other large hotel, the **Omni Shoreham** (*see* Upper Connecticut Avenue in Chapter 7) on Calvert Street west of Connecticut Avenue. The Shoreham was known for the entertainers who appeared here, including Rudy Vallee, who performed at its grand opening in 1930. The Shoreham and the nearby Sheraton-Washington are two of the city's main convention hotels; you'll notice that many of the people on the streets around you have plastic name badges pinned to their lapels.

The nearest Metro station is Woodley Park/Zoo, at Connecticut Avenue and Woodley Road.

## Tour 10: Arlington

*Numbers in the margin correspond with points of interest on the Arlington map.*

The Virginia suburb of Arlington County was once part of the District of Columbia. Carved out of the Old Dominion when Washington was created, it was returned to Virginia along with the rest of the land west of the Potomac in 1845. Washington hasn't held a grudge, though, and there are three attractions in Arlington—each linked to the military—that should be a part of any complete visit to the nation's capital: Arlington National Cemetery, the U.S. Marine Corps War Memorial, and the Pentagon. All are accessible by Metro, and a trip across the Potomac makes an enjoyable half day of sightseeing.

Begin your exploration in **Arlington National Cemetery.** To get there, you can take the Metro to the Arlington Cemetery station, travel on a Tourmobile bus, (*see* Essential Information), or walk across Memorial Bridge from the District (southwest of the Lincoln Memorial). Your first stop should be new skylit **Visitors Center,** on Memorial Drive. A free brochure includes a detailed map that will help you make sense out of the 612 acres of land. (If you're looking for a specific grave the staff will consult microfilm records and give you directions on how to find it. You should know the deceased's full name and, if possible, his or her branch of service and year of death.)

Tourmobile tour buses leave from just outside the Visitors Center. You can buy tickets here (adults $2.50, children $1.25) for the 40-minute tour of the cemetery, which includes stops at the Kennedy gravesites, the Tomb of the Unknowns, and Arlington House. Touring the cemetery on foot means a fair bit of hiking, but it will give you a closer look at some of the 200,000 graves spread out over these rolling Virginia hills. If you decide to walk, head west from the Visitors Center on Roosevelt Drive and then turn right on Weeks Drive.

While you are at Arlington you will probably hear the clear, doleful sound of a trumpet playing *Taps* or the sharp reports of a gun salute. Approximately 15 funerals are held here daily. It is projected the cemetery will be filled in 2020. While not the largest cemetery in the country, Arlington is certainly the best known, a place where visitors can trace America's history through the aftermath of its battles.

It was in Arlington that the two most famous names in Virginia history—Washington and Lee—became intertwined. George Washington Parke Custis—raised by Martha and George Washington, his grandmother and step-grandfather—built **Arlington House** (also known as the Custis-Lee Mansion) between 1802 and 1817 on his 1,100-acre estate overlooking the Potomac. After his death, the property went to his daughter, Mary Anna Randolph Custis. In 1831 Mary Custis married Robert E. Lee, a recent graduate of West Point. For the next 30 years the Custis-Lee family lived at Arlington House.

In 1861 Lee was offered command of the Union forces. He declined, insisting that he could never take up arms against his native Virginia. The Lees left Arlington House that spring, never to return. Union troops soon occupied the estate, making it the headquarters of the officers who were charged with defending Washington. When Mrs. Lee was unable to appear in person to pay a $92.07 property tax the government had assessed, the land was confiscated and a portion set aside as a military cemetery.

# Tour 10: Arlington

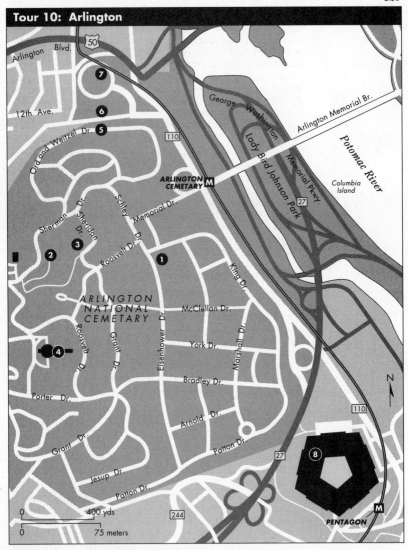

Arlington House, **2**

Kennedy graves, **3**

Netherlands
Carillon, **6**

Pentagon, **8**

Section 27, **5**

Tomb of the
Unknowns, **4**

U.S. Marine Corps
War Memorial, **7**

Visitors Center, **1**

Its heavy Doric columns and severe pediment make Arlington House one of the area's best examples of Greek-Revival architecture. The plantation home was designed by George Hadfield, a young English architect who for a while supervised construction of the Capitol. The view of Washington from the front of the house is superb. In 1955 Arlington House was designated a memorial to Robert E. Lee. It looks much as it did in the 19th century, and a quick tour will take you past objects once owned by the Custises and the Lees. *Between Lee and Sherman drs., tel. 703/557-0613. Open daily Apr.-Sept. 9:30-6, Oct.-Mar. 9:30-4:30. Closed Christmas.*

In front of the house, next to a flag that flies at half staff whenever there is a funeral in the cemetery, is the flat-topped grave of Pierre L'Enfant, designer of the Federal City. L'Enfant died in 1825, a penniless, bitter man who felt he hadn't been recognized for his planning genius. He was originally buried in Maryland, but his body was moved here with much ceremony in 1909.

On a hillside just below Arlington House to the east are the **❸ Kennedy graves.** John F. Kennedy is buried under an eternal flame near his two infant children, across from a low wall engraved with quotations from his inaugural address. JFK's grave was opened to the public in 1967 and since that time has become the most-visited gravesite in the country. The nearby grave of Robert Kennedy is marked by a simple white cross.

After visiting Arlington House and the Kennedy graves, walk west on Crook Walk past the seemingly endless rows of simple white headstones—arranged like soldiers on parade—and fol-**❹** low the signs to the **Tomb of the Unknowns.** The first burial at the Tomb of the Unknowns was on November 11, 1921, when the Unknown soldier from World War I was interred under the large white-marble sarcophagus. Servicemen killed in World War II and Korea were buried in 1958. The Unknown serviceman from the Vietnam War was laid to rest on the plaza on Memorial Day 1984. Soldiers from the Army's U.S. 3rd Infantry ("The Old Guard," portrayed in the movie *Gardens of Stone*) keep watch over the tomb 24 hours a day, regardless of weather conditions. Each sentinel marches exactly 21 steps, then faces the tomb for 21 seconds, symbolizing the 21-gun salute, America's highest military honor. The guard is changed with a precise ceremony during the day every half hour from April 1 to September 30, and every hour the rest of the year. At night the guard is changed every two hours. The **Memorial Amphitheater** west of the tomb is the scene of special ceremonies on Veterans Day, Memorial Day, and Easter. Decorations awarded to the Unknowns by foreign governments and U.S. and foreign organizations are displayed in an indoor trophy room.

Across from the amphitheater are memorials to the astronauts killed in the Challenger shuttle explosion and to the servicemen killed in 1980 while trying to rescue American hostages in Iran. Rising beyond that is the mast from the U.S.S. Maine, the American ship that was sunk in Havana Harbor in 1898, killing 299 men.

Below the Tomb of the Unknowns is **section 7A,** where you can find the graves of many distinguished veterans, including boxing champ Joe Louis, ABC newsman Frank Reynolds, actor

Lee Marvin, and World War II fighter pilot Col. "Pappy" Boyington.

To reach the sites at the northern end of the cemetery and to make your way into the city of Arlington, first walk north along Roosevelt Drive to Schley Drive (you'll pass the Memorial Gate), then turn right on Custis Walk to the Ord & Weitzel Gate. On your way you'll pass **section 27**, where 3,800 former slaves are buried. They lived at Freedman's Village, established at Arlington in 1863 to provide housing, education, and employment training to ex-slaves who had traveled to the capital. The headstones are marked with their names and the words "Civilian" or "Citizen." Buried at grave 19 in section 27 is William Christman, a Union private who died of peritonitis in Washington on May 13, 1864. He was the first soldier interred at Arlington National Cemetery during the Civil War. *West end of Memorial Bridge, Arlington, VA, tel. 703/692–0931. Open daily Apr.–Sept. 8–7, Oct.–Mar. 8–5. Arlington House open daily Apr.–Sept. 9:30–6, Oct.–Mar. 9:30–4:30.*

Leaving the cemetery through the Ord & Weitzel Gate, cross Marshall Drive carefully, and walk to the **Netherlands Carillon.** The 49-bell carillon was presented to the United States by the Dutch people in 1954 as thanks for aid received during World War II. For one of the most inclusive views of Washington, look to the east across the Potomac. From this vantage point, the Lincoln Memorial, the Washington Monument, and the Capitol are bunched together in a side-by-side formation. *Carillon information, tel. 703/285–2601. Performances June–Aug., Sat. 6:30 PM.; Sept., Sat. 2.*

To the north is the **United States Marine Corps War Memorial,** honoring Marines who have given their lives since the Corps was formed in 1775. The memorial statue, sculpted by Felix W. de Widdon, is based on Joe Rosenthal's Pulitzer Prize-winning photograph of five Marines and a Navy corpsman raising a flag atop Mount Suribachi on Iwo Jima on February 19, 1945. By executive order, a real flag flies 24 hours a day from the 78-foot-high memorial. On Tuesday evenings at 7 PM from late May to late August there is a Marine Corps sunset parade on the grounds of the Memorial. You can catch a free shuttle bus from the Arlington Cemetery visitor parking lot (for information, tel. 202/433–6060). A word of caution: It is dangerous to visit the memorial after dark.

The Arlington neighborhood of Rosslyn is north of the memorial. Like parts of downtown Washington and Crystal City further to the south, Rosslyn is almost empty at night once the thousands of people who work there have gone home. Its tall buildings do provide the preturnaturally horizontal Washington with a bit of a skyline, but this has come about not without some controversy: Some say the silvery, wing-shaped Gannett Buildings are too close to the flight path followed by jets landing at National Airport.

**Time Out**  Picnicking is not allowed at Arlington National Cemetery, and there are no restaurants open to the public at the next stop on the tour, the Pentagon. If you're hungry at this point in the tour, it's necessary to venture into Rosslyn. Walk north on Meade Street, turn left on Wilson Boulevard, then right onto Moore Street. Here you'll find some dependable fast food (McDonald's and Roy Rogers). For something more interesting, try the **Tivoli Restaurant** (1700 N. Moore St.). You can get an Italian sit-down meal or lighter fare at the restaurant's deli. The pastries are good, too.

**8** To get to the **Pentagon,** take the Metro to the Pentagon station, which is right alongside the humongous office building. The headquarters of the Department of Defense, the Pentagon was completed in 1943 after just two years of construction. The five-sided building is an exercise in immensity: 23,000 military and civilian employees work here; it is as wide as three Washington Monuments laid end to end; inside are 17½ miles of corridors, 7,754 windows, and 691 drinking fountains. The 45-minute tour of the Pentagon takes you past only those areas that are meant to be seen by outside visitors. In other words, you won't see situation rooms, communications centers, or gigantic maps outlining U.S. and Soviet troop strengths. A uniformed serviceman or woman (who conducts the entire tour walking backwards, lest anyone slip away down a corridor) will take you past hallways lined with the portraits of past and present military leaders, scale models of Air Force planes and Navy ships, and the Hall of Heroes, where the names of all the Congressional Medal of Honor winners are inscribed. Occasionally you will catch a glimpse through an interior window of the Pentagon's five-acre interior courtyard. In the center—at ground zero—is a hotdog stand. *Pentagon, off of Rte. I-395, Arlington, VA, tel. 202/695-1776. Tours Mon.–Fri. every half hour 9:30–3:30.*

## Tour 11: Alexandria

*Numbers in the margin correspond with points of interest on the Alexandria map.*

Just a short Metro ride (or bike ride) away from Washington, Old Town Alexandria today attracts visitors seeking a break from the monuments and hustle-and-bustle of the District and interested in an encounter with America's Colonial heritage. Founded in 1749 by Scottish merchants eager to capitalize on the booming tobacco trade, Alexandria emerged as one of the most important ports in Colonial America. The city's history is linked to the most significant events and personages of the Colonial and Revolutionary periods. This colorful past is still alive in restored 18th- and 19th-century homes, churches, and taverns; in the cobbled streets; and on the revitalized waterfront, where clipper ships dock and artisans display their wares.

The quickest way to get to Old Town is to take the Metro to the King Street stop (about 25 minutes from Metro Center). If you're driving you can take either the George Washington Memorial Parkway or Jefferson Davis Highway (Route 1) south from Arlington.

**1** The best place to start a tour of Old Town is at the **Alexandria Convention & Visitors Bureau,** which is in **Ramsay House,** the home of the town's first postmaster and lord mayor, William Ramsay. The structure is believed to be the oldest house in Alexandria. Ramsay was a Scotsman, as a swath of his tartan on the door proclaims. Travel counselors here provide information, brochures, and self-guided walking tours of the town. *221 King St. 22314, tel. 703/838-4200. Open daily 9–5. Closed Thanksgiving, Christmas, and New Year's Day. Out-of-*

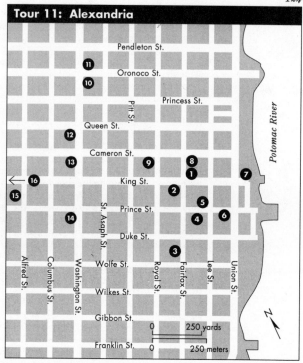

**Tour 11: Alexandria**

*towners are given a 72-hour courtesy parking permit that allows them to park free at any 2-hr. metered spot.*

**2** Across the street, at the corner of Fairfax and King streets, is the **Stabler-Leadbeater Apothecary Shop,** the second-oldest apothecary in the country. It was patronized by George Washington and the Lee family, and it was here, on October 17, 1859, that Lt. Col. Robert E. Lee received orders to move to Harper's Ferry to suppress John Brown's insurrection. The shop now houses a small museum of 18th-century apothecary memorabilia, including one of the finest collections of apothecary bottles in the country (some 800 bottles in all). *105–107 S. Fairfax St., tel. 703/836–3713. Closed for renovations until mid-1990; call for information.*

**3** Two blocks south on Fairfax Street, just beyond Duke Street, stands the **Old Presbyterian Meeting House** (321 S. Fairfax St., tel. 703/549–6670). Built in 1774, this was an important meeting place for Scottish patriots during the Revolution. Eulogies for George Washington were delivered here on December 29, 1799. In a corner of the churchyard you'll find the **Tomb of the Unknown Soldier of the American Revolution.**

**4**
**5** Next walk back up Fairfax Street one block and turn right on Prince Street. The block between Fairfax and Lee streets is known as **Gentry Row.** One of the most noteworthy structures in the city is the **Atheneum,** at the corner of Prince and Lee streets. The striking, reddish-brown Greek Revival edifice was built as a bank in the 1850s. Today the Atheneum houses the gallery of the Northern Virginia Fine Arts Association, which

displays the work of local artists. *201 Prince St., tel. 703/548–0035. Open Sept.–June, Tues.–Sat. 10–4, Sun. 1–4; July and Aug., Tues.–Fri. 10–4, Sat. and Sun. 1–4. Also open at other times for special exhibits.*

**6** The next block of Prince Street to the east (between Lee and Union streets) is known as **Captain's Row** because this was where many of the city's sea captains built their homes. The cobblestones in the street were allegedly laid by Hessian mercenaries who fought for the British during the Revolutionary War and who were being held in Alexandria as prisoners of war.

**7** Continuing east on Prince Street you'll come to Alexandria's lively waterfront. Two blocks to the north up Union Street (at the foot of King Street) is one of the most popular destinations in the city, the **Torpedo Factory Arts Center.** This former munitions plant (yes, naval torpedoes were actually manufactured here during World War I and World War II) has now been converted into studios and galleries for some 175 professional artists. Almost every imaginable medium is represented, from printmaking and sculpture to jewelry making, pottery, and stained glass. Visitors can view the artisans' workshops, and most of the artworks are for sale at reasonable prices. *105 N. Union St., tel. 703/838–4565. Open daily 10–5.*

The Torpedo Factory complex also houses the **Alexandria Archaeology Program,** a city-operated research facility devoted to urban archaeology and conservation. Artifacts from excavations dug in Alexandria are on display. *105 N. Union St., tel. 703/838–4399. Open Tues., Wed., and Thurs. 10–3, Fri. and Sat. 10–5.*

**8** Moving back into the town, a two-block walk up Cameron Street brings you to the grandest of the older houses in the town, **Carlyle House,** at the corner of North Fairfax Street. Patterned after a Scottish country manor house, the structure was completed in 1753 by Scottish merchant John Carlyle. This was General Braddock's headquarters and the place where he met with five Royal Governors in 1755 to plan the strategy and funding of the early campaigns of the French and Indian War. *121 N. Fairfax St., tel. 703/549–2997. Open Tues.–Sat. 10–5, Sun. noon–5.*

**9** One block west on Royal Street is **Gadsby's Tavern Museum,** housed in the old City Tavern and Hotel, which was a center of political and social life in the late 18th century. George Washington attended birthday celebrations in the ballroom here. A tour of the facilities takes you through the taproom, game room assembly room, ballroom, and communal bedrooms. *134–138 N. Royal St., tel. 703/838–4242. Open Tues.–Sat. 10–5, Sun. 1–5.*

**10** Continue west on Cameron Street for three blocks and turn right on Washington Street. The corner of Washington and Oronoco streets (three blocks north) is known as **Lee Corner** because at one time a Lee-owned house stood on each of the four corners. Two survive. One is the **Lee-Fendall House,** the home of several illustrious members of the Lee family, including Richard Henry Lee, signer of the Declaration of Independence, and cavalry commander "Light Horse Harry" Lee. *614 Oronoco St., tel. 703/548–1789. Open Tues.–Sat. 10–4, Sun. noon–4.*

⑪ Directly across the street is the **boyhood home of Robert E. Lee,** a fine example of a 19th-century town house. It features Federal architecture and antique furnishings and paintings. *607 Oronoco St., tel. 703/548–8454. Open Mon.–Sat. 10–4, Sun. noon–4. Closed Dec. 15–Feb. 1.*

⑫ Two blocks south, at the corner of Queen and Washington streets, is the **Lloyd House,** a fine example of Georgian architecture. Built in 1797, it is now operated as part of the Alexandria Library and houses a collection of rare books and documents relating to city and state history. *220 North Washington St., tel. 703/838–4577. Open Mon.–Sat. 9–5.*

⑬ At the corner of Cameron and Washington streets, one block south, stands **Christ Church** (118 N. Washington St., tel. 703/549–1450. Open Mon.–Sat. 9–4, Sun. 1–4.), where both Washington and Lee were pewholders (Washington paid 36 pounds and 10 shillings, a lot of money in those days, for Pew 60). Built in 1773, it is a fine example of an English, Georgian country-style church. The interior features a fine Palladian window, interior balcony, and a wrought-brass-and-crystal chandelier brought from England at Washington's expense.

⑭ From Christ Church, walk two blocks south to the **Lyceum** at the corner of Washington and Prince streets. Built in 1839, the structure served alternately as the Alexandria Library, a Civil War hospital, a residence, and an office building. It was restored in the '70s and now houses two art galleries, a gift shop, and a museum devoted to the area's history. A limited amount of travel information for the entire state is also available here. *201 S. Washington St., tel. 703/838–4994. Open daily 10–5. Closed Thanksgiving, Christmas, and New Year's Day.*

⑮ Two blocks to the west on South Alfred Street is the **Friendship Fire Company.** George Washington was a founder of the volunteer company and was its honorary captain. On display is a replica of the $400 fire engine that Washington bought, considered at the time to be the finest obtainable. *107 S. Alfred St. Irregular operating hours.*

⑯ A little far to walk but well worth visiting is the **George Washington Masonic National Memorial** on Callahan Drive at King Street, a mile west of the center of the city. The memorial's spire dominates the surroundings, and from the entryway visitors get a spectacular view of Alexandria and Washington in the distance. Among other things, the building contains furnishings from the first Masonic lodge in Alexandria, in which George Washington was Worshipful Master at the same time he served as president. *101 Callahan Dr., tel. 703/683–2007. Open daily 9–5. Closed Thanksgiving, Christmas, and New Year's Day. Free guided tours of the building and observation deck daily 9:10–4.*

## Washington for Free

Visitors will have a hard time finding attractions and events in Washington that are *not* free. There are no admission fees to any of the Smithsonian museums—including the National Zoo—and entry to many other museums and galleries is also without charge. The ride to the top of the Washington Monument used to cost a dime, but today, like admission to the rest of the memorials, that's free, too.

**Concerts**  **Fort Dupont Summer Theater** (Minnesota Ave. and F St. SE, tel. 202/485–9666) hosts well-known jazz artists Friday and Saturday evenings at 8:30 during the summer.
**The National Building Museum's** impressive Pension Building (F St. between 4th and 5th sts. NW, tel. 202/272–2448) is the site of lunchtime concerts.
**The National Symphony Orchestra** (tel. 202/785–8100) presents free concerts on the West Terrace of the Capitol on Memorial Day and Labor Day weekends and on July 4th. The orchestra also offers free classical concerts at the National Gallery of Art (6th St. and Constitution Ave. NW, tel. 202/737–4215) Sunday evenings from October to June.
**The Sylvan Theater** (tel. 202/485–9666), on the grounds of the Washington Monument, is the site of numerous military and big-band concerts from mid-June to August.

**Festivals**  **The Festival of American Folklife,** a celebration of home-grown crafts, music, and food, is sponsored by the Smithsonian and is held on the Mall each year in late June or early July (tel. 202/357–3700).
**The Hispanic-American Cultural Festival** (tel. 202/789–7000) is a day-long carnival of music, dance, and arts and crafts that is held in late July or early August in the city's Latino Adams-Morgan and Mt. Pleasant neighborhoods. Adams-Morgan heats up again in September for **Adams-Morgan Day,** a similarly ethnic celebration (tel. 202/789–7000).

**Lectures**  **The Library of Congress** (tel. 202/707–5394) sponsors periodic literary lectures and poetry readings by well-known poets, usually on Monday and Tuesday evenings.
**The Martin Luther King Memorial Library's** "Lunchtime Author Series" (901 G St. NW, tel. 202/727–1186) features readings and discussions with local and national authors every Tuesday at noon, except during the month of June.

The "Weekend" section in Friday's *Washington Post* is an excellent source of other free events in and around the District.

## What to See and Do with Children

Kids who have been learning about the early days of America or how its government works will find much to see and enjoy in Washington. History that seems dusty and boring in a textbook comes alive at the White House, the Senate Chamber, and the Supreme Court. For younger children (or less politically-minded tykes) numerous museums encourage hands-on learning.

**Adventure Theater** (MacArthur Blvd. and Goldsboro Rd., Glen Echo, MD, tel. 301/320–5331). Delightful plays for children ages four and up are performed year-round at the Glen Echo Park. The 1990 season will include *Rikki-Tikki-Tavi, Black Beauty, Raggedy Ann and Andy,* and *The House at Pooh Corner.* Performances are Saturday and Sunday at 1:30 and 3:30. Reservations suggested.

**Capital Children's Museum** (*see* Museums and Galleries, below). Youngsters immediately feel at home in this museum that's designed just for them. *Metro stop, Union Station.*

**Carousel** (*see* Tour 1: The Mall) *Metro stop, Smithsonian.*

**Dolls House and Toy Museum of Washington** (*see* Museums). *Metro stop, Friendship Heights.*

**National Air and Space Museum, National Museum of American History, National Museum of Natural History.** (*see* Tour 1: The Mall). *Metro stop, Smithsonian or Federal Triangle.*

**National Aquarium** (*see* Tour 5: Old Downtown and Federal Triangle). *Metro stop, Federal Triangle.*

**National Geographic Explorers Hall** (*see* Tour 7: Dupont Circle) *Metro stop, Farragut North.*

**The National Zoo** (*see* Tour 9: Cleveland Park/Zoo). *Metro stop, Cleveland Park or Woodley Park/National Zoo.*

**Tidal Basin paddle boats** (*see* Tour 2: The Monuments). *Metro stop, Smithsonian.*

**The Washington Monument** (Tour 2: The Monuments). *Metro stops, Federal Triangle or Smithsonian.*

## Off the Beaten Track

**The Ansel Adams Collection,** a permanent exhibit of the famed photographer's most important landscapes, is on display at the Wilderness Society's headquarters. *1400 I St. NW, tel. 202/ 842–3400. Open Mon.–Fri. 10–5. Closed holidays and day after Thanksgiving. Large groups should call ahead. Metro stop, McPherson Square.*

**Intelsat,** the international satellite cooperative, has its headquarters in a striking glass building that looks as if it itself had come down from space. Although no tours of the building are given, twice a week a brief film about the work of the organization is shown. Visitors also get a chance to see the models of rockets and satellites that adorn the main lobby, and the control and operations centers where satellite traffic is monitored. The last is like something out of a James Bond movie. Space and science buffs will enjoy the visit. *Connecticut Ave. and Van Ness St. NW, tel. 202/944–7500. Reservations required. Metro stop, Van Ness/UDC.*

**Two outdoor murals** have become fixtures in Washington. The unmistakable face of Marilyn Monroe gazes from the side of a beauty shop in Woodley Park, on Connecticut Avenue just north of Calvert Street NW. *Metro stop, Woodley Park/Zoo.* Painted on a monolithic exhaust tower on H Street between 2nd and 3rd streets NW, just north of Massachusetts Avenue, is a trompe l'oeil "hole" through which you can see the Capitol dome. *Metro stop, Judiciary Square.*

**The National Theater** is housed in a building that was constructed in 1922, though there has been a National Theater on this spot since 1835. After seeing her first play here at the age of six, first lady of the theater Helen Hayes vowed to become an actress. Free tours of the historic theater are offered every Monday and take in the house, stage, backstage, wardrobe room, dressing rooms, the area under the stage, the Helen Hayes Lounge, and the memorabilia-filled archives. *1321 Pennsylvania Ave. NW, tel. 202/783–3370. Make reservations at least a week ahead. Metro stop, Metro Center.*

# Sightseeing Checklists

## Historical Buildings and Sites

This list of Washington's principal buildings and sites includes both attractions that were covered in preceding tours and additional attractions that are described here for the first time.

**American Red Cross** (Tour 3: The White House) *Metro stop, Farragut West.*

**Anderson House** (Tour 7: Dupont Circle) *Metro stop, Dupont Circle.*

**Barney Studio House** (Tour 7: Dupont Circle) *Metro stop, Dupont Circle.*

**Clara Barton National Historic Site.** Home of the American Red Cross and its founder from 1897 to 1904, this 41-room building is furnished with original period artifacts, including large supply cabinets (where relief supplies were stockpiled), antique typewriters, and roll-top desks. *5801 Oxford Rd., Glen Echo, MD, tel. 301/492–6254. Open daily 10–5.*

**Blair House** (Tour 3: The White House) *Metro stop, McPherson Square.*

**Cox's Row** (Tour 6: Georgetown).

**Custom House** (Tour 6: Georgetown).

**Decatur House** (Tour 3: The White House) *Metro stop, McPherson Square.*

**District (of Columbia) Building** (Tour 5: Old Downtown and Federal Triangle) *Metro stop, Federal Triangle.*

**Frederick Douglass National Historic Site.** Cedar Hill, the Anacostia home of noted abolitionist Frederick Douglass, was the first place designated by Congress as a Black National Historic Site. Douglass, an ex-slave who delivered fiery abolitionist speeches at home and abroad, was 60 when he moved here, in 1877. He lived at Cedar Hill until his death, in 1895. The house has a wonderful view of the Federal City, across the Anacostia, and contains many of Douglass's personal belongings. A short film on Douglass's life is shown at a nearby visitors center. *1411 W St. SE, tel. 202/426–5961. Open fall and winter, daily 8:30–4:30; spring and summer, daily 9–5. Tours given on the hour.*

**Dumbarton House.** (Tour 6: Georgetown).

**Dumbarton Oaks** (Tour 6: Georgetown).

**Eastern Market.** Built in 1873, Eastern Market has always been a bustling center of activity on Capitol Hill. It was designed by Adolph Cluss, the architect of the Smithsonian Arts and Industries Museum. Inside are shops, restaurants, and galleries. There is a flea market outside on weekends. *7th and C sts. SE. Metro stop, Eastern Market.*

**Evermay** (Tour 6: Georgetown).

**Folger Shakespeare Library** (Tour 4: Capitol Hill) *Metro stop, Capitol South.*

**Ford's Theater** (Tour 5: Old Downtown and Federal Triangle) *Metro stop, Metro Center.*

**Heurich Mansion/Columbia Historical Society** (Tour 7: Dupont Circle) *Metro stop, Dupont Circle.*

**J. Edgar Hoover FBI Building** (Tour 5: Old Downtown and Federal Triangle) *Metro stop, Federal Triangle.*

**John F. Kennedy Center for the Performing Arts** (Tour 8: Foggy Bottom) *Metro stop, Foggy Bottom.*

**Marine Corps Barracks.** Each Friday evening at 8:45 from May to September the Marine Corps Drum and Bugle Corps, the

Marine Band, and the Silent Drill Team present a dress parade filled with martial music and precision marching. *8th and I sts. SE, tel. 202/433–6060. Reservations required. Call three weeks in advance.*

**Martin Luther King Memorial Library** (Tour 5: Old Downtown and Federal Triangle) *Metro stop, Gallery Place.*

**Library of Congress, Jefferson Building** (Tour 4: Capitol Hill) *Metro stop, Capitol South.*

**Meridian House and the White-Meyer House.** Meridian House International, a nonprofit institution promoting international understanding, now owns these two handsome mansions designed by John Russell Pope. The 30-room Meridian House was built in 1920 by Irwin Boyle Laughlin, scion of a Pittsburgh steel family and former ambassador to Spain. The Louis XVI-style home features parquet floors, ornamental iron grillwork, handsome mouldings, period furniture, tapestries, and a garden planted with European Linden trees. Next door is the Georgian-style house built for Henry White (former ambassador to France) that was later the home of the Meyer family, publishers of the *Washington Post*. The first floors of both houses are open to the public and are the scene of periodic art exhibits with an international flavor. *1630 and 1624 Crescent Pl. NW, tel. 202/667–6800. Open Mon.–Fri. 1–4; also Sun. 1–4 if an exhibition is in progress.*

**National Archives** (Tour 5: Old Downtown and Federal Triangle) *Metro stop, Archives.*

**Octagon House** (Tour 3: The White House) *Metro stop, Farragut West.*

**Old Executive Office Building** (Tour 3: The White House) *Metro stop, Farragut West.*

**Old Post Office** (Tour 5: Old Downtown and Federal Triangle) *Metro stop, Federal Triangle.*

**Old Stone House** (Tour 6: Georgetown).

**Organization of American States** (Tour 3: The White House) *Metro stop, Farragut West.*

**Pension Building** (Tour 5: Old Downtown and Federal Triangle) *Metro stop, Judiciary Square.*

**Peirce Mill.** Using the water power of Rock Creek, Isaac Peirce ground flour here from 1820 until 1897, when the mill shaft broke. The mill has been restored, and National Park Service employees grind wheat into flour that is then sold to visitors. *Rock Creek Park at Tilden St. and Beach Dr. tel. 202/426–6908. Open Wed.–Sun. 8–4. Closed holidays. Metro stop, Van Ness/ UDC.*

**Prospect House** (Tour 6: Georgetown).

**Sears House** (Tour 5: Old Downtown and Federal Triangle) *Metro stop, Archives.*

**Sewell-Belmont House** (Tour 4: Capitol Hill) *Metro stop, Union Station.*

**Sumner School** (Tour 7: Dupont Circle) *Metro stop, Farragut North.*

**Supreme Court of the United States** (Tour 4: Capitol Hill). *Metro stop, Capitol South.*

**Treasury Building** (Tour 3: The White House) *Metro stop, McPherson Square.*

**Union Station** (Tour 4: Capitol Hill) *Metro stop, Union Station.*

**United States Capitol** (Tour 4: Capitol Hill) *Metro stop, Capitol South or Union Station.*

**Washington Navy Yard.** The yard is the Navy's oldest shore establishment, authorized in 1799 by Benjamin Stoddert, first secretary of the Navy. It was burned during the War of 1812 to prevent it from falling into the hands of British troops. Rebuilt after the war, the yard was for a time used for the construction of ships, then ordnance. The facility is now a supply and administrative center. A **Navy Museum** is housed in the former Breech Mechanism Shop of the old Naval Gun Factory. Moored nearby and on permanent display is the *Barry*, a former USN destroyer. *9th and M sts. SE, tel. 202/433-2651. Open Mon.-Fri. 9-4; Sat. and Sun. 10-5; Memorial Day and Labor Day 9-5; other holidays 10-5.*

**White House** (Tour 3: The White House) *Metro stop, McPherson Square.*

**Willard Hotel** (Tour 5: Old Downtown and Federal Triangle) *Metro stops, Federal Triangle and Metro Center.*

**Woodrow Wilson House** (Tour 7: Dupont Circle) *Metro stop, Dupont Circle.*

## Museums and Galleries

The Smithsonian dominates the public museum and gallery scene in Washington, but there are also many private art galleries that show and sell the work of local, national, and international artists. These galleries are concentrated near Dupont Circle, in Georgetown, and on 7th Street north of Pennsylvania Avenue. For a good overview of the small private and the large public galleries in the city, consult the magazine *Museum & Arts Washington.*

**Anacostia Neighborhood Museum.** Exhibits in this Smithsonian museum deal with African-American history and culture. Past exhibits have focused on black aviators, the Harlem Renaissance, and the development of African-American churches. *1901 Fort Pl. SE, tel. 202/287-3369. Open daily 10-5. Closed Christmas.*

**Armed Forces Medical Museum.** Opened more than 125 years ago, the Medical Museum features exhibits that illustrate medicine's fight against injury and disease. Included are displays on the Lincoln and Garfield assassinations and one of the world's largest collection of microscopes. Since some exhibits are fairly graphic (the wax surgical models and various organs floating in alcohol, for example) the museum may not be suitable for young children or the squeamish. *Walter Reed Army Medical Center, 6825 16th St. NW, tel. 202/576-2348. Open Mon.-Fri. 9:30-4:30, weekends and holidays 11:30-4:30. Closed Thanksgiving, Christmas Eve, Christmas, and New Year's Day.*

**Art, Science, and Technology Institute.** At this small museum, 60 three-dimensional holograms seem to jump off the walls and float in space. The laser-produced works of art are by international artists and include the world's largest hologram on display, three square feet. *2018 R St., N.W., tel. 202/667-6322. Open Tues.-Sun. 11-7. Closed Thanksgiving, Christmas, New Years, Easter. $3 suggested donation.*

**Arts and Industries Building** (Tour 1: The Mall) *Metro stop, Smithsonian.*

**Bethune Museum-Archives.** Born to ex-slaves in South Carolina, Mary McLeod Bethune went on to found Florida's Bethune-Cookman College, establish the National Council of Negro Women, and serve as an advisor to President Franklin D. Roosevelt. Exhibits in the museum reflect Bethune's ideals and focus on the achievements of black women. *1318 Vermont Ave. NW, tel. 202/332–1233. Open Mon.–Fri. 10–4. Metro stop, McPherson Square.*

**B'nai B'rith Klutznick Museum** (Tour 7: Dupont Circle) *Metro stop, Farragut North.*

**Capital Children's Museum.** In this hands-on museum children can send messages in Morse code, hoist cinder blocks with pulleys and levers, crawl through a mock sewer, climb on a fire engine, and learn about foreign countries by making traditional ethnic foods and crafts. *800 3rd St. NE, tel. 202/543–8600. Open daily 10–5. Closed Thanksgiving, Christmas, New Year's Day and Easter. Admission: $5 for ages 2–59, senior citizens $2, children under 2 free.*

**Corcoran Gallery of Art** (Tour 3: The White House) *Metro stop, Farragut West.*

**Daughters of the American Revolution Museum** (Tour 3: The White House) *Metro stop, Farragut West.*

**Dumbarton Oaks Collection** (Tour 6: Georgetown).

**Fonda Del Sol Visual Art and Media Center.** Located near Dupont Circle in a Victorian town house, this nonprofit center is devoted to the cultural heritage of the Americas. Changing exhibitions cover contemporary, pre-Columbian, and folk art. The center also offers a program of lectures, concerts, poetry readings, exhibit tours, and an annual summer festival featuring salsa and reggae music. *2112 R St. NW, tel. 202/483–2777. Open Tues.–Sat. 12:30–5:30. Metro stop, Dupont Circle.*

**Freer Gallery of Art** (Tour 1: The Mall) *Metro stop, Smithsonian.*

**Hillwood Museum.** Hillwood House, the 40-room Georgian mansion of cereal heiress Marjorie Merriweather Post, contains a large collection of 18th- and 19th-century French and Russian decorative art that includes gold and silver work, icons, lace, tapestries, china, and Fabergé eggs. Also on the estate are a dacha filled with Russian objects and an Adirondacks-style cabin that houses an assortment of Native American artifacts. The grounds are comprised of lawns; formal French and Japanese gardens; and paths that wind through plantings of azaleas, laurels, and rhododendrons. *4155 Linnean Ave. NW, 202/686–5807. Admission to museum and grounds: $7, children under 12 not admitted. Make reservations well in advance to tour the house. Metro stop, Van Ness/UDC.*

**Joseph H. Hirshhorn Museum and Sculpture Garden** (Tour 1: The Mall) *Metro stop, Smithsonian.*

**Interior Department Museum** (Tour 3: The White House) *Metro stop, Farragut West.*

**International Monetary Fund Visitors Center.** Exhibits and a 24-minute film outline the origin and functions of the IMF. International photographs, paintings, and sculpture are on display. The Center also hosts cultural events—readings, recitals, and films—with an international flavor. *700 19th St. NW, tel. 202/623–6869. Open Mon.–Fri. 10–6.*

**Museum of Modern Art of Latin America** (Tour 3: The White House) *Metro stop, Farragut West.*

**National Air and Space Museum** (Tour 1: The Mall) *Metro stop, Smithsonian.*

**National Aquarium** (Tour 5: Old Downtown and Federal Triangle) *Metro stop, Federal Triangle.*

**National Building Museum** (Tour 5: Old Downtown and Federal Triangle) *Metro stop, Judiciary Square.*

**National Gallery of Art** (Tour 1: The Mall) *Metro stop, Archives.*
**National Geographic Explorers Hall** (Tour 7: Dupont Circle) *Metro stop, Farragut North.*
**National Museum of African Art** (Tour 1: The Mall) *Metro stop, Smithsonian.*
**National Museum of American Art** (Tour 5: Old Downtown and Federal Triangle) *Metro stop, Gallery Place.*
**National Museum of American History** (Tour 1: The Mall) *Metro stop, Smithsonian.*
**National Museum of Natural History** (Tour 1: The Mall) *Metro stop, Smithsonian.*
**National Museum of Women in the Arts.** Housed in a 1907 Renaissance Revival Masonic temple, this museum displays the works of prominent female artists. The permanent collection of more than 500 works ranges from the Renaissance to the present and includes paintings, drawings, sculpture, prints, and photography. Artists represented include Georgia O'Keeffe, Mary Cassatt, Vigee Le Brun, and Judy Chicago. Art from women in particular states is exhibited in the State Gallery. *1250 New York Ave. NW, tel. 202/783–5000. Suggested donation: adults $2, students and senior citizens $1. Open Tues.– Sat. 10–5, Sun. noon–5. Metro stop, Metro Center.*
**National Portrait Gallery** (Tour 5: Old Downtown and Federal Triangle) *Metro stop, Gallery Place.*
**National Rifle Association** (Tour 7: Dupont Circle) *Metro stop, Farragut North.*
**Navy Museum.** The history of the U.S. Navy from the Revolution to the present is chronicled in exhibits that include the fully rigged foremast of the *USF Constitution* (better known as "Old Ironsides"), a model of America's first submarine (invented in 1776), and operating periscopes from more recent submarines. Children enjoy elevating and aiming the 40-millimeter guns and don't seem to mind much that the guns don't actually fire. *9th and M sts. SE, tel. 202/433–2651, 4882. Open Mon.–Fri. 9–4, Sat. and Sun. 10–5, Memorial Day and Labor Day 9–5, other holidays 10–5.*
**Phillips Collection** (Tour 7: Dupont Circle) *Metro stop, Dupont Circle.*
**Renwick Gallery** (Tour 3: The White House) *Metro stop, McPherson Square.*
**Sackler Gallery** (Tour 1: The Mall) *Metro stop, Smithsonian.*
**Smithsonian Institution Castle** (Tour 1: The Mall) *Metro stop, Smithsonian.*
**Textile Museum** (Tour 7: Dupont Circle) *Metro stop, Dupont Circle.*
**Trolley Museum.** Transportation buffs young and old enjoy this collection of restored trolleys from the United States and Europe. For a nominal fare you can go on a 2-mile ride through the country. *Bonifant Rd. between Layhill Rd. and New Hampshire Ave., Wheaton, MD, tel. 301/384–9797. Trolley-ride fare $1.50 adults, $1 children. Open Sat. and Sun. noon–5. Closed Dec. 15–Jan. 1.*
**Washington Dolls' House and Toy Museum.** Founded in 1975 by a dollhouse historian, this compact museum contains a charming collection of American and imported dolls, dollhouses, toys, and games, most from the Victorian period. Highlights of the collection include a miniature Teddy Roosevelt on safari and an 1884 model of the Capitol. Miniature accessories, dollhouse kits, and antique toys and games are on sale in the museum's shops. *5236 44th St. NW, tel. 202/244–0024. Admission: $2 ad-*

ults, *$1 children under 14. Open Tues.–Sat. 10–5, Sun.
noon–5. Metro stop, Friendship Heights.*

**Washington Project for the Arts** (Tour 5: Old Downtown and
Federal Triangle) *Metro stops, National Archives or Gallery
Place.*

## Parks and Gardens

**The Bishop's Garden.** This traditional English-style church-
garden is on the grounds of the Washington Cathedral. Boxwoods, ivy, tea roses, yew trees, and an assortment of arches,
bas reliefs, and stonework from European ruins provide a restful counterpoint to the nearby cathedral's Gothic towers.
*Wisconsin and Massachusetts aves. NW. Metro stop, Woodley
Park–Zoo.*

**Cabin John Regional Park.** Extensive playgrounds, ball fields,
picnic areas, and tennis courts can be found at this suburban-
Maryland park complex. Children enjoy the train ride and
Noah's Ark Zoo. *7400 Tuckerman Ln., Rockville, MD, tel. 301/
299–4555. Park open sunrise to sunset. Noah's Ark Zoo open 8
to half-hour before sunset. Train ride: 85 cents. For train
schedule tel. 301/469–7835.*

**Constitution Gardens** (Tour 2: The Monuments) *Metro stop,
Foggy Bottom.*

**East Potomac Park.** This 328-acre tongue of land hangs down
from the Tidal Basin between the Washington Channel to the
east and the Potomac River to the west. Facilities include playgrounds, picnic tables, tennis courts, swimming pools, a
driving range, two nine-hole golf courses, and an 18-hole golf
course. The park's miniature golf course, built during the
"midget golf" craze of the '20s, is the oldest in the area; its art
deco–ish architecture is a welcome contrast to the artificial
theme-park design of most miniature golf courses. Double-
blossoming cherry trees line Ohio Drive and bloom about two
weeks after the single-blossoming variety that attract throngs
to the Tidal Basin each spring. *The Awakening*, a huge, fantastical sculpture of a man emerging from the ground, sits on
Hains Point, at the tip of the park. *Approach park via Maine
Ave. SW, heading west; or from Ohio Drive, heading south.
Follow signs carefully. Metro stops, Smithsonian or L'Enfant
Plaza.*

**Fort Washington Park.** Built to protect the city from enemies
sailing up the Potomac, this 1808 fort was burned by the British
during the War of 1812. Rebuilt, it served as an Army post until
1945. The National Park Service maintains it now and holds historical programs there every weekend. *From the Capital
Beltway (Rte. 95) take the Indian Head Hwy. exit (Rte. 210)
and drive 4½ miles south; look for sign on right. Entrance fee:
$3 per vehicle. Park open summer, daily 7:30 AM–8 PM, winter,
daily 7:30–5. Fort open daily 9–5.*

**Glen Echo Park.** This park was once the site of the Chautauqua
Assembly, built in 1891 to promote liberal and practical education among the masses. It served a stint as an amusement park
and is now run by the National Park Service, which offers space
to a variety of artists, who conduct classes year-round. Monthly exhibits of artists' work are shown in a stone tower left over
from the Chautauqua period. An antique carousel is open in the
summer, and there is big band– and square dancing in the
Spanish ballroom. On weekends, Adventure Theater presents
shows for children. *MacArthur Blvd., Glen Echo, MD, tel. 301/*

*492–6282. Carousel open summer, Sat. and Sun. 12–6, Wed. 10–2.*

**Great Falls Park.** The waters of the Potomac River cascade dramatically over a steep, jagged gorge on this 800-acre park in Virginia. Inside the park are a visitors center and the ruins of George Washington's unsuccessful Potowmack Canal, designed to skirt unnavigable portions of the river. The area is ideal for hiking, picnicking, climbing, and fishing. *9200 Old Dominion Dr., Great Falls, VA, tel. 703/285–2966. Open daily 8–sunset.*

**Hillwood Museum.** The grounds of Marjorie Merriweather Post's Georgian-style Hillwood House feature a French-style *parterre*, a rose garden, a Japanese garden, paths that wind through azaleas and rhododendrons, and a greenhouse in which 5,000 orchids bloom. Tours of the Hillwood Museum are often booked up months in advance, but reservations are not needed for the garden. *4155 Linnean Ave. NW, tel. 202/686–5807. Admission: $2; children under 12 not admitted. Open daily, 11–3. Metro stop, Van Ness–UDC.*

**Kenilworth Aquatic Gardens.** Exotic water lilies, lotuses, hyacinths, and other water-loving plants thrive in this 12-acre sanctuary of quiet pools and marshy flats. In a pool near the visitors center bloom East Indian lotus plants grown from 350-year-old seeds recovered from a dry Manchurian lake-bed. The gardens are home to a variety of wetland animals, including turtles, frogs, muskrats, and some 40 species of birds. The best time to visit is early in the morning, when day-bloomers are just opening and night-bloomers have yet to close. *Kenilworth Ave. and Douglas St. NE, tel. 202/426–6905. Open daily 7–3:30. Garden walks held on summer weekends at 9, 11, and 1.*

**Lafayette Park** (Tour 3: The White House) *Metro stop, McPherson Square.*

**Meridian Hill Park.** Landscape architect Horace Peaslee created this often-overlooked park after a 1917 study of the parks of Europe. It contains elements of France (a long, straight mall bordered with plants), Italy (terraces and wall fountains), and Switzerland (a lower-level reflecting pool based on one in Zurich). Visit this park during daylight hours only. *16th and Euclid sts. NW.*

**National Arboretum.** During the azalea season, from the middle of April to the end of May, this 444-acre oasis is a blaze of color. In the summer, clematis, ferns, peonies, rhododendrons, and roses bloom. Paths and roadways make the arboretum an ideal place to visit for either a relaxing stroll or a scenic drive. Also popular are the National Bonsai Collection and National Herb Garden. *3501 New York Ave. NE, tel. 202/475–4815. Open weekdays 8–5, weekends and holidays 10–5.*

**National Zoological Park** (Tour 9: Cleveland Park) *Metro stops, Cleveland Park or Woodley Park–Zoo.*

**Pershing Park** (Tour 3: The White House) *Metro stop, Federal Triangle.*

**Rock Creek Park.** The 1,800 acres of park on either side of Rock Creek have provided a cool oasis for Washington residents since Congress set them aside in 1890. There's a lot to enjoy here. Thirty picnic areas are scattered throughout the park. Bicycle routes and hiking and equestrian trails wend through the groves of dogwoods, beeches, oaks, and cedar. Rangers at the **Nature Center and Planetarium** (south of Military Rd. at 5000 Glover Rd. NW, tel. 202/426–6834) will acquaint you with the park and advise you of scheduled activities. Highlights include: **Peirce Mill,** a restored 19th-century gristmill powered by the falling water of Rock Creek; **Fort Reno,** one of the original ring of forts that guarded Washington during the Civil War; and the **Rock Creek Golf Course,** an 18-hole public course. *Between 16th St. and Connecticut Ave. NW. Park open daylight hours only; hours for individual sites vary.*

**Theodore Roosevelt Island.** This 88-acre island wilderness-preserve in the Potomac River is a living tribute to the conservation-minded 26th president. It features 2½ miles of nature trails through marshland, swampland, and upland forest. Cattails, arrowarum, pickerelweed, willow, ash, maple, and oak all grow on the island, providing a habitat for frogs, raccoons, birds, squirrels, and the occasional red or gray fox. There is also a 17-foot bronze statue of Roosevelt, executed by Paul Manship. *A pedestrian bridge connects the island to a parking lot on the Virginia shore and is accessible from the northbound lanes of the George Washington Memorial Parkway. From downtown, take Constitution Ave. west across the Theodore Roosevelt Bridge to GW Memorial Parkway north and follow signs. Tel. 202/426–6922 or 703/285–2598.*

**United States Botanic Garden** (Tour 4: Capitol Hill) *Metro stop, Federal Center SW.*

**West Potomac Park** (Tour 3: The Monuments) *Metro stop, Smithsonian.*

## Churches, Temples, and Mosques

**Adas Israel Synagogue.** This red-brick, Federal Revival–style building is the oldest synagogue in Washington. Dedicated in 1876, the structure originally stood at 6th and G streets NW but was moved to its present location in 1969 to make way for the construction of the Metro headquarters. Exhibits in the Albert and Lillian Small Jewish Museum inside explore Jewish life in Washington. *3rd and G sts. NW, tel. 202/881–0100. Open Sundays 11–3 and by appointment. Metro stop, Judiciary Square.*

**All Souls' Unitarian Church.** The design of this church, erected in 1924, is based on that of St. Martin-in-the-Fields in London. *16th and Harvard sts. NW, tel. 202/332–5266.*

**Franciscan Monastery and Gardens.** Not far from the Shrine of the **Immaculate Conception,** this Byzantine-style monastery contains fascimiles of such Holy-Land shrines as the Grotto of Bethlehem and the Holy Sepulcher. Underground are reproductions of the catacombs of Rome. The gardens are especially beautiful, planted with roses that bloom in the summer. *14th and Quincy sts. NE, tel. 202/526–6800. Metro stop, Brookland–Catholic University.*

**Grace Episcopal Church** (Tour 6: Georgetown).

**Islamic Mosque and Cultural Center.** The Moslem faithful are called to prayer five times a day from atop this mosque's 162-foot-high minaret. Each May, the Moslem Women's Association sponsors a bazaar, with crafts, clothing, and food for sale. *2551 Massachusetts Ave. NW, tel. 202/332–8343. Center open daily 10–5; mosque open for all five prayers, from dawn until past sunset.*

**Metropolitan African Methodist Episcopal Church.** Completed in 1886, this Gothic-style church became one of the most influential black churches in the city. Abolitionist orator Frederick Douglass worshipped here. *1518 M St. NW, tel. 202/331–1426. Metro stop, Farragut North.*

**Mt. Zion United Methodist Church** (Tour 6: Georgetown).

**National Shrine of the Immaculate Conception.** This is the largest Catholic church in the United States, begun in 1920 and built with funds contributed by every parish in the country. Dedicated in 1959, the shrine is a blend of Romanesque and Byzantine styles, with a bell tower that reminds many of St. Mark's in Venice. *Michigan Ave. and 4th St. NE, tel. 202/526–8300. Open spring and summer, daily 7–7; fall and winter, daily 7–6. Sunday mass at 7:30, 9, 10:30, noon, 1:30 (in Latin), and 4:30. Metro stop, Brookland–Catholic University.*

**St. John's Episcopal Church** (Tour 3: The White House) *Metro stop, McPherson Square.*

**St. Matthew's Cathedral** (Tour 7: Dupont Circle) *Metro stop, Farragut North.*

**Saint Sophia.** (Massachusetts Ave. and 36th St. NW, tel. 202/333–4730) This Greek Orthodox cathedral is noted for the handsome mosaic work on the interior of its dome. Saint Sophia holds a festival of Greek food and crafts each May.

**Scottish Rite Temple** (1733 16th St. NW.). This dramatic Masonic shrine is patterned after the Mausoleum of Halicarnassus.

**Washington National Cathedral.** Construction of this stunning Gothic church—the sixth largest cathedral in the world—started in 1907. It is scheduled to be consecrated on September 30, 1990. Like its 14th-century counterparts, Washington's Cathedral Church of St. Peter and St. Paul has flying buttresses, naves, transepts, and barrel vaults that were built stone by stone. It is adorned with fanciful gargoyles created by skilled stone carvers. The tomb of Woodrow Wilson, the only president buried in Washington, is on the south side of the nave. The expansive view of the city from the Pilgrim Gallery is exceptional. The cathedral is under the governance of the Episcopal church but has played host to services of many denominations. *Wisconsin and Massachusetts Ave. NW, tel. 202/537–6200. Open fall, winter, and spring, daily 10–4:30; May 1 to Labor Day, weekdays 10–9, weekends 10–4:30. Sunday services at 8, 9, 10, and 11; evensong at 4 PM.*

**Temple of the Church of Jesus Christ of Latter-Day Saints.** This striking Mormon temple in suburban Maryland—one of its white towers is topped with a golden angel—has become a Washington landmark. It is closed to nonMormons, but a visitors center offers a lovely view of the white-marble church and has a film about the temple and what takes place inside. Tulips, dogwoods, and azaleas bloom in the 57-acre grounds each spring. *9900 Stoneybrook Dr., Kensington, MD, tel. 301/587–0144. Church open daily 10–9:30. Grounds open Tues.–Fri. 10–9:30, Sat. 10–6.*

## Statues and Monuments

Washington, perhaps more than any other city in the United States, is filled with allegorical outdoor art. Examples can be found in the middle of traffic circles and on dozens of Neoclassical public buildings. *The Outdoor Sculpture of Washington, D.C.*, by architectural historian James M. Goode provides readable histories of the well-known and little-known works to be found in the nation's capital.

**The Awakening.** Children love this giant sculpture of a bearded man emerging from the ground near Hains Point. Adults are captivated, too. *Hains Point, East Potomac Park.*

**Bartholdi Fountain** (Tour 4: Capitol Hill) *Metro stop, Federal Center SW.*

**Columbus Statue** (Tour 4: Capitol Hill) *Metro stop, Union Station.*

**Dumbarton Bridge** (Tour 7: Dupont Circle) *Metro stop, Dupont Circle.*

**Dupont Fountain** (Tour 7: Dupont Circle) *Metro stop, Dupont Circle.*

**Albert Einstein** (Tour 8: Foggy Bottom) *Metro stop, Foggy Bottom.*

**Freedmen's Memorial.** This bronze statue of Abraham Lincoln standing above a newly freed slave who has just broken his chains was dedicated on April 14, 1876, the 11th anniversary of the president's assassination. Money for its construction was donated by hundreds of ex-slaves. *Lincoln Park, Massachusetts Ave. between 11th and 13th streets NE. Metro stop, McPherson Square.*

**Albert Gallatin** (Tour 3: The White House) *Metro stop, McPherson Square.*

**James Garfield** (Tour 4: Capitol Hill) *Metro stop, Capitol South.*

**Grand Army of the Republic** (Tour 5: Old Downtown and Federal Triangle) *Metro stop, Archives.*

**Grant Memorial** (Tour 4: Capitol Hill) *Metro stop, Federal Center SW.*

**Alexander Hamilton** (Tour 3: The White House) *Metro stop, Federal Triangle.*

**General Winfield Scott Hancock** (Tour 5: Old Downtown and Federal Triangle) *Metro stop, Archives.*

**Andrew Jackson** (Tour 3: The White House) *Metro stop, McPherson Square.*

**Jefferson Memorial** (Tour 2: The Monuments).

**John F. Kennedy** (Tour 9: Foggy Bottom) *Metro stop, Foggy Bottom.*

**Thaddeus Kosciuszko** (Tour 3: The White House) *Metro stop, McPherson Square.*

**Marquis de Lafayette** (Tour 3: The White House) *Metro stop, McPherson Square.*

**Lincoln Memorial** (Tour 2: The Monuments).

**Marine Corps War Memorial** (Tour 10: Arlington) *Metro stop, Arlington Cemetery.*

**Navy Memorial** (Tour 5: Old Downtown and Federal Triangle) *Metro stop, Archives.*

**Navy and Marine Memorial** (Tour 10: Arlington) *Metro stop, Arlington Cemetery.*

***The Peace of God that Passeth Understanding.*** Henry Adams commissioned Augustus Saint-Gaudens to create this memorial to Adams's wife, who had committed suicide. Known by the nickname "Grief," this figure of a shroud-draped woman is thought by many to be the most moving sculpture in the city. *In Rock Creek Cemetery, Rock Creek Rd. and Webster St. NW.*

**Peace Monument** (Tour 4: Capitol Hill) *Metro stop, Union Station.*

**Comte de Rochambeau** (Tour 3: The White House) *Metro stop, McPherson Square.*

**General Casimir Pulaski** (Tour 5: Old Downtown and Federal Triangle) *Metro stop, Federal Triangle.*

**Franklin Delano Roosevelt Memorial** (Tour 5: Old Downtown and Federal Triangle) *Metro stop, Archives.*

**General Winfield Scott** (Tour 7: Dupont Circle) *Metro stop, Dupont Circle.*

**General Philip Sheridan** (Tour 7: Dupont Circle) *Metro stop, Dupont Circle.*

**General William Tecumseh Sherman** (Tour 3: The White House) *Metro stop, Federal Triangle.*

**Baron von Steuben** (Tour 3: The White House) *Metro stop, McPherson Square.*

**Temperance Fountain** (Tour 5: Old Downtown and Federal Triangle) *Metro stop, Federal Triangle.*

**Vietnam Veterans Memorial** (Tour 2: The Monuments) *Metro stop, Foggy Bottom.*

**Washington Monument** (Tour 2: The Monuments) *Metro stop, Federal Triangle or Smithsonian.*

# 4 Shopping

*by Deborah Papier*

Not long ago, a shopping trip in the Washington area really was a trip—a long trek to one of the suburban shopping malls, which offered far more than could be found in town. It is still true that many major national retailers are bypassing the city, so that a visitor wanting to check out Bloomingdale's, Nordstrom, or Macy's has to venture to White Flint Mall in Maryland (the White Flint stop on Metrorail's red line) or the twin megamalls in Tyson's Corner, Virginia (reachable by bus but not subway). In recent years, however, the city's shopping scene has been revitalized. The old Washington department stores have upgraded both their facilities and their merchandise; many of the smaller one-of-a-kind shops have managed to survive urban renewal; and interesting specialty shops and mini-malls are popping up all over town.

Store hours vary greatly, so it is safest to call ahead. In general, Georgetown stores are open late and on Sunday, while stores in the downtown district that cater to office workers close at 6 PM and may not be open at all on Saturday. Some stores extend their hours on Thursday.

Sales tax is 6%, and the major credit cards are accepted everywhere.

## Shopping Districts

**Georgetown** remains Washington's favorite shopping area. Though it is not on a subway line, and parking is impossible, people still flock here. The attraction (aside from the lively street scene) is the profusion of specialty shops, which offer wares unavailable elsewhere in the city. Georgetown has most of the city's antiques dealers, craft shops, and high-style clothing boutiques.

The hub of Georgetown is the intersection of Wisconsin Avenue and M Street, with most of the stores lying to the west on M Street and to the north on Wisconsin. That intersection is also the location of **Georgetown Park** (tel. 202/342–8180, 8192), a three-level mall that looks like a Victorian ice cream parlor. Georgetown Park is anchored by Conran's (tel. 202/298–8300), which features reasonably priced, well-designed housewares, including furniture. In most of the stores in the Park, however, the emphasis is on the fantastical rather than the practical—cosmetics, chocolates, prints, and toys for adults as well as children.

**Dupont Circle** has some of the same flavor as Georgetown. Here, too, there is a lively mix of shops and restaurants, with most of the action on the major artery of Connecticut Avenue. There are many book and record stores in the neighborhood, as well as stores selling coffees, stationery, and bric-a-brac.

The city's department stores can be found in the "new" downtown, which is still being built. Its fulcrum is **Metro Center**, which spans 11th and 12th streets NW along G Street. The Metro Center subway stop takes you directly into the basements of downtown's two major department stores, Woodward & Lothrop, familiarly called "Woodies," and Hecht's. Take the 11th and G streets exit to Woodies; for Hecht's, follow the signs to the 12th or 13th street exits. A block away on 14th Street is Garfinckel's, which used to be known as the store of the presi-

# Shopping

Ann Taylor, **29**
Appalachiana, **8**
Arthur Adler, **25**
Bally, **28**
Bellini, **30**
Brooks Brothers, **24**
Burberrys, **20**
Camalier &
Buckley, **22**
Chapters, **31**

Charles Schwartz
& Son, **4**
Cherishables, **9**
The Chesire Cat, **6**
Church's, **27**
Crown Books, **12**
Eddie Bauer, **18**
Fahrney's, **32**
Garfinckel's, **33**
Hecht's, **34**
Hugo Boss, **17**

J. Press, **26**
The Kid's Closet, **16**
Kitchen Bazaar, **7**
Kramerbooks, **10**
Lord & Taylor, **2**
Marston Luce, **11**
Moon, Blossoms and
Snow, **37**
Music Box Center, **36**
Neiman Marcus, **3**

Pampillonia
Jewelers, **5**
Raleighs, **23**
Saks Fifth Avenue, **1**
Serenade Record
Shop, **19**
Shoe Scene, **15**
Talbots, **14**
The Tiny Jewel
Box, **21**
Tower Records, **13**
Woodward &
Lothrop, **35**

NW ◀▶ NE

N

0 ____ 500 yards
0 ____ 500 meters

T St.
S St.
R St.
Q St.
O St.
N St.
M St.
L St.
I St.
H St.
G St.
F St.
E St.
D St.

Vermont Ave.
Rhode Island Ave.
Florida Ave.
New Jersey Ave.
3rd St.
New York Ave.
1st St.
North Capitol St.
Lincoln Rd.
S St.
R St.
Q St.
P St.
O St.
M St.

12th St.
11th St.
10th St.
9th St.
8th St.
7th St.
6th St.
5th St.
4th St.

Massachusetts Ave.
Mt. Vernon Square

2nd St.

GALLERY PLACE
JUDICIARY SQUARE
I-395

Union Station
Columbus Fountain

Stanton Park

METRO CENTER
34
35
36

ARCHIVES
Pennsylvania Ave.
Louisiana Ave.
New Jersey Ave.

NE
SE

1

Madison Dr.
Smithsonian Institution
National Gallery of Art
National Air and Space Museum
US Capitol
East Capitol St.

THE MALL
Jefferson Dr.
Independence Ave.
Maryland Ave.
C St.

37

3rd St.
4th St.
2nd St.

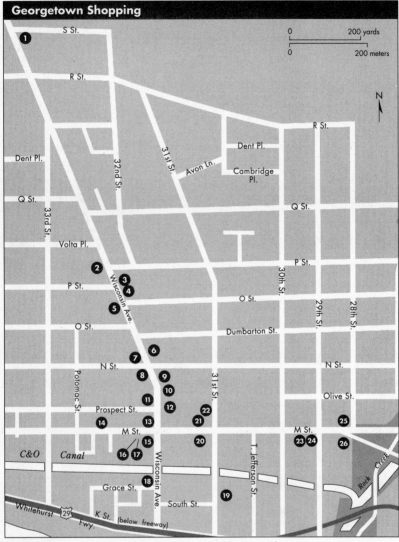

## Georgetown Shopping

The American
Hand, **24**
Appalachian Spring, **3**
Banana Republic, **15**
Benetton, **20**
Britches, **10**
The Coach Store, **13**
Commander
Salamander, **5**
Earl Allen, **21**

F.A.O. Schwarz, **16**
The Gap, **9**
Georgetown Antiques
Center, **23**
Georgetown Leather
Design, **14**
G.K.S. Bush, **26**
Indian Craft Shop, **18**
Kemp Mill Record
Shops, **8**
The Limited, **17**
Little Caledonia, **4**
Martin's, **7**

Miller & Arney
Antiques, **1**
Mineral Kingdom, **11**
Old Print Gallery, **22**
Olsson's Books &
Records, **12**
The Phoenix, **2**
Save the Children's
Craft Shop, **25**
Susquehanna, **6**
Yes!, **19**

dents and still has something of the elegance of Old Washington.

Catty-corner from Garfinckel's is the new downtown mall, **The Shops at National Place** (13th and F streets NW, tel. 202/783–9090). Taking up three levels, one of which is devoted to food stands, The Shops is oriented primarily to younger consumers. This is a good place to drop off teenagers weary of the Smithsonian and more in the mood to buy compact discs or T-shirts. Banana Republic, Victoria's Secret, and The Sharper Image are three of the catalogue stores that have outlets here.

Although Washington doesn't have anything on the order of Boston's Faneuil Hall, it does have **The Pavilion at the Old Post Office** (12th St. NW and Pennsylvania Ave., tel. 202/289–4224), a renovated building dating from the last century. The Pavilion's 21 small shops include Caswell & Massey (for toiletries and perfumes) and The Last Wound-Up (selling wind-up toys). An observation deck in the building's clock tower offers an excellent view of the city.

An even newer project is the renovation of **Union Station,** at Massachusetts Ave. NE, near North Capitol Street. Resplendent with marble floors and gilded, vaulted ceilings, this is now both a working train station and a mall with three levels of stores, including one level of food stands. Union Station is full of trendy clothing boutiques, including Cignal, Chico's, and Martinaro. Other stores worthy of special mention are Political America, The Nature Company, and B. Galleries, which features sophisticated kitchen designs.

The final major shopping district is on the outskirts of the city, on Wisconsin Avenue, straddling the Maryland border. Here is the **Mazza Gallerie** (5300 Wisconsin Ave. NW, tel. 202/966–6114) a four-level mall anchored by the ritzy Neiman Marcus department store. Its other stores include Williams-Sonoma's kitchenware and Pierre Deux's provincial fabrics. Three other department stores are close by: Lord & Taylor, Woodward & Lothrop, and Saks Fifth Avenue (*see* Department Stores, below). The neighborhood also contains an eclectic array of upscale shops, and more are being built all the time.

## Department Stores

**Garfinckel's** (1401 F St. NW, tel. 202/628–7730). To walk into Garfinckel's is to step back in time. The grand first floor has been entirely refurbished. It's lost a little bit of its fusty splendor, but it still brings back memories of more gracious and elegant days, when a shopping trip was an occasion. Garfinckel's calls itself a specialty store, rather than a department store, and its focus is on clothing (classic in look, with many private labels) and giftware not readily available elsewhere.

**Hecht's** (12th and G streets NW, tel. 202/628–6661). When the Hecht company decided to abandon its store on 7th Street and build a new one, they did the job right. The new downtown Hecht's is bright and spacious, and its sensible groupings and attractive displays of merchandise make shopping relatively easy on the feet and the eyes. The clothes sold here are a mix of conservative and trendy lines, with the men's department assuming increasing importance. Cosmetics, lingerie, and housewares are also strong departments.

**Lord & Taylor** (5255 Western Ave., tel. 202/362–9600). Like Garfinckel's, Lord & Taylor lets other stores be all things to all people, while it focuses on nonutilitarian housewares and classic clothing by such designers as Anne Klein and Ralph Lauren. All of the clothing is American-designed and manufactured. The store has a strong dress department that includes evening dresses, and there is an expanded selection of women's clothing in larger sizes. The men's department is equally well stocked.

**Neiman Marcus** (Mazza Gallerie, tel. 202/966–9700). If you have to ask how much it costs, you probably shouldn't shop at Neiman Marcus, which caters to the customer who values quality above all. The carefully selected merchandise includes couture clothes, furs, precious jewelry, crystal, and silver.

**Saks Fifth Avenue** (5555 Wisconsin Ave., tel. 301/657–9000). Though not strictly a Washington department store, since it is located just over the Maryland line, Saks is nonetheless a Washington institution. The major draw is the wide selection of European and American couture clothes; other attractions are the shoe, jewelry, fur, and lingerie departments.

**Woodward & Lothrop** (11th and F streets NW, tel. 202/347–5300). The largest of the downtown stores, Woodies has eight floors of merchandise that can accommodate just about any need or whim. There are two floors of women's clothing in a variety of style and price ranges, another floor for juniors, one for men, and a large children's department. In addition, just about anything you could need for the home can be found here, including gourmet food. There is also a branch across the border in Maryland at Wisconsin and Western avenues (tel. 301/654–7600).

## Specialty Stores

**Antiques** **Cherishables** (1608 20th St. NW, tel. 202/785–4087) offers American 18th- and 19th-century furniture and decorative arts, with emphasis on the Federal period.

**Georgetown Antiques Center** (2918 M St. NW, tel. 202/338–3811). Three dealers share space in this Victorian townhouse: Cherub Gallery (tel. 202/337–2224) specializes in art glass and Icart etchings; Michael Getz (tel. 202/338–3811) sells fireplace equipment and silverware; Justine Mehlman has one gallery of jewelry (tel. 202/337–0613) from the 18th century through the Art Deco period and another gallery of prints (tel. 202/337–8645).

**G.K.S. Bush** (2828 Pennsylvania Ave. NW, tel. 202/965–0653). Formal American furniture from the 18th and early 19th centuries, plus related accessories such as candlesticks, porcelain, and globes.

**Marston Luce** (1314 21st St. NW, tel. 202/775–9460). The specialty here is American folk art, including quilts, weather vanes, and hooked rugs. There is also furniture, primarily American, but some English and French as well.

**Miller & Arney Antiques** (1737 Wisconsin Ave. NW, tel. 202/338–2369). English, American, and European furniture and accessories from the 18th and early 19th centuries, plus Oriental porcelain.

**Old Print Gallery** (1220 31st St. NW, tel. 202/965–1818). The area's only store specializing in old prints and maps, including Washingtoniana.

**Susquehanna** (1319 Wisconsin Ave. NW, tel. 202/333–1511) The largest antique shop in Georgetown, specializing in American furniture and paintings.

**Books**  **Chapters** (1613 I St. NW, tel. 202/861–1333). Calling itself a "literary bookstore," Chapters eschews cartoon collections and diet guides, filling its shelves instead with the sort of books that are meant to be read—serious contemporary fiction, classics, and poetry.

**The Cheshire Cat** (5512 Connecticut Ave. NW, tel. 202/244–3956). A bookstore just for children.

**Crown Books** (1200 New Hampshire Ave. NW, tel. 202/822–8331. Also at 3131 M St. NW, tel. 202/333–4493; 2020 K St. NW, tel. 202/659–2030; and 1710 G St. NW, 202/789–2277). This large local chain sells hardback best-sellers at significant discounts.

**Kramerbooks** (1517 Connecticut Ave., tel. 202/387–1400). Sharing space with a café that offers late-night dining and entertainment on weekends, Kramer's is an always-bustling hangout with a small but well-selected stock.

**Olsson's Books & Records** (1239 Wisconsin Ave., tel. 202/338–9544. Also at 1307 19th St. NW, tel. 202/785–1133; and 1200 F St. NW, tel. 202/347–3686). With its large and varied collection, this is undoubtedly the area's preeminent general bookstore.

**Yes!** (1035 31st St. NW, tel. 202/338–7874). A bookstore geared to self-development, Yes! has an unusual stock of volumes on spiritual growth, psychology, mythology, and travel. While the emphasis is on Asian modes of thought, the collection of Western philosophy is one of the best in town.

**Children's Clothing and Toys**  **Bellini** (1722 I St. NW, tel. 202/659–4144). Bellini is a designer and manufacturer of children's furniture, but the store also carries bedding, wall hangings, infant clothing, and stuffed toys.

**F.A.O. Schwarz** (3222 M St. NW, tel. 202/342–2285). The most upscale of toy stores, carrying such items as a toy car (a Mercedes, of course) that costs almost as much as the real thing. Among the other imports are stuffed animals (many larger than life), dolls, and children's perfumes.

**The Kid's Closet** (1226 Connecticut Ave. NW, tel. 202/429–9247). This is downtown DC's only children's clothing store. The focus is on clothes for newborns, plus other items that make suitable baby-shower gifts.

**Crafts and Gifts**  **The American Hand** (2906 M St. NW, tel. 202/965–3273). One-of-a-kind functional and nonfunctional pieces from America's foremost ceramic artists, plus limited-edition objects for home and office, such as architect-designed dinnerware.

**Appalachian Spring** (1415 Wisconsin Ave., tel. 202/337–5780, and Union Station, tel. 202/682–0505). Traditional and contemporary crafts, including quilts, jewelry, weavings, pottery, and blown glass.

**Appalachiana** (2633 Connecticut Ave., tel. 202/483–8334). A full assortment of moderately priced American pottery, jewelry, fiber, and glass.

**Fahrney's** (1430 G St. NW, tel. 202/628–9525). Fahrney's started out as a pen bar in the Willard Hotel, a place to fill your fountain pen before embarking on the day's business. Today it offers pens in silver, gold, and lacquer by the world's leading manufacturers.

**Indian Craft Shop** (1050 Wisconsin Ave., tel. 202/342–3918.

Also at Dept. of Interior, 1800 C St. NW, tel. 202/343–4056).
Handicrafts, including jewelry, pottery, sand paintings, weavings, and baskets, from a dozen Native American tribal traditions.

**Moon, Blossoms and Snow** (225 Pennsylvania Ave. NE, tel. 202/543–8181). Wearable art is the specialty of this store, one of the relatively few shops on Capitol Hill. In addition to hand-painted, hand-woven garments, the store sells contemporary American ceramics, glass, jewelry, and wood.

**Music Box Center** (918 F St. NW, tel. 202/783–9399). Choose from over 500 melodies played by boxes made of marble, glass, porcelain, pewter, and inlaid woods.

**The Phoenix** (1514 Wisconsin Ave., tel. 202/338–4404). Mexican crafts, including folk art, masks, silver jewelry, fabrics, and native garments.

**Save the Children's Craft Shop** (2803 M St. NW, tel. 202/342–8096). Part of a program to help families supplement their income and at the same time preserve their cultural heritage, this store sells crafts from over 20 countries, including the United States. Wood carvings, masks, weavings, and wall hangings are among the moderately priced offerings.

**Jewelry**  **Charles Schwartz & Son** (Mazza Gallerie, tel. 202/363–5432). A full-service jeweler specializing in precious stones in traditional and modern settings. Fine watches are also offered.

**Mineral Kingdom** (3251 Prospect St. NW, tel. 202/338–5505). Tucked into the Georgetown Court, this shop sells jewelry with a European look—clean, modern designs in 18-karat gold with bezel-set stones. Some of the pieces are Italian imports; others are designed and made by the husband and wife who own the store.

**Pampillonia Jewelers** (Mazza Gallerie, tel. 202/363–6305. Also at 1213 Connecticut Ave. NW, tel. 202/628–6305). Traditional designs in 18-karat gold and platinum, including many pieces for men.

**The Tiny Jewel Box** (1143 Connecticut Ave., tel. 202/393–2747). A well-chosen collection of estate jewelry.

**Kitchenware**  **Kitchen Bazaar** (4401 Connecticut Ave. NW, tel. 202/244–1550). This emporium carries just about everything one could possibly need to equip a kitchen.

**Little Caledonia** (1419 Wisconsin Ave., tel. 202/333–4700). A "Tom Thumb department store" for the home, this old Georgetown store consists of nine rooms crammed with almost 100,000 items, with candles, cards, fabrics, and lamps rounding out the stock of decorative kitchenware.

**Martin's** (1304 Wisconsin Ave., tel. 202/338–6144). A long-established Georgetown purveyor of china, crystal, and silver, including antique silver.

**Leather Goods**  **Camalier & Buckley** (1141 Connecticut Ave., tel. 202/347–7700. Also at 1260 F St. NW, tel. 202/347–2400). The city's largest collection of briefcases in a variety of skins, plus luggage, desk accessories, stationery, clocks, crystal, and porcelain.

**The Coach Store** (1214 Wisconsin Ave., tel. 202/342–1772). The complete line of Coach's rugged, well-made handbags, briefcases, belts, and wallets.

**Georgetown Leather Design** (3265 M St. NW, tel. 202/333–9333. Also at 5300 Wisconsin Ave. NW, tel. 202/363–9710; and 1150 Connecticut Ave. NW, tel. 202/223–1855). A full line of leather goods, most of them made for the store, including jackets, briefcases, wallets, gloves, and handbags.

**Men's Clothing**  **Arthur Adler** (1805 L St. NW, tel. 202/872–8850. Also at 1270 F St. NW, tel. 202/347–0841; and 5530 Wisconsin Ave., tel. 301/656–1505). In business for almost half a century, this Washington clothier offers what used to be called the Ivy League look in suits, sportcoats, and formal and casual wear.

**Britches of Georgetown** (1247 Wisconsin Ave., tel. 202/338–3330. Also at 1219 Connecticut Ave. NW, tel. 202/223–9023). Britches carries an extensive selection of traditional but trend-conscious designs in natural fibers.

**Brooks Brothers** (1840 L St. NW, tel. 202/556–6566. Also at 5500 Wisconsin Ave. NW, tel. 301/654–8202). The oldest men's store in America, Brooks Brothers has offered traditional formal and casual clothing since 1818. It is the largest men's specialty store in the area and has a small women's department as well.

**Hugo Boss** (1201 Connecticut Ave., tel. 202/887–5081. Also at 1517 Wisconsin Ave. tel. 202/338–0120). The Washington area has the only U.S. collection of clothes from this German designer and manufacturer, noted for his classic fabrics and unique silhouettes.

**J. Press** (1801 L St. NW, tel. 202/291–4222). Founded in 1902 as a custom shop for Yale University, J. Press is a stalwartly traditional clothier. Shetland-wool sportcoats are a specialty.

**Men's and Women's Clothing**  **Banana Republic** (3200 M St. NW, tel. 202/333–2554. Also at 529 14th St. NW, tel. 202/783–1400). Safari-style clothing for those who fancy themselves tropical explorers—a fairly accurate description of those who travel in Washington during the summer.

**Burberrys** (1155 Connecticut Ave., tel. 202/463–3000). It made its reputation with the trench coat, but this British company also manufactures traditional men's and women's sportswear, a good selection of which is available here.

**Commander Salamander** (1420 Wisconsin Ave., tel. 202/333–9599). This is about as funky as Washington gets—leather, chains, silver skulls. As much entertainment as shopping, Commander Salamander is open until midnight on weekends.

**Eddie Bauer** (1800 M St. NW, tel. 202/331–8009). Though it calls itself an outdoor outfitter, Eddie Bauer no longer sells much camping gear. The focus instead is on clothing and footwear that combines function with fashion.

**The Gap** (5430 Wisconsin Ave., tel. 202/657–3380. Also at 1217 Connecticut Ave., tel. 202/638–4603; and 1267 Wisconsin Ave. NW, tel. 202/333–2657). Well-designed and well-made jeans, T-shirts, and other casual clothing in natural fibers.

**Raleighs** (1133 Connecticut Ave., tel. 202/785–7071). A specialty store catering to men and noted for its well-tailored suits, Raleighs also has a small women's department.

**Records**  **Kemp Mill Record Shops** (1260 Wisconsin Ave., tel. 202/333–1392. Also at 1518 Connecticut Ave. NW, tel. 202/332–8247; 4304 Connecticut Ave. NW, tel. 202/362–9262; 2459 18th St. NW, tel. 202/387–1011; and 4000 Wisconsin Ave. NW, tel. 202/364–9704). This local chain store concentrates on popular music (New Age is a particular specialty) and keeps its prices low. Also at several locations in the suburbs.

**Olsson's Books & Records** (1239 Wisconsin Ave., tel. 202/338–6712. Also at 1307 19th St. NW, tel. 202/785–2662; and 1200 F

St. NW, tel. 202/393–1853). A full line of compact discs and cassettes can be found in this broad-spectrum record store.

**Serenade Record Shop** (1800 M St. NW, tel. 202/452–0075. Also at 1710 Pennsylvania Ave. NW, tel. 202/638–5580; and 1713 G St. NW, tel. 202/638–6648). A full-catalogue record store with a strong classical collection. The G Street store sells classical music only.

**Tower Records** (2000 Pennsylvania Ave. NW, tel. 202/331–2400). With 16,000 square feet of selling space, Tower offers the area's best selection of music in all categories.

**Shoes**   **Bally** (1020 Connecticut Ave. NW, tel. 202/429–0604). The Swiss manufacturer of high-quality leather goods is expanding its line of women's shoes, but the focus is still on footwear for men, primarily European-style loafers. The store also sells handbags, briefcases, and belts.

**Church's** (1742 L St. NW, tel. 202/296–3366). Church's is an English company whose handmade men's shoes are noted for their comfort and durability. This is their only store in the United States.

**Shoe Scene** (1330 Connecticut Ave. NW, tel. 202/659–2194). A good selection of moderately priced, fashionable shoes for women.

**Women's Clothing**   **Ann Taylor** (1720 K St. NW, tel. 202/466–3544. Also at 3222 M St. NW, tel. 202/338–5290; 5300 Wisconsin Ave. NW, tel. 202/244–1940; and Union Station, tel. 202/371–8010). Sophisticated fashions for the woman who has broken out of the dress-for-success mold. Ann Taylor also has an excellent shoe department.

**Benetton** (3108 M St. NW, tel. 202/333–7839. Also at 1234 Wisconsin Ave. NW, tel. 202/337–0632; 3501 Connecticut Ave. NW, tel. 202/785–4607; and Union Station, tel. 202/289–8422). A line of Italian sportswear, primarily knits, in bright colors and mix-and-unmatch patterns.

**Earl Allen** (3109 M St. NW, tel. 202/338–1678). Earl Allen caters to the professional woman, offering conservative but distinctive dresses and sportswear, much of it made exclusively for this shop.

**The Limited** (Georgetown Park, tel. 202/342–5150. Also at 1331 Pennsylvania Ave. NW, tel. 202/628–8221; and Union Station, tel. 202/682–0416). Moderately priced casual clothing with European flair. The store also has suburban locations.

**Talbots** (1227 Connecticut Ave., tel. 202/887–6973. Also at 3222 M St. NW, tel. 202/338–3510; and 4801 Massachusetts Ave. NW, tel. 202/966–2205). Traditional classic clothing, most of it private-label. There is also a large selection in petite sizes.

# 5 Sports and Fitness

*by Tom Carter*

*A sports reporter for the* Washington Times, *Tom Carter contributes frequently to national and regional publications.*

When the experts at the local bar begin to discuss the nation's great sports towns, Washington is not often high on the list. The honors usually go to New York, Los Angeles, or Boston. Nevertheless, Washington is home to an impressive variety of opportunities for both spectators and participants. According to national surveys, the residents of metropolitan Washington are more active than the nation as a whole. Washingtonians jog, cycle, swim, fish, lift weights, play tennis, and sail more than the residents of any other major city in the United States. One reason may be that Washington's climate is generally mild year-round. Another reason is that there are plenty of parks, trails, and athletic facilities throughout the area to entice an active population.

Whether you're coming to Washington for a few days of sightseeing or a few days of business, don't forget to bring your sweats. There is more to the District than national monuments and boardrooms.

## Participant Sports and Fitness

**Biking**  Bicycling is one of the most popular activities in Washington for locals and visitors alike. The numerous trails in the District and the surrounding areas are well-maintained and clearly marked, which makes for pleasant and safe bike-touring. Most of the paths described below in the section on jogging—the Mall, the C & O Canal, the Mount Vernon Trail, and Rock Creek Park—are also well-suited for use by bikers.

**The Greater Washington Bicycle Atlas,** published by the American Youth Hostels Association, is the complete guide to tours within 100 miles of Washington. It is available for $10 at most Washington area bookstores or from the Washington Area Bicyclist Association (1015 31st Street NW, 20007, tel. 202/944-8567).

Bicycles can be rented at the following locations:

**Big Wheel Bikes** (1034 33rd St. NW, Georgetown, tel. 202/337-0254; and 1004 Vermont Ave. NW, tel. 202/638-3301).
**Fletcher's Boat House** (C & O Canal Towpath, near Reservoir Rd. NW, tel. 202/244-0461).
**Metropolis Bike & Scooter** (719 8th St. SE, Capitol Hill, tel. 202/543-8900).
**Proteus Bicycle Shop** (2422 18th St. NW, Adams-Morgan, tel. 202/332-6666).
**Thompson's Boat House** (Virginia Ave. and Rock Creek Park, behind Kennedy Center, tel. 202/333-4861).
**Tow Path Cycle** (823 S. Washington St., Alexandria, VA, tel. 703/549-5368).

Cyclists interested in serious training might want to try the three-mile loop around the golf course in East Potomac Park, Hains Point (the entryway is near the Jefferson Memorial). This is a favorite training course for dedicated local racers and would-be triathletes. A note of caution, though: Restrict your workouts to the daytime; the area is not safe after dark.

**Boating**  Canoeing, sailing, and powerboating are all popular in the region. There are several places to rent boats along the Potomac River north and south of the city. The two boat houses listed here are convenient for tourists.

**Fletcher's Boat House** (tel. 202/244–0461), about two miles north of Georgetown on the C & O Canal, rents rowboats and canoes for use in the canal.

**Thompson's Boat House** (tel. 202/333–9543), at Virginia Avenue and Rock Creek Parkway behind the Kennedy Center, rents canoes, rowboats, rowing shells, and sailboards.

**Paddle boats** are available on the east side of the **Tidal Basin** in front of the Jefferson Memorial (Tel. 202/484–0845).

If you're interested in **sailing,** consider taking a day trip to Annapolis, Maryland (about an hour's drive from the District). Annapolis is one of the best sailing centers on the East Coast, and the Chesapeake Bay is without a doubt one of the great sailing basins of the world. The **Annapolis Sailing School** (tel. 301/267–7205) is a world-renowned school and charter company.

If you can't make time for a day on the Bay, the **Washington Sailing Marina** (tel. 703/548–9027), just south of National Airport on the George Washington Parkway, and the **Bell Haven Marina** (tel. 703/768–0018), just south of Old Town Alexandria on the George Washington Parkway, rent Sunfish, Windsurfers, and larger boats to those qualified to charter.

Although it is not widely known, Washington is home to some of the best whitewater **kayakers** and whitewater **canoeists** in the country. On weekends they can be seen practicing below Great Falls in **Mather Gorge,** a canyon carved by the Potomac River just north of the city, above Chain Bridge. The water there is deceptive and dangerous, and only top-level kayakers should consider kayaking there. Every year since 1975 there have been four or five drownings. It is, however, safe to watch the experts at play from a post above the gorge. For information call the **ranger station** at Great Falls, Virginia (tel. 703/285–2966) or Great Falls, Maryland (tel. 301/443–0024).

**Fishing**  A five-mile stretch of the Potomac River—running roughly from the Wilson Memorial Bridge in Alexandria south to Fort Washington National Park—is one of the best spots for largemouth bass fishing in the country. It has, in fact, become something of an East Coast mecca for anglers in search of this particular fish. But the simple act of renting a boat and going fishing is complicated by the fact that this stretch of the Potomac is divided among three jurisdictions: Virginia, Maryland, and the District of Columbia. It's not always easy to determine in whose water you're fishing or which licenses you should have. The best solution is to hire a guide. **Outdoor Life Unlimited** (tel. 301/572–5688), run by nationally known fisherman and conservationist Ken Penrod, is an umbrella group of area fishing guides. Thirty of the area's best guides are listed with Penrod, and for about $150 to $250 a day a professional guide will take care of all your needs, from licenses to tackle to boats. Penrod's guides are all professionals and will teach novices or guide experts.

Other fish species found in the region include striped bass, shad, and white and yellow perch. The area around Fletcher's Boat House on the C & O Canal is one of the best spots for perch.

The two best tackle shops in the area are both in Alexandria, Virginia: **Delta Tackle** (1437 Powhatan Street, tel. 703/549–

5729) and **Potomac Sports Center** (6231 Richmond Highway, tel. 703/765–2220).

**Gene Mueller,** a nationally known hunting and fishing writer, has a column three times a week (Mon., Wed., and Fri.) in the *Washington Times*. He takes readers' telephone calls Thursday mornings at 202/636–3268.

**Golf**  Serious golfers must resign themselves to driving out of the District to find a worthwhile course. There are two public courses in town, but the greens and fairways are in poor shape and should be considered only for hitting practice and only if there is no alternative.

The **Hains Point course** (tel. 202/863–9007) in East Potomac Park near the Jefferson Memorial is a flat, wide, 6,303-yard, par-72 course. Its greatest claim to fame is that professional golfer and Washington resident Lee Elder got his start there. The fee is $7 for 18 holes.

**Rock Creek Park** (16th and Rittenhouse Sts. NW, tel. 202/723–9832) has a 4,798-yard, par-65 course with an easy front-nine and challenging back. It is not in good condition. The fee is $7 for 18 holes.

There are several excellent courses within a half hour of downtown:

**Reston South** (11875 Sunrise Valley Dr., Reston, VA, tel. 703/620–9333) is a four-star, 6,480-yard, par-71 course widely considered the best public course in the metropolitan area. Well-maintained, it is heavily wooded but not too difficult for the average player. The fee is $9 weekdays and $12 weekends.

Also 30 minutes from town is **Northwest Park** (15701 Layhill Rd., Wheaton, MD, tel. 301/598–6100). This 6,732-yard, par-72 course is extremely long, making for slow play, but it is immaculately groomed and fair. The fee is $9.50 weekdays, $10.50 weekends, for 18 holes.

If you are flying in or out of Dulles Airport and want to fit in a round of golf, try **Penderbrook** (at Rt. 50 and I-66, tel. 703/339–8585). A short but imaginative 5,927-yard, par-72 course, it is one of the best public greens in the area. The 5th, 11th, and 15th holes are exceptional. The fee is $9 for 18 holes.

**Health Clubs**  In recent years the number of health clubs in Maryland and northern Virginia has doubled, while the number within the District has declined. All of the clubs in Washington require that you be a member—or at least a member of an affiliated club—in order to use their facilities. Some hotels, however, have made private arrangements with neighboring health clubs to enable hotel guests to use the club's facilities (in some cases guests pay a daily fee). Check with your hotel when making reservations. A number of downtown hotels are associated with the **Westin Fitness Center.** One of the best hotel clubs in the world and definitely the fanciest fitness center in Washington, this is the place where celebrities like Cybill Sheperd, Holly Hunter, and Arnold Schwarzennegger come to sweat. (The Westin Hotel, 2401 M St. NW, tel. 202/457–5070).

Card-carrying members of the **International Racquet Sports Association (I.R.S.A.)** can use the facilities at one of the many member clubs in Washington for a daily fee. You must present your membership card from your home club. The I.R.S.A. "Passport" lists member clubs.

The **National Capital YMCA** (1711 Rhode Island Ave. NW, tel. 202/862–9622) offers just about everything a body could want, from basketball, weights, racquetball, and swimming to exercise equipment. Usage fees run from $5 to $10 a day depending on the time. Members of out-of-town Ys are welcome; simply show your membership card.

**Horseback Riding** **Rock Creek Park Equestrian Center** (Military Rd. and Glover Rd. NW, tel. 202/362–0117) is open all year; the hours vary according to season.

**Ice Skating** The **Sculpture Garden Outdoor Rink** (Constitution Ave. between 7th and 9th streets NW, tel. 202/371–5343) appears each winter with the cold weather. **Pershing Park Ice Rink** (Pennsylvania Ave. between 14th and 15th streets NW) is also popular. Skates can be rented at both locations. **Fort Dupont Park** (37th and Ely Pl. SE, tel. 202/581–0199) has a beautiful rink; the park itself, though, is in a less-than-wonderful section of town. Equally close to the downtown area is the **Mount Vernon Ice Rink** (2017 Belle View Blvd., Alexandria, VA 22307, tel. 703/768–3222). It too has rentals.

**Jogging** If you really want to know who runs Washington, go for a jog. Congressmen, senators, and Supreme Court justices can often be spotted on the Mall, running loops around the monuments. Georgetown power brokers are seen hoofing the towpaths along the C & O Canal or the meandering trails in Rock Creek Park. And at lunchtime in Arlington, the Pentagon empties out along the Mount Vernon Trail.

Whatever your reason for coming to Washington, don't leave your running shoes at home. Downtown Washington and nearby northern Virginia offer some of the most scenic running trails in the country, and running is one of the best ways to take in the vistas of the city. The most popular paths are presented below. A word of caution: Joggers unfamiliar with the city should not go out at night, and, even in daylight, it's best to run in pairs if you venture beyond the most public areas and the more heavily used sections of the trails.

For information on weekend races, check the calendar in the "Weekend" section of the Thursday *Washington Times* or the Friday *Washington Post*. For general information about running and races in the area, contact the national headquarters of **Road Runners Clubs of America** in Alexandria (tel. 703/836–0558).

**The Mall.** The loop around the Capitol and past the Smithsonian museums, the Washington Monument, the Reflecting Pool, and the Lincoln Memorial is the most popular of all Washington running trails. At any time of day, hundreds of joggers, speed walkers, bicyclists, and tourists can be seen making their way along the gravel pathways of this 4.5-mile loop. If you're looking for a longer run, you can veer south of the Mall on either side of the Tidal Basin and head for the Jefferson Memorial and East Potomac Park, the site of many races.

**The Mount Vernon Trail.** Just across the Potomac in Virginia, this trail is another favorite with Washington runners. The northern (shorter) section begins near the pedestrian causeway leading to Theodore Roosevelt Island (directly across the river from the Kennedy Center), goes past National Airport and on to Old Town Alexandria. This stretch is approximately

3.5 miles one-way. You can get to the trail from the District by crossing either the Theodore Roosevelt Bridge (at the Lincoln Memorial) or the Rochambeau Memorial Bridge (also known as the 14th Street Bridge, at the Jefferson Memorial). South of National Airport, the trail runs down to the Washington Marina. The final mile of the trail's northern section meanders through protected wetlands before ending in the heart of Old Town Alexandria. The longer southern section of the trail (approximately nine miles) takes you along the coast of the Potomac from Alexandria all the way to George Washington's home, Mount Vernon.

For over ten years, on Tuesday evenings year-round, the **Fairfax Running Center** (tel. 703/549–7688) in Old Town Alexandria has sponsored informal runs along the Mount Vernon Trail.

**Rock Creek Park.** A miraculously preserved bit of wilderness in the middle of Washington, Rock Creek Park has 15 miles of trails, a bicycle path, bridle path, picnic groves, playgrounds, and a boulder-strewn rolling stream from which it gets its name (the creek is not safe for swimming). Starting at P Street on the edge of Georgetown, Rock Creek Park runs all the way to Montgomery County, Maryland. The most popular run in the park is a trail along the creek extending from Georgetown to the National Zoo (about a 4-mile loop). In summer, there is considerable shade, and there are water fountains at an exercise station along the way. The roadway is closed to traffic on weekends. On Sunday morning, **Fleet Feet Triathlete** in Adams-Morgan near the National Zoo, sponsors five-mile runs in Rock Creek Park (tel. 202/387–3888).

**The C & O Canal.** Now maintained by the National Park Service, the Chesapeake and Ohio Canal National Historical Park is a favorite spot with both runners and bikers. A pancake-flat gravel trail leads from Georgetown through wooded areas along the Potomac and northward into Maryland. The most popular loop is from a point just north of Key Bridge in Georgetown to Fletcher's Boat House (approximately four miles round-trip).

**Swimming** There are no beaches in the Washington area. If you want to swim during your visit, it's best to stay at a hotel that has a pool. A few years ago it was possible to gain entry to some hotel pools for a small fee, but that practice has by and large been discontinued. Health-club pools, too, are open only to members. The only alternative is public pools. The District of Columbia maintains eight indoor pools and 18 large outdoor pools. For more information and a list of public facilities, contact the Aquatic Department of the DC Department of Recreation (1230 Taylor St. NW 20011, tel. 202/576–6436).

**Tennis** Tennis being the sport of the rich, powerful, and famous, it's no surprise the sport is extremely popular in Washington. The District of Columbia maintains 144 outdoor courts. Some of these courts are located in rather seedy parts of town, however, so it is best to check on the neighborhood in question before heading out. Free permits, required at all public courts, are issued by the Department of Recreation. Send a self-addressed, stamped envelope for a permit and a list of all city-run courts. You can also call for information on specific courts (3149 16th St. NW 20010, tel. 202/673–7646).

The best courts in the area are at two locations: **Hains Point** (East Potomac Park, tel. 202/554–5962) has outdoor courts as well as courts under a bubble for wintertime play. Fees run from $8 to $23 an hour depending on the time and season. The **Washington Tennis Center** (16th and Kennedy sts. NW, tel. 202/ 667–1233) has clay and hard courts. The fees are the same as at Hains Point.

## Spectator Sports

Tickets for all Capital Centre, Patriot Centre, and Baltimore Arena events can be purchased through **TicketCenter** (tel. 202/ 432–0200 in DC, tel 301/481–6000 in Baltimore, or tel. 800/448– 9009 in other areas).

**Baseball**    Because the District does not have its own professional base- ball team, baseball fans from the area go to Baltimore to root for the **Orioles.** Tickets range from $4.75 for general admission seats to $9.94 for lower box seats (tel. 301/432–0200).

If you prefer Class A baseball à la Bull Durham, you might want to make a trip just south of the Beltway to the County Stadium Complex in Woodbridge, Maryland, to watch the **Prince Wil- liam Cannons.** Tickets range from $2 to $4. (tel. 301/690–3622).

**Basketball**    The **Washington Bullets'** home games are held at the Capital Centre in Landover, Maryland, just outside the Beltway. Their schedule runs from September to April. For tickets, tel. 800/ 448–9009.

Among the Division I **college basketball** teams in the area, for- mer NCAA national champion Georgetown University's Hoyas are the best known. Their home games are played at the Capital Centre (tel. 202/687–2270 or TicketCenter, 800/448–9009). Other Division I schools include the University of Maryland (tel. 301/454–2121), George Mason University (tel. 703/323– 2672), George Washington University (tel. 202/994–3865), American University (tel. 202/885–7328), the Naval Academy (tel. 301/268–6226), and Howard University (tel. 202/636– 7173).

**Football**    Washington is a football-crazy town—never, *never* say any- thing bad about the **Redskins.** Unfortunately, unless you happen to be a relative of the team's owner you may as well for- get about trying to get tickets to a home game. Since 1966, all Redskins games at the 55,750-seat Robert F. Kennedy Stadi- um on the eastern edge of Capitol Hill have been sold out to season-ticket holders. Tickets are occasionally advertised in the classified section of the Sunday *Post*, but expect to pay con- siderably more than face value.

The **area colleges** offer an excellent alternative for frustrated football fans. Teams from the University of Maryland (tel. 301/ 454–2121), the Naval Academy (tel. 301/268–6226) in Annapo- lis, and Howard University (tel. 202/636–7173) all play a full schedule of college football.

**Ice Hockey**    The **Washington Capitals'** season runs from October through April. In recent years the team has come close to greatness, but they've always choked at playoff time. Washingtonians love them nonetheless. Home games are played at the Capital Cen- tre. For tickets call 301/350–3400 or TicketCenter at 800/448– 9009.

**Lacrosse** The **Washington Waves** play in the Capital Centre from January through March. For tickets call 301/432–0200 or TicketCenter at 800/448–9009.

**Soccer** The **Washington Stars'** home games are played at the H.T. Woodson High School (9325 Main St., Fairfax, VA, tel. 703/352–4625). The **Washington Diplomats** play a season from April to August at Robert F. Kennedy Stadium (tel. 202/543–8503). Tickets for either team—$9 for adults—can also be purchased through TicketCenter (tel. 800/448–9009).

# 6 Dining

## Introduction

*by Deborah Papier*

It is often said of Washington's weather that if you don't like it, all you have to do is wait a minute. The same applies to the city's restaurant scene. Every week, at least, a restaurant opens or closes or changes ownership, chef, or menu. In the space of a month whole categories of cuisine can appear or disappear.

This can be frustrating, since it means that a restaurant you have enjoyed visiting—or were looking forward to visiting—may be transformed or gone when you arrive. But it's also exhilarating, since there are always new places to discover.

And although a particular restaurant may falter or fall, in general, Washington's restaurants are getting better and better. In the last few years Italian restaurants have come to rival French establishments, which for a long time set the standard in fine dining. There has also been an explosion of the kind of cooking usually called New American. Its practitioners don't much like that label, but whatever you call the cuisine, it has brought considerable style and energy to the area's restaurant scene.

Despite the dirth of ethnic neighborhoods in Washington and the corresponding lack of the kinds of restaurant districts found in many cities, you *can* find almost any type of food here, from Nepalese to Salvadoran to Ethiopian. In only one category of food is the city falling short these days, and that's Chinese. The restaurants that for years were considered preeminent in the city's minuscule **Chinatown** (centered on G and H streets between 6th and 8th) have been slipping, and no new ones have emerged to fill their place. (Though by the time you read this, that may no longer be the case.)

Aside from Chinatown, there are four areas of the city where restaurants are concentrated:

Most of the deluxe restaurants are on or near **K Street NW,** also the location of many of the city's blue-chip law firms. These are the restaurants that feed and feed off of expense-account diners and provide the most elegant atmosphere, attentive service, and often the best food. Needless to say, this restaurant row is not renowned for its bargains.

The other area of town long known as a restaurant district is **Georgetown,** whose central intersection is Wisconsin Avenue and M Street. Georgetown contains some of the city's priciest houses as well as some of its cheesiest businesses, and its restaurants are similarly diverse, with white-tablecloth dining places right next door to hole-in-the-wall carryouts. Almost every kind of ethnic cuisine can be found here—Argentinian, Afghani, Indian, Indonesian, Ethiopian, Vietnamese—and many of the restaurants serve good food at reasonable prices. Georgetown also houses the city's trendiest dining spots, whose high style makes them the places to see and be seen, at least until their cutting edge is dulled.

Now emerging as a culinary competitor to Georgetown is **Adams-Morgan.** Eighteenth Street extending south from Columbia Road is wall-to-wall restaurants, with new ones opening so fast it's almost impossible to track them. Although the area has retained some of its Hispanic identity, the new eating establishments tend to be either Italian or New American.

Despite (or perhaps because of) the proliferation of eating places, it is hard to be sure of getting a good meal in Adams-Morgan. The inconsistency that once characterized kitchens elsewhere in the city is now manifest here. It will probably be a few years before things settle down and before the Adams-Morgan restaurants can match the professionalism of those in Georgetown. Before you venture to the area for a meal, be warned: Adams-Morgan is not served by the subway, and parking here can be a problem.

South from Adams-Morgan and north from K Street is **Dupont Circle,** around which a number of restaurants are clustered. Some of the city's best Italian places can be found here as well as a variety of cafés, most boasting outdoor seating.

**Capitol Hill** has a number of bar/eateries that cater to congressional types in need of fortification after a day spent running the country. Many of these serve good bar fare, and some of them can turn out quite a credible meal. But for some reason there is a paucity of first-class restaurants on the Hill whose cooking can justify a cross-town trip.

Outside the city limits are some thriving restaurant districts. **Bethesda, Maryland,** offers a wealth of possibilities, from diners on up; a number of successful D.C. restaurants have opened branches here. Virginia has its Georgetown equivalent, in **Old Town Alexandria,** as well as some of the area's best Oriental restaurants.

Highly recommended restaurants in each price category are indicated by a star ★.

| Category | Cost* |
|---|---|
| Very Expensive | over $35 |
| Expensive | $25–35 |
| Moderate | $15–25 |
| Inexpensive | under $15 |

*average cost of a 3-course dinner, per person, excluding drinks, service, and (9%) sales tax*

The following credit card abbreviations are used: AE, American Express; CB, Carte Blanche; DC, Diners Club; MC, MasterCard; and V, Visa.

### Adams-Morgan

**Ethiopian**    **Meskerem.** Adams-Morgan may well have more Ethiopian restaurants than Ethiopia itself—about a dozen in a three-block stretch of 18th Street. While all of them have virtually identical menus, Meskerem is distinctive for its bright, appealingly decorated dining room. Another attractive feature: The restaurant has a balcony where you can eat Ethiopian-style—seated on the floor on leather cushions, with large woven baskets for tables. But whether it is served atop baskets or on conventional tables, an Ethiopian meal is definitely exotic. There is no silverware; instead, the food is scooped up with *injera,* a spongy flat bread that also does duty as the platter on which the meal is presented. The country's main dish is the *watt,* or stew, which may be made with chicken, lamb, beef, or shrimp in either a

# Dining

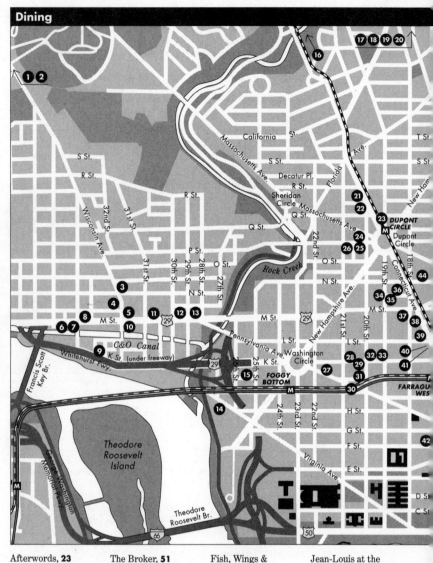

Afterwords, **23**
American Cafe, **5**
Austin Grill, **1**
Bacchus, **36**
Bamiyan, **6**
Bistro Francais, **10**
Bombay Palace, **32**
Bradshaw's, **20**

The Broker, **51**
La Chaumière, **13**
La Colline, **50**
La Fourchette, **18**
Las Pampas, **8**
Le Gaulois, **27**
Le Lion D'Or, **38**
Le Pavillon, **41**
Devon Bar & Grill, **30**
Duke Zeibert's, **40**

Fish, Wings &
Tings, **19**
Foggy Bottom
Cafe, **15**
Galileo, **26**
Gary's, **37**
Geppetto, **12**
Georgetown Seafood
Grill, **11**
i Ricchi, **34**

Jean-Louis at the
Watergate Hotel, **14**
Jean-Pierre, **33**
Maison Blanche, **42**
Marrakesh, **49**
McPherson Grill, **45**
Meskerem, **17**
Morton's of Chicago, **4**
New Heights, **16**
Obelisk, **24**

spicy or a mild sauce. Several vegetarian watts are also available. Those seeking a truly authentic experience should order their injera made with *teff*, a green grown only in Ethiopia and Idaho that imparts a distinctive sourness to the bread. *2434 18th St. NW, tel. 202/462–4100. Reservations advised. Dress: casual but neat. AE, CB, DC, MC, V. Closed lunch Mon.– Thurs. Inexpensive.*

**French**   **La Fourchette.** Located on a block in Adams-Morgan where new restaurants are opening almost weekly and closing just as fast, La Fourchette has stayed in business for over a decade by offering good bistro food at reasonable prices. Most of the menu consists of daily specials, but you can pretty much count on finding bouillabaisse and rabbit on the list. The most popular entrées on the regular menu are the hearty veal and lamb shanks. La Fourchette also looks the way a bistro should, with an exposed brick wall, tin ceiling, bentwood chairs, and quasi-post-impressionist murals. *2429 18th St. NW, tel. 202/332– 3077. Reservations advised. Dress: casual but neat. AE, CB, DC, MC, V. Closed lunch Sat. and Sun. Moderate.*

**Jamaican**   **Fish, Wings & Tings.** You don't go to this wild-and-woolly restaurant for a quiet meal, any more than you put on a reggae record for background music. This Caribbean café (or *mini kafe*, according to the menu) is the brilliantly idiosyncratic creation of a husband-and-wife team. She's from Jamaica and works in the kitchen. He's a Panamanian with dreadlocks who keeps a semblance of order in the tiny dining room, which is barely able to contain the crowds that wait for carryout or for one of the few tables. The menu includes stewed oxtail and curry goat, but most people come here for the curry-ginger chicken wings, or the jerk (barbecued) thighs. Marinated and grilled rainbow trout is another popular item from the regular menu, which is supplemented by two or three daily specials, usually poultry or fish. *2418 18th St. NW, tel. 202/234–0322. Reservations not accepted. Dress: casual. Closed Sun. AE. Inexpensive.*

**New American**   **New Heights.** With its precise geometrical design softened by pastel colors, New Heights is one of Washington's most attractive restaurants. The food is New American but not radically so; in response to customer preference the restaurant is taking a more traditional approach. The menu varies seasonally but always includes a vegetarian entrée, such as asparagus strudel. Salmon, a frequent offering, might be cooked in a black-bean sauce with sprouts and bell peppers. Also worth ordering if it is available is the grilled beef with horseradish cream. New Heights is a good choice for Sunday brunch. *2317 Calvert St. NW (1 block from Woodley Park/Zoo Metro stop), tel. 202/234– 4110. Reservations advised. Dress: casual but neat. AE, CB, DC, MC, V. Closed lunch Sat. Expensive.*

**Bradshaw's.** A standout in the burgeoning restaurant row of 18th Street in Adams-Morgan, Bradshaw's is a New American restaurant that looks as trendy as it cooks. The menu, which draws from Oriental, Eastern European, and Southwestern traditions, is heavy on fish and poultry. Two of the best offerings are jade shrimp and scallions; and duck smoked in the house, roasted, and served with blueberry chutney. The extensive list of appetizers includes several dishes unavailable elsewhere in town, such as smoked salmon dumplings and wild mushroom blinis. Bradshaw's also features numerous wines by the glass, creative weekend brunches, and a selection of sandwiches and salads for those not wanting a full meal. *2319 18th St. NW, tel. 202/462–8330. Reservations advised. Dress: casual but neat. AE, CB, DC, MC, V. Closed lunch weekdays. Moderate.*

## Capitol Hill

**French** **La Colline.** Even before Washington became a contender in the
★ U.S. restaurant ring, it did have its heavyweight chefs, such as Robert Gréault, originally of Le Bagatelle. For the past nine years Gréault has worked to make La Colline into one of the city's best French restaurants and the best of any type on Capitol Hill. When it first opened, La Colline was also one of the city's great bargains. That's no longer the case; unless you order the special fixed-price dinner, a meal at La Colline is likely to be pricey. But it's worth it. The menu changes daily, and it seems always to strike the perfect balance between innovation and tradition. The emphasis is on seafood, with offerings ranging from simple grilled preparations to fricassees and gratins with imaginative sauces. The non-seafood menu usually offers duck with an orange or cassis sauce and veal with chanterelles. Desserts are superb, as is the wine list. *400 N. Capitol St. (3 blocks from Union Station Metro stop), tel. 202/737–0400. Reservations required. Jacket and tie advised. AE, CB, DC, MC, V. Closed lunch Sat. and Sun. Free parking in underground lot. Expensive.*

**Swiss** **The Broker.** There can be no arguing over which is the best Swiss restaurant in Washington, since at the moment there is only one. But even when the city had several, The Broker still had no real competition—this is as good as Swiss food gets. The Swiss cheese standards, like fondue and raclette, are available, as are *bündnerfleisch* and *rosti* potatoes. The most popular entrées, however, are the *emince de veau Zurichoise,* a rich veal stew, and the lamb chops. Daily low-calorie specials and a pretheater menu are also offered. The wine list leans toward Switzerland and Germany. Don't come here expecting Swiss kitsch—the dining room is decorated in Scandinavian modern and doesn't even have a cuckoo clock. *713 8th St. SE (2 blocks from Eastern Market Metro stop), tel. 202/546–8300. Reservations advised. Jacket and tie advised. AE, DC, MC, V. Closed lunch Sat. and Sun. Expensive.*

## Downtown

**American** **The Palm.** Food trends come and go, but the Palm pays no attention; it offers the same he-man food it always has—gargantuan steaks and lobsters, several kinds of potatoes, New York cheesecake. The staff's been packing them in for 17 years with this kind of fare, and they're not about to let the calorie- and cholesterol-counters spoil the party. The look of the restaurant is basement basic—acoustic ceiling tiles, wooden fans—nothing to distract one from the serious business of chowing down. In addition to the beef and lobsters it is famous for, the Palm also offers lamb chops, two veal and two poultry entrées, fresh fish, and linguini with clam sauce. *1225 19th St. NW, tel. 202/293–9091. Reservations advised. Dress: casual but neat. Closed Sat. lunch and Sun. AE, CB, DC, MC, V. Very Expensive.*

★ **Prime Rib.** Despite its name, the Prime Rib is no longer really a
steakhouse. In response to the increasing popularity of seafood, it now devotes half its menu to fish and shellfish, some of it
shipped express from Florida. The most popular of the seafood
dishes is the imperial crab, made only of jumbo lump-crabmeat;
the crab imperial is also stuffed in a two-pound lobster. The
aged beef from Chicago includes a steak au poivre in addition to
New York strip, porterhouse, filet mignon, and the restaurant's namesake, for which you might need to reserve ahead.
Also served are simple preparations of veal, pork, lamb, and
chicken. Prime Rib is an unusually attractive restaurant; its
black walls, leather chairs, and leopardskin print rugs give it a
timeless sophistication. *2020 K St. NW. (1 block from Farragut
West Metro stop), tel. 202/466–8811. Reservations advised.
Jacket and tie required. AE, CB, DC, MC, V. Closed Sat.
lunch and Sun. Very Expensive.*

**Duke Zeibert's.** At lunch, this 450-seat restaurant is filled with
regulars who come to talk sports with Duke and eat heartily
from a menu that essentially hasn't changed in 39 years—
boiled beef and chicken in a pot, deli sandwiches, and specials
like corned beef and cabbage. At dinner, only the front room is
used, and the restaurant becomes a different place, with couples and families replacing the deal makers. In the evening the
signature chicken and beef in a pot are still available, but the
menu leans more toward broiler items like lamb chops and sirloin, not to mention two dishes for which the restaurant is
famous—prime rib and crab cakes. This may also be the only
place in town where you can get chicken soup with matzo balls,
and potato pancakes. *1050 Connecticut Ave. NW (on the mezzanine of the Washington Square Building at Farragut North
Metro stop), tel. 202/466–3730. Reservations required. Jacket
and tie advised. AE, CB, DC, MC, V. Closed lunch Sun.
Closed Sun. during July and Aug. Validated parking at Washington Square lot. Expensive.*

**Gary's.** Though it is located in a claustrophobic new shopping
complex, Gary's is a spacious, elegant restaurant with an old-
money look. Furnished with rich wood paneling, etched glass,
and Oriental carpets, the dining room is reminiscent of an English men's club, but the food is American, with some Italian
accents. The regular menu is heavy on meat—rack of lamb and
pork, in addition to steaks and prime ribs—and Gary's is generally thought of as a steakhouse. But the daily specials
emphasize fish in a variety of preparations, from blackened
redfish to soft-shell crabs to linguine pesto with shrimp. In addition, Gary's will prepare lobster any way the customer wants
it, which makes the restaurant popular among transplanted
New Englanders seeking their regional specialty of lobster
stuffed with lobster. *1800 M St. NW (Metro stop, Farragut
North) tel. 202/463–6470. Reservations advised. Dress: casual
but neat. AE, CB, DC, MC, V. Closed Sat. lunch and Sun.
Closed Sat. during July and Aug. Expensive.*

**Foggy Bottom Café.** Because of zoning restrictions, the area
around the Kennedy Center is almost bereft of dining options.
One possibility for a hungry theatergoer who doesn't want to
eat at the center's own restaurants (which tend to be seriously
overcrowded) is the Foggy Bottom Café. A small, pleasant
eatery located in the River Inn, about a five-block walk from
the center, the Foggy Bottom Café is a place where you can
have either a snack—a hamburger, sandwich, or salad—or a

full meal. Though the entrée list is not extensive, it is diverse, with Oriental, Southwestern, and Middle Eastern traditions represented. The most popular items are the shrimp and vegetable tempura, the barbecued spareribs, and the fresh salmon. Keep the Foggy Bottom Café in mind if you're looking for a place for breakfast—the sunny room and the muffins baked fresh every morning are good incentives for getting out of bed. *924 25th St. NW (2 blocks from Foggy Bottom Metro stop), tel. 202/338–8707. Reservations required. Dress: casual but neat. AE, CB, DC, MC, V. Moderate.*

**Old Ebbitt Grill.** It doesn't have the charm of the old Old Ebbitt, which was urban-renewed out of existence, but this incarnation of Washington's longest-lived restaurant is obviously doing something right—it does more business than any other eating place in town. People flock here to drink at the several bars, which seem to go on for miles, and to enjoy carefully prepared bar food that includes buffalo chicken wings, hamburgers, and reuben sandwiches. But this is not just a place for casual nibbling; the Old Ebbitt offers serious diners homemade pastas and a list of daily specials, with the emphasis on fish dishes like Shenandoah trout in a champagne sauce. Despite the crowds, the restaurant never feels crowded, thanks to its well-spaced, comfortable booths. *675 15th St. NW (2 blocks from Metro Center Metro stop), tel. 202/347–4800. Reservations advised. Dress: casual but neat. AE, CB, DC, MC, V. Moderate.*

**French** **Jean-Louis at the Watergate Hotel.** A showcase for the cooking
★ of Jean-Louis Palladin, who was the youngest chef in France ever to be recognized with two stars by the Michelin raters, this small restaurant is often cited as one of the best in the United States. The contemporary French fare is based on regional American ingredients—crawfish from Louisiana, wild mushrooms from Oregon, game from Texas—combined in innovative ways. There are two limited-choice fixed-price dinners: one with five courses, for $75 per person, the other with six courses (the additional course is a foie-gras dish), for $90. There is also a pre-theater menu of four courses for $38, designed for but not limited to those attending the nearby Kennedy Center. In general, the first course is a soup or terrine; corn soup with oysters and lobster quenelles is a signature offering. Next comes a shellfish preparation, perhaps a potato stuffed with lobster mousseline; then a fish course, such as snapper with braised cabbage; and last, a meat dish, perhaps rack of lamb with artichoke ragout. The wine cellar is said to be the largest on the East Coast. *2650 Virginia Ave. NW (downstairs in the Watergate Hotel, which can be entered from Virginia or New Hampshire aves; 3 blocks from Foggy Bottom Metro stop). tel. 202/298–4488. Reservations required. Jacket and tie required. AE, DC, MC, V. Closed lunch, Sun. and the last 2 weeks in Aug. Validated parking. Very Expensive.*

★ **Jean-Pierre.** This restaurant ushered in a new era of haute cusine in Washington when it opened 20 years ago, and it still serves exquisite food in exquisite surroundings. The menu, which combines dishes from the classic repertory with newer approaches, changes twice yearly. Winter brings such hearty fare as cassoulet and game dishes, while the summer list features such temptations as salmon with shiitake mushrooms. The menu is further enlivened by some Morrocan offerings, such as couscous and tagine (a stew cooked in a clay pot) of duck with honey and dates. Unlike most Washington restaurants,

Jean-Pierre was clearly designed for romantic dinners rather than power lunches. Its peach and lavender hues and opalescent tiles make your dinner partner look almost as good as what's on your plate. *1835 K St. NW, tel. 202/466–2022. Reservations advised. Jacket and tie advised. AE, CB, DC, MC, V. Closed Sat. lunch and Sun. Free parking in lot next door at dinner. Very Expensive.*

★ **Le Lion D'Or.** Other French restaurants may flirt with fads, but this one sticks to the classics—or at any rate the neoclassics—and does them so well that its popularity remains undiminished year after year. Aside from the owner's collection of faience and the abudant floral arrangements, the decor doesn't do much to entertain the eye. But the palate is another story. This is the sort of food that makes the French posture of cultural superiority almost defensible: lobster soufflé, crêpes with oysters and caviar, ravioli with foie gras, salmon with crayfish, roast pigeon with mushrooms, lamb with green peppercorns. The long list of daily specials can get rather confusing unless you take notes while the waiter recites them. But don't forget to place an order for a dessert soufflé—it will leave you breathless. *1150 Connecticut Ave. NW (at Farragut North Metro stop), tel. 202/296–7972. Reservations required. Jacket and tie required. AE, CB, DC, MC, V. Closed Sat. lunch and Sun. Free parking in lot next door at dinner. Very Expensive.*

★ **Le Pavillon.** Chef Yannick Cam is the man who brought nouvelle cuisine to America, first at New York's Le Coup de Fusil, then, in 1978, at Le Pavillon in Washington. Cam, like most of his fellow innovators, now repudiates the nouvelle cuisine label; he calls his creations "cuisine personalisée." The heart of this cuisine, however, remains reductions of sauces, whose intense flavors provide the foundation on which dishes of great complexity are built. Meals are fixed-price, ranging from $48 to $85 per person at dinner. For that you get either two or three appetizers of your choice, a main course, and dessert. The offerings change daily, but entrées always include lamb with olives and turnips, beef in a garlic-cream sauce, and a pigeon, perhaps roasted with figs and ginger. The dish for which Cam is most famous, however, is an appetizer: an ambrosial beet ravioli with caviar. The dozen or so desserts he makes each day are extraordinary (in particular the white-chocolate mousse), as is the wine list. The setting is as elegant as the food—etched glass, handmade wallpaper, and a Lalique table refracting the light that fills the room. *1050 Connecticut Ave. NW (on the mezzanine of the Washington Square Building, at Farragut North Metro stop), tel. 202/833–3846. Reservations advised. Jacket and tie advised. Closed Sat. lunch and Sun. AE, CB, DC, MC, V. Very Expensive.*

**Maison Blanche.** No matter whether Democrats or Republicans are in power, Maison Blanche is the restaurant elected by the city's power brokers and those who enjoy gawking at them. It owes its bipartisan popularity in large part to its location near the White House and executive office buildings, but also to its Old World elegance, the friendliness of the family that runs it, and its large repertory of classic and modern French dishes. The menu, which changes four times a year, is supplemented by a large number of daily specials, primarily fish. Maison Blanche goes to great lengths to obtain Dover sole, which it serves simply grilled in butter. This is perhaps the restaurant's most popular dish, but also exceptional are the rack of lamb and the pasta dishes, such as shrimp sautéed with tomatoes and garlic, served over angelhair. The pastry chef has a proper reverence for chocolate, and the wine list is extensive, with California wines well represented. *1725 F St. NW (4 blocks from Farragut West Metro stop), tel. 202/842–0070. Reservations advised. Jacket and tie suggested. AE, CB, D, DC, MC, V. Closed Sat. lunch and Sun. Free valet parking at dinner. Very Expensive.*

**Le Gaulois.** This vinyl-tablecloth café offers the kind of unpretentious Gallic fare that is becoming hard to find these days—omelets, quiche, hearty stews, and casseroles. The specialty of the house is the *pot au feu,* beef and chicken boiled with vegetables. Other hallmark dishes are quenelles, which inexplicably have fallen off the menus of most of the city's French establishments; and zucchini and seafood in a cream-and-brandy sauce. But Le Gaulois, while it favors the tried-and-true over the trendy, is not simply into retro cuisine. Although most of the daily specials are classics, like coquilles St. Jacques and beef Bordelaise, the kitchen does make occasional forays into nouvelle offerings—such as sweetbreads with shiitake mushrooms and breast of duck with black currants. *2133 Pennsylvania Ave. NW. (3 blocks from Foggy Bottom Metro stop), tel. 202/466–3232. Reservations advised. Dress: casual but neat. AE, MC, V. Closed Sat. lunch and Sun. Moderate.*

**Indian**  **Bombay Palace.** As the number of Indo-Pakistani restaurants dwindles in Washington, this one stands out. An international operation that trains all its chefs in New York to maintain consistency throughout the chain, it offers authentic Indian food in a cosmopolitan setting. The descriptive menu makes clear which dishes are hot and which are mild, though all can be adjusted to the diner's taste. Among the recommended entrées are the chicken and prawns cooked in the tandoor oven, the *gosht patiala* (a stew of meat, potatoes, and onion in a ginger sauce), and the butter chicken (tandoori chicken in a tomato sauce). At lunch, the restaurant offers "executive" specials—meals that can be prepared quickly, at discount prices. *1835 K St. NW (3 blocks from Farragut West Metro stop), tel. 202/331–0111. Reservations advised. Dress: casual but neat. AE, CB, DC, MC, V. Moderate.*

**Italian**  **i Ricchi.** Every once in a while a new restaurant opens that
★ makes even the most level-headed food critics swoon. Last year it was i Ricchi, which features the earthy cuisine of the Tuscany region of Italy. There are two menus, one for spring and summer, one for fall and winter. The spring list includes such offerings as rolled pork and rabbit roasted in wine and fresh herbs, and skewered shrimp, while winter brings grilled goat chops and spare ribs. But whatever the calendar says, it always feels like spring in this airy dining room, which is decorated with terra cotta tiles, cream-colored archways, and floral frescoes. *1220 19th St. NW, tel. 202/835–0459. Reservations required. Jacket and tie advised. AE, DC, MC, V. Closed Sat. lunch and Sun. Expensive.*

**Primi Piatti.** A meal here is like a taxi ride in Rome at rush hour—the crowds and the noise are overwhelming, but you'll never forget the trip. What makes eating at Primi Piatti a memorable experience—aside from the manic exuberance of the dining room—is the food. The restaurant makes a point of serving dishes that are both authentically Italian, and light and healthful. There's a wood-burning grill, on which several kinds of fish are cooked each day—tuna with fresh mint sauce is one preparation—as well as lamb and veal chops. Meat is also done to a succulent turn on the rotisserie. Pastas, made in house, are outstanding, as are the pizzas, which come with such contemporary twists as sun-dried tomatoes. The wine list is unusually descriptive, identifying the grape, color, and taste of each of its offerings, as well as suggesting complementary dishes. *2013 I St. NW (2 blocks from Farragut West and Foggy Bottom Metro stops), tel. 202/223–3600. Reservations accepted only during certain hours. Jacket and tie suggested. AE, CB, DC, MC, V. Closed Sat. lunch and Sun. Moderate.*

**Moroccan** **Marrakesh.** This is one of Washington's most delightful sur-
★ prises: a bit of Morocco located in a part of the city otherwise given over to auto-supply shops. A knock on the carved wooden door summons a caftanned figure, who ushers you past a splashing fountain into the dining room, where you are seated on a couch piled with pillows in front of a low table. The waiter pours warm water over your hands, then explains the menu—a fixed-price, seven-course feast shared by everyone at your table and eaten without silverware. The first course is a platter of three salads; the second, *b'stella*, the pigeon-stuffed pie (Marrakesh substitutes chicken) that is one of the glories of Moroccan cuisine. For the first main course, you choose among several chicken preparations; first-time visitors are usually advised to have the chicken with lemon and olives. For the second main course, the options are beef shish kebab and two lamb preparations. Then come a vegetable couscous, fresh fruit, mint tea, and pastries. Belly dancers put on a nightly show, and when the moon is full and the mood is right the waiters coax the diners onto their feet for a line dance. *617 New York Ave. NW, 202/393–9393. Reservations required. Jacket and tie advised. No credit cards. Closed lunch. Valet parking. Moderate.*

**New American** **Occidental and Occidental Grill.** The historic 1906 Occidental
★ restaurant, which re-opened in 1987 after a 16-year hiatus, is now two separate restaurants. Upstairs is the formal restaurant, called simply Occidental; downstairs is the small, casual grill room. Both are preeminent among the city's New American restaurants, but the Occidental management prefers to consider the establishments simply American, with the emphasis on Chesapeake Bay seafood. The small list of offerings upstairs changes seasonally but always includes a steak (perhaps a filet sauteed with artichokes and wild mushrooms), a veal dish (perhaps stuffed with fresh mozzarella and garlic purée), and various preparations of crabmeat and scallops. The Grill menu changes frequently, but you can count on chicken, fish, and steak as grilled options (the steak might be served with mustard seed, thyme, and bourbon sauce), plus salads and sandwiches. The upstairs room has parquet floors, red velvet booths, and etched glass; the downstairs is done in dark wood and brown banquettes, with 900 photos of the formerly famous animating the walls. *1475 Pennsylvania Ave. NW (3 blocks from Metro Center Metro Stop), tel. 202/783–1475. Reservations advised for the Occidental, but only accepted for certain times at the Grill; count on a long wait otherwise. Jacket and tie advised upstairs. AE, CB, DC, MC, V. Occidental closed Sat. lunch and Sun.; Grill closed Sun. Occidental, Very Expensive; Grill, Expensive.*

★ **Twenty-One Federal.** Offering New American cuisine in a sophisticated setting, Twenty-One Federal is one of the city's hottest restaurants. The menu changes seasonally but always includes a spit-roasted chicken; lamb, pheasant, and rabbit are also prepared on the rotisserie. The New England–born chef has a way with seafood, as exemplified in his grilled oysters and pancetta. But meat eaters will find much to satisfy them as well —such dishes as beef in a marrow-shallot crust, and a lamb plate that includes a rack chop, a loin stuffed with veal, and a grilled, butterflied slice of leg. A pianist plays nightly in the large dining room, which is decorated primarily in black and gray, with marble tiles and brass gridwork adding a touch of class. *1736 L St. NW (½ block from Farragut North Metro stop), tel. 202/331–9771. Reservations advised. Jacket and tie advised. AE, CB, DC, MC, V. Closed Sat. lunch and Sun. Free valet parking at dinner. Very Expensive.*

★ **The Willard.** An exact replica of the 1904 dining room of the historic Willard Hotel, this restaurant exudes a turn-of-the-century splendor. The food, however, is strictly contemporary and includes seafood medley with wilted spinach and angelhair pasta; lamb chops with eggplant and goat cheese; and veal with orzo, pearl onions, and black olives. The unusual wine list emphasizes regional American varieties drawn from the vineyards of Virginia and the Pacific Northwest as well as California; an extensive selection of cognacs is presented on a rolling cart. As one might expect, such luxury does not come cheap; even the ostensibly affordable chef's sampler menu, a limited-selection list, is a pricey $42 for a full dinner. But this is one place where a meal really is an occasion. *1401 Pennsylvania Ave. NW (2 blocks from Metro Center Metro stop), tel. 202/637–7440. Reservations required. Jacket and tie required. AE, CB, DC, MC, V. Free valet parking at dinner. Very Expensive.*

**McPherson Grill.** It is said that nothing is riskier than opening a new restaurant. But there does seem to be one sure-fire formula for success in the restaurant business: Find a central location, hire decorators who know how to fill a room with light, install a grill, and concentrate on seafood. At the McPherson Grill, the seafood includes what may be the most sublime salmon in town—a grilled or steamed fillet with lobster, roast corn, and rosemary butter. Other fish preparations you might encounter on the seasonal menu are tuna steak with coriander, wilted greens, and red bell pepper coulis; and swordfish with dill-butter. Meat possibilities include grilled chicken with cumin, lamb steak with olives and goat cheese, and pork chops with charred tomato relish. Desserts are homey: peach cobbler, coconut-custard pie. *950 15th St. NW (1 block from McPherson Square Metro stop), tel. 202/638–0950. Reservations advised. Jacket and tie advised. AE, CB, DC, MC, V. Closed Sat. lunch and Sun.; closed Sat. and Sun. during Aug. Expensive.*

**Tex-Mex** **Devon Bar & Grill.** Recently expanded, this is one of the city's largest restaurants; but its series of rooms, furnished in modernized traditional—stained glass, dark woods, velvet, and brass—give it a cozy feel. The specialty here is mesquite-grilled fish; the diner can choose from about a dozen seasonal possibilities. There are also live lobsters, and crab cakes with black bean relish. Unlike most seafood restaurants, the Devon does not discriminate against meat-eaters; it buys the highest grade of beef available for its three steak offerings. *2000 Pennsylvania Ave. NW (1 block from Foggy Bottom and Farragut West Metro stops), tel. 202/833–5660. Reservations advised. Dress: casual but neat. AE, CB, DC, MC, V. Expensive.*

**Thai** **Thai Kingdom.** At most of the restaurants on K Street an expense account is essential. At the Thai Kingdom, you need little
more than some loose change. The authentic Thai fare is evenly
divided between mild and hot dishes. Diners with incendiary
inclinations should try "Anna and the King"—scallops
wrapped in minced chicken and served in a basil sauce—or the
crispy chili fish. Among the milder dishes, the grilled chicken
and the *Pad Thai* (shrimp with noodles and bean sprouts) are
outstanding. Fresh squid, served in several guises, is sweet
and tender, without the rubberiness that comes from doing
hard time in the freezer. *2021 K St. NW (3 blocks from Farragut West Metro stop), tel. 202/835–1700. Reservations advised.
Dress: casual but neat. AE, CB, DC, MC, V. Closed weekend
lunch. Validated parking in lot next door. Inexpensive.*

## Dupont Circle

**Italian** **Galileo.** When Galileo opened six years ago, its combination of
★ authentic Italian cuisine and modest prices proved so irresisti-
ble to a city oversaturated with French restaurants that it was
all but impossible to get a table here. The stampede has ended
—largely because the cost of eating at the restaurant has risen
steeply. You can now have a meal without making a reservation
weeks in advance and find out what all the fuss was about. The
menu changes daily, but there is always risotto; a long list of
grilled fish; a game bird, such as quail, guinea hen, or wood-
cock; and one or two beef or veal dishes. Preparations are
generally simple. For example, the veal may be served with
mushroom-and-rosemary sauce, the beef with tomato sauce
and polenta. Everything is made in house, from the breadsticks
to the mozzarella, and it all tastes terrific. *2041 P St. NW (2
blocks from Dupont Circle Metro stop), tel. 202/293–7991. Reservations advised. Jacket and tie advised. AE, CB, DC, MC,
V. Closed Sat. and Sun. lunch. Valet parking at dinner. Very
Expensive.*
**Vincenzo.** Vincenzo has relaxed somewhat since its early days,
when it was so determined to be authentically Italian that it refused to serve butter with the bread. Butter is now available
(on request), and the once exclusively seafood menu has been
supplemented with a few meat dishes—game in autumn, pork
in winter, lamb in spring. But it is still a restaurant for purists
who appreciate its commitment to finding the best fish it can
and serving it as simply as possible. Dinner is fixed-price and
includes an appetizer, first course, main dish, side dish, and
dessert; lunch is à la carte. Along with its enlarged menu,
Vincenzo has expanded its dining space, adding a glassed-in
courtyard. Already light and airy, Vincenzo now more than
ever seems touched by Mediterranean breezes. *1601 20th St.,
NW (1 block from Q St. exit of Dupont Circle Metro stop), tel.
202/667–0047. Reservations advised. Jacket and tie advised.
AE, CB, DC, MC, V. Closed Sat. lunch and Sun. Very Expensive.*
★ **Obelisk.** One of the most exciting new restaurants in Washington, Obelisk serves eclectic Italian cuisine, with a small, fixed-
price menu that includes both traditional dishes and the chef's
imaginative innovations. The list, which changes daily, usually
offers one meat, one fish, and one poultry entrée. The meat is
likely to be lamb, with garlic and sage or perhaps anchovies;
fish might be a pompano stuffed with bay leaves; a typical poultry selection is the hardly typical pigeon with chanterelles. In

winter there is lasagne, but what lasagne—layered with wild mushrooms or with artichokes and sweetbreads. The minimally decorated dining room is tiny, with tables so closely spaced that even whispers can be overheard. But it doesn't matter, because with food like this, who needs conversation? *2029 P St. NW (3 blocks from Dupont Circle Metro stop), tel. 202/872–1180. Reservations advised. Dress: casual but neat. AE, MC, V, and personal checks. Dinner only. Closed Sun. and Aug. Expensive.*

**Odeon.** Like the country as a whole, Washington is in the midst of a fourth Italian invasion. First to arrive were the red-tablecloth southern-Italian restaurants. Then came white-tablecloth northern-Italian places, which teetered on the borderline of French. Third, and still moving in, are the elegant and authentic regional-Italian restaurants. Last have come the new-wave Italians, slick pizza-and-pasta parlors whose food is more or less true to its roots, but whose sensibility is strictly New York. Odeon is a preeminent example of this type. On the surface Odeon seems all surface—glossy to the point of being almost intimidating. But amid all the glass and marble and the resultant din is some very good food. Pasta and pizza dough are made in house and topped with first-class ingredients. In addition, there is a good list of grilled dishes, and specials change every two weeks. *1714 Connecticut Ave. NW (2 blocks from Q Street exit of Dupont Circle Metro stop), tel. 202/329–6228. Reservations advised on weekdays, not accepted on weekends. Dress: casual but neat. AE, MC, V. Closed lunch Sat. and Sun. lunch. Moderate.*

**Middle Eastern** **Bacchus.** The name is somewhat misleading; Bacchus is a Middle Eastern restaurant, specifically Lebanese, that has no real competition in Washington. In the Lebanese tradition, appetizers far outnumber entrées; it is possible to put together a feast just from the list of hot and cold first courses, which include impeccable versions of such standards as hummus and baba ghannouj, as well as more exotic concoctions of ground beef, eggplant, and yogurt. Among the main courses, *ouzi* (lamb with spiced rice, mushrooms, almonds, and pine kernels), *kafta* (grilled logs of ground beef), and *shish taouk* (grilled chunks of marinated chicken) are outstanding, but you really can't go wrong with anything served here. *1827 Jefferson St. NW (8 blocks from Dupont Circle and Farragut North Metro stops), tel. 202/785–0734. Reservations advised. Dress: casual but neat. AE, MC, V. Closed Sat. lunch and Sun. Moderate.*

**Skewers.** Depending on your point of view, Skewers is an American restaurant with a strong Middle Eastern influence or an avant-garde Middle Eastern restaurant. In either case, it offers fresh, flavorful meals at reasonable prices. This is where Ralph Nader eats both lunch and dinner, so you know you're getting healthful food and good value. As the name implies Skewers's specialty is kebabs. The lamb with eggplant and the chicken with roasted pepper are the most popular, but filet mignon and shrimp are equally tasty. For those wanting less meat—perhaps to leave room for scrumptious desserts like Key-lime pie or chocolate cake—mini kebobs are available, either served with pita bread or in a salad. Just as the menu favors imagination over ostentation, so does Skewers's decor which uses a few lengths of shimmering cloth to create an Arabian Nights fantasy. *1633 P St. NW (1½ blocks from the Dupon*

*Circle Metro stop), tel. 202/387-7400). Reservations advised on weekends. Dress: casual. AE, DC, MC, V. Moderate.*

**New American**  **Tabard Inn.** With its artfully artless decor, absent-minded waiters, and quasi–health-food menu, the Tabard is an idiosyncratic restaurant that has a devoted clientele of baby-boomers with '60s values and '80s incomes. The lounge looks like a garage sale waiting to happen, and the two dining rooms are likewise somewhat shabby. But the courtyard may be Washington's prettiest outdoor eatery, and the Tabard's New American cuisine, although it doesn't always quite come off, is fresh and interesting. The Tabard raises much of its produce, without pesticides, on its own farm; meat is additive-free. Most of the menu changes daily; complicated preparations of fish are a specialty. Desserts are not to be missed. And in a city where finding a good breakfast—or any breakfast at all—can be a major challenge the Tabard is outstanding for the quantity and quality of its offerings. *1739 N St. NW (5 blocks from Dupont Circle or Farragut North Metro stops), tel. 202/833-2668. Reservations advised. Dress: casual. MC, V. Very Expensive.*

**Afterwords.** Though some people have been known to say snidely that Afterwords serves pretty good food for a bookstore, this café annex to Kramerbooks is one of Washington's liveliest spots. And its New American cuisine is, in fact, pretty good—often very good. In addition to the predictable quiches and salads, Afterwords has inventive pastas and stir fries, its own smoked meats, a superb selection of cakes and pies, and a good list of wines available by the glass. The menu changes frequently but always includes such Southwestern-inspired dishes as quesadillas. *1517 Connecticut Ave. NW (Metro stop, Dupont Circle), tel. 202/387-1462. Reservations not accepted. Dress: casual. AE, MC, V. Breakfast, lunch, and dinner daily; open all night Fri. and Sat. Moderate.*

**Thai**  **Sala Thai.** This is not the sort of Thai restaurant where you go for the burn; the Sala Thai will make the food as spicy as you wish, but the chef is interested in flavor, not fire. Among the subtly seasoned offerings are *panang goong* (shrimp in curry-peanut sauce), chicken sautéed with ginger and pineapple, and flounder with a choice of four sauces. The *Pad Thai* P Street is an exceptional treatment of that signature dish, which consists of noodles with shrimp and bean sprouts in a peanut sauce. Sala Thai is decorated in the currently fashionable minimalist style, but colored lights take the harsh edges off its industrial look. *2016 P St. NW (3 blocks from Dupont Circle Metro stop), tel. 202/872-1144. Reservations accepted. Dress: casual but neat. AE, DC, MC, V. Closed Sun. lunch. Inexpensive.*

## Georgetown

**Afghani**  **Bamiyan.** Because not many people are vacationing in Afghanistan these days, Afghani food is largely unknown in the West. That's a pity, because the country's cuisine is quite appealing, unusual enough to be interesting but not so strange as to be intimidating. Bamiyan is the oldest and arguably the best Afghanian restaurant in the area, even though it does look like a motel that has seen better days. Kebabs—of chicken, beef, or lamb—are succulent. More adventurous souls should try the *quabili palow* (lamb with saffron rice, carrots, and raisins) or the *aushak* (dumplings with scallions, meat sauce, and yogurt). For a side vegetable, order the sautéed pumpkin; it will make you forget every other winter squash dish you've ever had. *3320 M St. NW, tel. 202/338–1896. Reservations accepted. Dress: casual. AE, MC, V. Closed lunch. Moderate.*

**American** **Morton's of Chicago.** Unless you come early, you'll have to wait up to an hour for a table at the Washington branch of this national steakhouse chain, which claims to serve the country's best beef. The claim must have merit, because the crowds patiently doing time at the bar clearly have not come for the restaurant's ambience—there are bus stations that have more class than this vinyl-boothed dining room. In the classic steakhouse tradition, Morton's emphasizes quantity as well as quality. The New York strip and porterhouse steaks, two of the most popular offerings, are well over a pound each. For diners with even larger appetites, there's a 3-pound porterhouse. Morton's also includes lamb, veal, chicken, lobster, and grilled fish on its menu—which for some reason is not printed, but instead recited by a waiter who displays the raw ingredients on a cart. *3251 Prospect St., tel. 202/342–6258. Reservations accepted before 7 P.M. Jacket and tie advised. AE, CB, DC, MC, V. Closed lunch and Sun. Very Expensive.*

**Georgetown Seafood Grill.** For years you would never have guessed that the Chesapeake Bay was in Washington's back yard, so landlocked were the kitchens in most of the city's restaurants. That's changed, but the city still has very few of the sort of restaurants you expect to find near water—unpretentious places where your oysters are shucked in front of you. The Georgetown Seafood Grill does not have unpretentious prices, but in every other respect it is the perfect seafood eatery. It has an appropriately weathered visage—old tilework and exposed brick decorated with nautical photographs—and its menu casts a wide net. There are four or five kinds of oysters at the raw bar, plus clams, spiced shrimp, and crab claws. Crab cakes are made with jumbo lump-meat and no filler, and soft shell crabs are served in season. On weekends you can order steamed lobsters, and each night you can choose among about seven fish specials—everything from fried catfish to broiled red snapper with macadamia pesto. *3063 M St. NW, tel. 202/333–7038. Reservations accepted for large parties. Dress: casual but neat. AE, CB, DC, MC, V. Expensive.*

**American Café.** Thirteen years ago someone had the bright idea of opening a Georgetown restaurant that would serve fresh, healthy food—but not health food—at affordable prices in a casual but sophisticated environment. And so the American Café empire, which now numbers 13 restaurants in the Washington area, was born. Sandwiches, such as the namesake roast beef on a humongous croissant, are still the mainstay of the café, with salads and nibbles rounding off the regular menu. But the list of specials, which changes every two weeks, offers intriguing possibilities for those wanting a larger meal. There's always a fresh fish, a seafood pie, a chicken dish, and barbecued ribs. Weekend brunches offer temptations like strawberry-banana-nut waffles and stuffed French toast. *1211 Wisconsin Ave. NW (also at 227 Massachusetts Ave. NE, 1331 Pennsylvania Ave. NW, and 5252 Wisconsin Ave. NW) tel. 202/944–9464. Reservations accepted only for large parties. Dress: casual. AE, CB, DC, MC, V. Inexpensive.*

**Argentinian** **Las Pampas.** Fish is edging meat off the menu at most of the ★ city's restaurants, but there's no danger of that happening at Las Pampas, an Argentinian restaurant many think serves the best steak in town. The beef, which is fresh, not aged, is cooked over a special grill that simulates charcoal heat; the result is a firm-textured steak with a crusty surface and a juicy interior. The familiar New York strip and filet mignon are available from the grill, but the preferred choice is the *churrasco*, a special Argentinian cut. Other options from the limited regular menu are a whole boneless chicken that is first roasted then grilled; and a combination plate of chicken, short ribs, and sausage. Daily specials usually include swordfish, brochettes of beef, seafood, lamb, or chicken, and a pasta. The wine list includes a preponderance of Argentinian vintages. The restaurant's South American authenticity does not extend to its ambience— aside from a couple of wall hangings. Las Pampas is decorated in international nondescript. *3291 M St. NW, tel. 202/333– 5151. Reservations advised. Dress: casual but neat. AE, CB, DC, MC, V. Closed Sat. lunch, Sun., and first week of Aug. Moderate.*

**French**  **Bistro Français.** A longtime fixture on M Street, this French country restaurant is a favorite among the city's chefs. What do the professionals order when they want to eat someone else's cooking? The Minute Steak Maitre d'Hotel, a sirloin with herb butter, accompanied by french fries. Among amateur eaters, the big draw is the rotisserie chicken. While the Bistro excels at such simple fare, it also does well with the more complicated dishes it offers on the extensive list of daily specials, such as supreme of salmon with cauliflower mousse and beurre blanc. The restaurant is divided into two parts, the café side and the more formal dining room. Both have the same comfortable, lived-in look, but the café menu includes sandwiches and omelettes in addition to the entrées. The Bistro also offers fixed-price lunches and early- and late-night dinner specials and stays open until 3 A.M. on weekdays, 4 A.M. on weekends. *3128 M St. NW, tel. 202/338–3830. Reservations advised. Dress: casual but neat. AE, CB, DC, MC, V. Moderate.*

**La Chaumière.** A longtime favorite of Washingtonians seeking an escape from the hurly-burly of Georgetown, La Chaumière has the rustic charm of a French country inn, particularly during the winter, when its central stone fireplace warms the room. The food is country French, with an emphasis on seafood —crab meat in a crêpe, mussels, and scampi are on the regular menu, and there is usually a grilled fish special and a seafood brochette. The restaurant also has a devoted following for its meat dishes, which include such hard-to-find entrees as blood sausage and calves brain. Many local diners plan their meals around La Chaumière's rotating specials, particularly the couscous on Wednesday and the cassoulet on Thursday. *2013 M St. NW., tel. 202/338–1784. Reservations required. Jacket and tie advised. AE, CB, DC, MC, V. Closed Sat. lunch. and Sun. Validated parking at dinner at Four Seasons Hotel lot. Moderate.*

**Indian**  **Tandoor.** The crucible of Indian cuisine is the *tandoor*, a charcoal-burning clay oven. Meat is cooked on skewers held upright by the coals, and bread is baked directly on the oven walls. This namesake restaurant was the first in town to install a tandoor and consequently the first to give area diners a taste of the real India. The ovens are still rare in town (the fire department doesn't much like them), which means the Tandoor has retained its popularity among aficionados of Indian food. Chicken, lamb filet, and minced lamb, beef, and shrimp are available from the oven, as is a combination platter. The tandoor-cooked meats are also used in a variety of curries, with chicken tikka masala one of the best. This restaurant is not as luxurious as some of the newer Indian restaurants, but its prints of Indian dancers and orange tablecloths make it cheerful. *3316 M St. NW, tel. 202/333–3376, and 2623 Connecticut Ave. NW, tel. 202/483–1115. Reservations advised. Dress: casual but neat. AE, DC, MC, V. Moderate.*

**Italian** **Paolo's.** This glitzy pizza-and-pasta emporium is one of Georgetown's most bustling restaurants. The action revolves around the central wood-burning pizza oven, out of which emerges an endless parade of new- and old-style pies. One version has four cheeses, red peppers, and smoked salmon; another has goat cheese, sun-dried tomatoes, and duck sausage. Customers can also create a "personal pie" by picking three ingredients from the cornucopia arrayed around the oven. Pastas are equally eclectic: capelli with shrimp and scallops, penne in vodka, as well as the traditional bolognese and carbonara. There's also a short list of entrées that includes grilled homemade sausage and shrimp scampi. *1305 Wisconsin Ave. NW, tel. 202/333–7353. No reservations. Dress: casual but neat. AE, CB, DC, MC, V. Moderate.*

**Geppetto.** Although in most parts of Washington you can choose among half a dozen establishments eager to deliver a pizza to your home or hotel, people still wait in line for pizza at Geppetto—a clear indication that the restaurant delivers quality. The pizza here comes in either a thick- or a thin-crust version. There's also a white pizza (cheese, garlic, and shallot; no tomato sauce) and a geppino, which is essentially a pizza sandwich. Geppetto also serves homemade pastas, several veal and chicken entrées, and a half dozen sandwiches. Named after the creator of Pinocchio and decorated with puppets and cuckoo clocks, this is a good restaurant for children, as long as they can be persuaded to look, not touch. *2917 M St. NW, tel. 202/333–2602. No reservations. Dress: casual. AE, CB, DC, MC, V. Inexpensive.*

**Japanese** **Sushi-Ko.** This was Washington's first sushi bar, and 12 years later it continues to hold its own against the competition. In addition to the à la carte items and assortments of sushi and sashimi, which vary according to the availability of fish that meets Sushi-Ko's stringent standards for freshness, the menu includes seafood and vegetable tempuras, fish teriyaki, and udonsuki (noodles with seafood and vegetables). Sushi novices might want to test the waters by ordering tuna or yellowtail as an appetizer, followed by one of the cooked dishes. Those looking for more exotic fare will find it on the back of the menu—printed in Japanese, but your waiter can be prevailed upon to translate. *2309 Wisconsin Ave. NW, tel. 202/333–4187. Reservations advised. Dress: casual but neat. AE, MC, V. Closed Mon. and weekend lunch. Moderate.*

**New American** **The River Club.** Until someone invents a time machine, there is
★ no better way to experience the Jazz Age than by taking a trip to The River Club, an art deco extravaganza in an out-of-the-way part of Georgetown. Decorated in ebony, silver, neon, and marble, The River Club is in fact a club, with a disc jockey who plays '30 and '40s music for the two dance floors. But this is more than just a place to feed your fantasies—it is a real restaurant that takes its cooking very seriously. Salmon is flown in

from Iceland and beef from Chicago. The inspiration for much of the food comes from the Orient—the salmon is served Thai style, with a basil sauce; lobster is smoked and comes with fried spinach with ginger and scallions. But the menu, which changes seasonally, is not limited to Asian-American creations. There might also be veal stuffed with wild mushrooms, swordfish with mint pesto, and grilled chicken stuffed with goat cheese. And of course there's always the option of nibbling on caviar while you dream the night away. *3223 K St. NW, tel. 202/333–8118. Reservations advised. Jacket and tie required. AE, CB, DC, MC, V. Closed lunch and Sun. Valet parking available. Very Expensive.*

**Tex-Mex** **Austin Grill.** Even before the 1988 election put a Texan, of
★ sorts, into the White House, Washington was big on Tex-Mex cooking—one of the city's hot-ticket social events is the annual congressional chili-off. But Washington didn't have a Tex-Mex restaurant of note until the opening of the Austin Grill, a small, lively spot in upper Georgetown whose popularity is well deserved. The Austin has a food-smoker out back, where ribs are prepared for dinner. The mesquite grill is always in operation, turning out fajitas and grilled fish and providing the starting point for what the Austin claims is the best chili in town—made with cubed meat, not ground, unadulterated by beans. With its multi-colored booths, the restaurant looks like a post-modern diner; a bright mural adds to the cheerful effect. Waiters are friendly and efficient, a rare combination. *2404 Wisconsin Ave. NW, tel. 202/337–8080. No reservations. Dress: casual. AE, MC, V. Closed Mon. lunch. Inexpensive.*

# 7 Lodging

## Introduction

*by Jan Ziegler*

*A free-lance writer and editor, DC resident Jan Ziegler contributes frequently to national publications.*

The nation's capital has been riding a hotel boom for more than a decade. Between 1976 and 1988, 49 new hotels were built, and it's estimated that more than 2,000 additional hotel rooms will open over the next few years. As a result, visitors who plan to spend the night, a week, or a month in DC can expect variety as well as quantity. Hostelries include grand hotels with glorious histories, quiet Victorian inns, the hotel and motel chains common to every American city, and small independently operated hotels that offer little more than good location, a smile, and a comfortable, clean place to lay your head.

Because Washington is an international city, nearly all hotel staffs are multilingual. All hotels in the Expensive and Very Expensive categories have concierges; some in the Moderate group do, too. All of the hotels here are air-conditioned. All the large hotels and many of the smaller ones offer meeting facilities and special features for business travelers, ranging from state-of-the-art teleconferencing equipment to modest conference rooms with outside catering.

In an effort to attract weekend business, many Washington hotels, particularly those downtown, offer special reduced rates and package deals. Some packages are available midweek; be sure to ask whether these are available at the hotel of your choice.

Not all the city's hotels are included here; there are simply too many to list. Most of the major chains have hotels at desirable locations throughout town. For a complete listing of hotels in the area, contact the Washington D.C. Convention and Visitors' Association (1212 New York Ave. NW, Washington, DC 20005, tel. 202/789–7000).

To find reasonably priced accommodations in small guest houses and private homes, contact either of the following bed-and-breakfast services: **Bed 'n' Breakfast Ltd. of Washington, D.C.** (Box 12011, Washington, DC 20005, tel. 202/328–3510) or **Bed and Breakfast League, Ltd.**, (3639 Van Ness St., Washington, DC 20008, tel. 202/363–7767).

A word about reservations: They are crucial. Hotels are often full of conventioners, politicians in transit, or families and school groups in search of cherry blossoms and monuments. If you're interested in visiting Washington at a calmer time—and if you can stand tropical weather—come in July or August, during the Congressional recess. You may not spot many VIPs, but hotels will have more rooms to offer, and you'll be able to relax.

The hotel reviews here are grouped according to price categories. Keep in mind that rates are variable and can be lower depending on season and whether they are part of a group, corporate, or weekend package. Also, some of the older hotels have a few smaller rooms that rent for prices in a lower category.

Unless otherwise noted below, hotels charge extra for parking. Rates range from $5 to $15 a night, depending on how close to downtown you are. The DC room tax will add 10% to your bill.

Highly recommended lodgings in each price category are indicated by a star ★.

| Category | Cost* |
| --- | --- |
| Very Expensive | over $190 |
| Expensive | $130–$190 |
| Moderate | $100–$130 |
| Inexpensive | under $100 |

*All prices are for a standard double room, excluding 10% room tax.*

The following credit-card abbreviations are used: AE, American Express; CB, Carte Blanche; DC, Diners Club; MC, MasterCard; and V, Visa.

## Capitol Hill

**Very Expensive**  **Hyatt Regency on Capitol Hill.** One of the chain's more spartan entries in Washington, this hotel has the typical Hyatt garden atrium but with high-tech edges. Close to Union Station and the Mall, this is a mecca for families and for businesspeople with dealings on the Hill. Rooms are plainly furnished; those on the south side have a view of the Capitol dome, which is just a few blocks away. Sunday brunch is popular. *400 New Jersey Ave. NW, 20001, tel. 202/737–1234 or 800/228–9000. 834 rooms, including 31 suites. Facilities: 24-hr room service; 3 restaurants; 2 bars; health club with weight equipment, steam room, sauna, pool; parking. AE, CB, DC, MC, V.*

**Washington Court.** This luxury hotel is one of the few hostelries in DC where it is possible to make a truly grand entrance. Guests descend three terraced tiers of polished steps into an atrium surmounted by a skylight. Until September 1988, this hotel was the Sheraton Grand. It shares its view of the Capitol with the Hyatt and others on the same street. Rooms are done in warm earth tones. *525 New Jersey Ave. NW, 20001, tel. 202/ 628–2100. 268 rooms, including 15 suites. Facilities: 24-hr room service, 2 restaurants, 2 bars, exercise equipment delivered to rooms, valet parking. AE, CB, DC, MC, V.*

**Expensive**  **Phoenix Park Hotel.** Just steps from Union Station and only four blocks from the Capitol, this high-rise hotel has an Irish club theme and is the home of the Dubliner, one of Washington's best bars. Leather, wood panelling, and leaded glass abound in the bar's re-creation of the decor favored by the 18th-century Irish gentry; but guest rooms are bright, traditionally furnished, and quiet. Penthouse suites have fireplaces. The Powerscourt Restaurant is named after an Irish castle. *520 North Capitol St. NW, 20001, tel. 202/638–6900 or 800/824–5419. 88 rooms, including 6 suites. Facilities: 2 restaurants, access to health club, complimentary newspaper, parking nearby. AE, CB, DC, MC, V.*

**Moderate**  **Bellevue Hotel.** In business for 61 years, the Bellevue is a charming and comfortable hotel. The public rooms on the main floor have balconies and are modeled after great halls in manor houses of yore. Accommodations here are standard modest-hotel fare, but the staff is friendly. The location is convenient, near Union Station and major Metrorail stations and within six blocks of the Supreme Court and the Smithsonian museums. *15 E St. NW, 20001, tel. 202/ 638–0900 or 800/327–6667. 140*

# Lodging

Bellevue Hotel, **43**
Braxton Hotel, **27**
Capitol Hilton, **32**
Channel Inn, **47**
Days Inn
Connecticut Avenue , **1**
Embassy Suites, **16**
Four Seasons
Hotel, **14**
Georgetown
Dutch Inn, **12**

Georgetown Inn, **10**
Georgetown Marbury
Hotel, **13**
Grand Hyatt, **37**
Guest Quarters, **18, 23**
Hay-Adams Hotel, **34**
Henley Park Hotel, **36**
Holiday Inn
Governor's House, **26**
Hotel Anthony, **24**
Hotel Tabard Inn, **25**

Hotel Washington, **38**
Hotel Windsor Park, **5**
Howard Johnson
Kennedy Center, **21**
Hyatt Regency on
Capitol Hill, **45**
Jefferson Hotel, **28**
J.W. Marriott, **40**
Kalorama Guest
House, **4**

Key Bridge
Marriott, **11**
Loew's L'Enfant
Plaza , **46**
The Madison Hotel, **31**
Mayflower Hotel, **29**
Morrison-Clark Inn
Hotel, **35**
Normandy Inn, **6**
Omni Shoreham
Hotel, **3**
Park Hyatt
Washington, **17**

Phoenix Park
Hotel, **42**

Quality Hotel Capitol
Hill, **44**

Quality Hotel
Central, **7**

The Ritz-Carlton, **9**

River Inn, **20**

Sheraton Carlton
Hotel, **33**

Sheraton Washington
Hotel, **2**

Vista International, **30**

Washington Court, **41**

The Washington Hilton
and Towers, **8**

Watergate Hotel, **22**

Westin Hotel, **15**

The Willard Inter-
Continental, **39**

Wyndham Bristol
Hotel, **19**

*rooms, including 2 suites. Facilities: restaurant, bar, library. AE, DC, MC, V.*

**Quality Hotel Capitol Hill.** A good value for the budget-minded traveler, this hotel shares the block with the Hyatt and offers the same views and convenience of location. *415 New Jersey Ave. NW, 20001, tel. 202/638–1616 or 800/228–5151. 341 rooms, including 5 suites. Facilities: room service 6:30 AM–11 PM, restaurant, outdoor rooftop pool, free parking. AE, CB, DC, MC, V.*

## Downtown

**Very Expensive**  **Capitol Hilton.** There are three advantages here: location, location, and location. The busy Capitol Hilton is not only just up the street from official Washington, including the White House and many monuments, it is smack in the middle of the K Street business corridor. Built in 1943 as a Statler Hotel, the building underwent a $55 million renovation that was completed in 1987. Rooms were enlarged by a third. Now the theme is neo–art deco, with torchères, winding staircases, and columns finished with milled cherrywood. Rooms are sleekly furnished in shades of camel, gray, or dusty rose. The new Towers section on the top four floors offers VIP accommodations. Fitness-conscious guests use the state-of-the-art health club. The hotel hosts the annual Gridiron Club dinner, at which the media have roasted every president since Franklin Roosevelt. *1001 16th St. NW, 20036, 202/393–1000 or 800/445–8667. 549 rooms, including 34 suites. Facilities: 24-hr room service; 2 restaurants; valet parking; florist; barber and beauty salon; health club with treadmills, Nautilus equipment, steam room, sauna, tanning bed. AE, CB, DC, MC, V.*

**Grand Hyatt.** Imagine a 1930s movie-musical set. Studio-built walls of a Mediterranean hillside village rise around a courtyard; a gazebo and curved lounge and dining areas surround a blue lagoon fed by waterfalls. On a small island in the lagoon is a man in black tie playing Cole Porter tunes on a white grand piano. The Hyatt has created just such a fanciful interior in this bustling new high-rise hotel that successfully compensates for the relative drabness of the neighborhood. Opened in June 1987, the Grand is across the street from the Washington Convention Center and just steps away from downtown shopping and theaters. Quiet, contemporary rooms are reached by glass-walled elevators; some suites have Jacuzzis or saunas. Conference suites are popular with businesspeople who may need to meet clients in their rooms. The Zephyr Deli is a popular lunch spot; the Grand Cafe features country breakfasts on weekends. A disco—Impulse—attracts local office workers and conventioners. *1000 H St. NW, 20001, tel. 202/582–1234 or 800/ 228–9000. 908 rooms, including 61 suites. Facilities: 24-hr room service, 3 restaurants, bar, multilingual staff, health club, valet parking. AE, CB, DC, MC, V.*

★ **Hay-Adams Hotel.** Built in 1927, the Hay-Adams sits upon the site of houses owned by John Hay and Henry Adams, social and political paragons in turn-of-the-century Washington. In its early days the hotel housed Charles Lindbergh and Amelia Earhart; now, corporate executives and lawyers occupy its rooms during the week, and couples and families come on weekends. Italian Renaissance in design, the hotel looks like a mansion in disguise. A 17th-century Medici tapestry graces one lobby wall, while the John Hay Room restaurant seems to belong to an English Tudor residence. The guest rooms are the most brightly colored in the city, decorated in 20 different English–country-house schemes. Rooms on the south side have a picture-postcard view of the White House. The hotel's afternoon tea is renowned, and the Adams Room is a popular spot for power breakfasts. The staff is dignified and friendly. *One Lafayette Square, 20006, tel. 202/638–6600 or 800/424–5054. 143 rooms, including 23 suites. Facilities: 24-hr room service, 3 restaurants, bar, valet parking. AE, CB, DC, MC, V.*

★ **Jefferson Hotel.** Incoming and outgoing administration officials have stayed at the Jefferson since it opened. The undistinguished exterior of this 1923 building is deceiving; past the tiny foyer the atmosphere is classically elegant and smacks of the 18th and early 19th centuries. Rooms are furnished with antiques and reproductions as well as original art. Double-glass windows assure quiet on a busy intersection. The Hunt Club bar is a dark den full of nooks and crannies and comfortable English furniture. The staff of this small hotel remembers guests' names and greets them by name; laundry is hand-ironed and delivered in wicker baskets. *1200 16th St. NW, 20036, tel. 202/347–2200 or 800/368–5966. 102 rooms, including 32 suites. Facilities: 24-hr room service, 2 restaurants, bar, multilingual staff, valet parking. AE, CB, DC, MC, V.*

**J.W. Marriott.** Opened in 1984, this large, glossy hotel is in a prime location on Pennsylvania Avenue, close to the White House and next door to the National Theater. The hotel may look impersonal, yet the concierge will gladly make a restaurant reservation for you. The Marriott has served as home-away-from-home for Joan Rivers, the prime minister of Israel, and Egyptian President Hosni Mubarak's delegation; but usually it lodges an equal mix of people traveling for business and pleasure. Rooms are furnished in hotel moderne and quiet colors. The best views are on the Pennsylvania Avenue side. On other sides, you may end up looking across a courtyard at the blank windows of another section of the complex. Guests have indoor access to the National Press Building and the shops and restaurants of National Place. The signature dessert at the Celadon restaurant is Painter's Palette, made of chocolate topped with fruit sorbets. *1331 Pennsylvania Ave. NW, 20004, tel. 202/393–2000 or 800/228–9290. 773 rooms, including 41 suites. Facilities: 24-hr room service, 4 restaurants, bar, health club with Universal weights and stationary bikes, indoor pool, valet parking. AE, CB, DC, MC, V.*

**The Madison Hotel.** Elegance and fine service are the hallmarks of the Madison. Deceivingly modernistic on the outside, the 14-story Madison was built to house not only guests from around the world but a world-class collection of antiques, oriental rugs, and fine art. Even the front lobby is graced by a rare antique Chinese altar table. The guest rooms are also furnished with antiques and reproductions, and the Madison's suites are among the most opulent and un-hotellike in Washington. *15th and M streets NW, 20005, tel. 202/862–1600 or 800/424–8577. 353 rooms, including 35 suites. Facilities: room service, 2 restaurants, 2 bars, access to health club with pool, valet parking. AE, CB, DC, MC, V.*

**Sheraton Carlton Hotel.** Entering the Sheraton Carlton is like stepping into an updated Italian Renaissance mansion: Gilt, carved wood, stone, plaster, and 19th-century details abound. This hotel is in a bustling business sector, yet the rooms are quiet and service is cordial and dignified. Built in 1926, the hotel underwent a $16 million face-lift in 1988, in the course of which all rooms were enlarged. The rooms are decorated in either flowers or stripes and are furnished with antiques and reproductions. Each room has a safe. Butler service is available. *923 16th St. NW, 20006, tel. 202/638–2626 or 800/325–3535. 200 rooms, including 15 suites. Facilities: 24-hr room service, restaurant, bar, exercise room, exercise equipment delivered to room, valet parking. AE, CB, DC, MC, V.*

★ **The Willard Inter-Continental.** "This hotel, in fact, may be much more justly called the center of Washington and the Union than either the Capitol, the White House, or the State Department," Nathaniel Hawthorne wrote while covering the Civil War. Indeed, the Willard, whose present building dates from 1901, welcomed every American president from Franklin Pierce in 1853 to Dwight Eisenhower in the 1950s. Martin Luther King wrote his "I have a dream" speech here. But the huge building fell on hard times and closed in 1968. When renovation began in 1984, grass grew in the rooms and a tree had sprouted in one of the restaurants. The new Willard is a faithful renovation, presenting an opulent, beaux-arts feast to the eye. Even DC residents drop in to stroll the famous "Peacock Alley," which runs between the front and back entrances. Rooms are furnished with mahogany Queen Anne reproductions; all have minibar. The sixth floor, which was designed with the help of the Secret Service and the State Department, has lodged 20 heads of state. Two restaurants, the Occidental and the Willard Room, have won nationwide acclaim. *1401 Pennsylvania Ave. NW, 20004, tel. 202/628–9100 or 800/327–0200. 365 rooms, including 65 suites. Eight rooms designed for the handicapped. Facilities: 24-hr room service, 3 restaurants, 2 bars, valet parking. AE, CB, DC, MC, V.*

**Expensive** **Henley Park Hotel.** Constructed as an apartment building in ★ 1918 and converted to a small hotel in 1983, the Henley Park offers a bit of Britain in a rapidly gentrifying neighborhood near the convention center. Though the architecture is Tudorstyle, the decor is Edwardian; a cozy sitting room with working fireplace could well have been transplanted from an English country house. Afternoon tea here is renowned. Guest rooms are warmly furnished with chintz and oriental porcelain lamps. The hotel is in a quiet neighborhood, close to the Washington Convention Center and only a short ride on public transportation to the major sites. It's best to take a cab if you're returning after dark. *926 Massachusetts Ave. NW, 20001, tel. 202/638–5200 or 800/222–8474. 96 rooms, including 17 suites. Facilities: 24-hr room service, restaurant, bar, access to health club, valet parking. AE, CB, DC, MC, V.*

**Hotel Washington.** Since its opening in 1918, this hostelry has been known as the hotel with a view. Washingtonians bring visitors to the outdoor rooftop bar for cocktails and a view of the White House grounds and the Washington Monument. The oldest continuously operating hostelry in the city and now a national landmark, the Hotel Washington sprang from the drawing boards of John Carrere and Thomas Hastings, who designed the New York Public Library. Renovated in 1987, the hotel has retained its Edwardian character; a Gibson girl would not feel out of place in the lobby. The guest rooms, some of which look directly onto the White House grounds, are furnished with antique reproductions; the windows are festooned with swags, heavy drapes, and lace underdrapes. Antique beiges predominate. Suite 506 is where Elvis Presley stayed on his trips to DC. *515 15th St. NW, 20004, tel. 202/638–5900. 350 rooms, including 17 suites. Facilities: room service 6 AM– midnight, restaurant, outdoor café, lounge. AE, CB, DC, MC, V.*

**Mayflower Hotel.** Now part of the Stouffer chain, the Mayflower was opened for Calvin Coolidge's inaugural and continues to be a central part of Washington life. Guests come from all walks of life; 8% of them are foreign. The ornate lobby gleams with gilded trim and cherubs supporting electrified candelabra. At press time, renovation was in progress. The older rooms are outfitted with plain, homey, English-style furniture, and newly decorated rooms (about half) have custom-designed reproduction furniture, warmly colored fabrics, and indirect lighting. Seventy-four suites have fireplaces. A Japanese-style breakfast is offered, and afternoon tea is popular. The Mayflower is steps from the K Street business corridor, the White House, and Dupont Circle. *1127 Connecticut Ave. NW, 20036, tel. 202/347–3000 or 800/468–3571. 724 rooms, including 83 suites. Facilities: 24-hour room service, 2 restaurants, bar, shops, access to National Capital YMCA, parking at nearby garage. AE, CB, DC, MC, V.*

★ **Morrison-Clark Inn Hotel.** Victorian with an airy, modern twist, this unusual historic inn was created by merging two 1864 townhouses. Appended to one of the houses is a 1917 Chinese Chippendale porch; oriental touches echo throughout the public rooms, which also boast marble fireplaces and 14-foot-high mirrors with original gilding. Antique-filled rooms— some with bay windows, fireplaces, or access to a porch—have different personalities; one called the "deer and bunny room" because of its decorative trim, harbors a bedspread once owned by the mistress of a fin-de-siècle mayor of New York. A new addition contains 42 rooms in the neoclassical style. Country rooms are plainly furnished with informal Victorian pieces. *Washington Post* food critic Phyllis Richman called the restaurant, which features southern fare, history in the making. A complimentary breakfast is served. Take a cab to the hotel after dark. *Massachusetts Ave. and 11th St. NW, 20001, tel. 202/ 898–1200 or 800/332–7898. 54 rooms, including 14 suites. Facilities: room service during meal periods, restaurant, valet parking, complimentary limousine service to downtown and Capitol Hill. AE, CB, DC, MC, V.*

**Vista International.** This 14-story member of the Hilton family is located in one of downtown's fastest-developing areas and is a few blocks from the White House, the Washington Convention Center, and the K Street business corridor. Designed to look like an urban town square, the Vista features a garden-courtyard lobby that is flooded by light from a 130-foot window facing M Street. Guest rooms and restaurants are located in the surrounding towerlike structures. Opened in 1983, the hotel has hosted Elizabeth Taylor, Kirk Douglas, and countless business travelers from the United States and abroad. Rooms are contemporary in design and decorated in earth tones, burgundy, and green. Some face an alley; the hotel doesn't rent these out unless all other rooms are occupied, and even then guests are warned. The Presidential Suite and six other suites were designed by Hubert de Givenchy; these have Jacuzzis, French-silk and cotton-blend wall coverings, and original artwork from France. *1400 M St. NW, 20005, tel. 202/429–1700 or 800/445– 8667. 398 rooms, including 14 suites. Facilities: 24-hr room* *service, 2 restaurants, bar, health club with sauna, multilingual staff, baby-sitting service, valet parking. AE, CB, DC, MC, V.*

**Moderate** **Holiday Inn Governor's House.** A deluxe Holiday Inn with a sweeping staircase in the lobby, this hotel is close to the White House and Dupont Circle. The staff is friendly. *1501 Rhode Island Ave. NW, 20036, tel. 202/296–2100 or 800/821–4367. 152 rooms, including 9 suites; 24 rooms have kitchenettes. Facilities: room service 7 AM–midnight, restaurant, bar, outdoor pool, access to health club, parking. AE, CB, DC, MC, V.*

**Hotel Anthony.** A good value, this small hotel has a courteous staff, offers the basics in the midst of the K and L streets business district, and is close to the White House. Some rooms have a full kitchen, some a wet bar; king, queen, or extra-long double beds are available. *1823 L St. NW, 20036, tel. 202/223–4320 or 800/424–2970. 99 rooms. Facilities: room service 7 AM–10 PM, 2 restaurants, access to health club, parking. AE, CB, DC, MC, V.*

**Inexpensive** **Braxton Hotel.** Billed as Washington's newest small hotel, the Braxton offers budget basics in a central location. The newly refurbished rooms in this older building have stucco walls and are small but quiet and clean. Take a cab to the hotel after dark. *1440 Rhode Island Ave. NW, 20005, tel. 202/232–7800. 65 rooms. AE, MC, V.*

## Dupont Circle

**Very Expensive** **The Ritz-Carlton.** One of the nicest things to do at the Ritz on a
★ winter day (aside from stay there) is to have a drink or afternoon tea in front of the fire in the warm, woody Fairfax Bar. Exclusive and intimate, the hotel has an English hunt-club theme. European furnishings abound and an extensive collection of 18th- and 19th-century English art, heavy on horses and dogs, graces the walls. This is the home of the pricey Jockey Club restaurant, where crowned heads of Washington like to have lunch (it was one of Nancy Reagan's favorite spots). Lee Iacocca, Carol Burnett, and Eddie Murphy have stayed here. At press time, the new owners were planning to renovate the hotel between January and June 1990. *2100 Massachusetts Ave. NW, 20008, tel. 202/293–2100 or 800/241–3333. 230 rooms, including 27 suites. Facilities: 24-hr room service, restaurant, access to health club. AE, CB, DC, MC, V.*

**Expensive** **The Washington Hilton and Towers.** One of the city's busiest
★ convention hotels, this 24-year-old establishment is as much an event as a place to stay. President George Bush made two appearances here in one week. At any moment, you could run into a leading actor, a cabinet official, six busloads of teenagers from Utah, 500 visiting heart surgeons, or Supreme Court Justice Sandra Day O'Connor, who is among the notables who play tennis here. Though this Hilton specializes in large groups, individual travelers who like to be where the action is also check in. A $27 million refurbishment was completed in 1988. The light-filled, pastel-colored guest rooms are furnished in hotel moderne and have marble bathrooms. In back of the hotel is a miniresort with a café. Dancing and live music are the draw at Ashby's Club. The hotel is a short walk from the shops and restaurants of Dupont Circle, Embassy Row, the National Zoo, and the Adams Morgan neighborhood. *1919 Connecticut Ave.*

NW, 20009, tel. 202/483–3000 or 800/445–8667. 1,150 rooms, including 85 suites. Facilities: 24-hr room service, 3 restaurants (one seasonal), 2 bars, 3 lighted tennis courts, outdoor pool, whirlpool, weight-training equipment, pro shop, flower shop, valet parking. AE, CB, DC, MC, V.

**Inexpensive** ★ **Hotel Tabard Inn.** Three Victorian townhouses were linked 70 years ago to form an inn, and the establishment is still welcoming guests. Named after the hostelry of Chaucer's *Canterbury Tales,* the hotel is furnished throughout with broken-in Victorian and American Empire antiques. A Victorian-inspired carpet cushions the hallways, which run in intriguing labyrinthine patterns. Rooms have phone but no TV. There is no room service, but the Tabard Inn Restaurant serves breakfast, lunch, and dinner; menus feature local ingredients whenever possible. Located on a quiet street, the hotel is a quick walk to Dupont Circle and the K Street business district. Reserve at least two weeks in advance. *1739 N St. NW, 20036, tel. 202/785–1277. 40 rooms, 23 with private bath. Facilities: restaurant. MC, V.*

★ **Quality Hotel Central.** A Holiday Inn until 1988, this high-rise just down the street from Dupont Circle is one of the city's best values for travelers on a budget. Travelers who can't find rooms at the Washington Hilton stay here, as well as families and businesspeople. Rooms are clean, quiet, and decorated with light colors and blond wood. Rooms on the western and southern sides have good views. *1900 Connecticut Ave. NW, 20009, tel. 202/332–9300 or 800/842–4211. 149 rooms. Facilities: room service 7 AM–10 PM, restaurant, outdoor pool, access to health club, free parking. AE, CB, DC, MC, V.*

## Georgetown

**Very Expensive** ★ **Four Seasons Hotel.** A polished staff is at your service the moment you approach the doors of this contemporary hotel conveniently situated between Georgetown and Foggy Bottom. The Four Seasons is a gathering place for Washington's elite. Rooms, all of which have a minibar, are traditionally furnished in light colors. The quieter rooms face the courtyard; others have a view of the C & O Canal. The restaurant, Aux Beaux Champs, is highly esteemed by locals. Afternoon tea is served in the Garden Terrace Lounge. The Four Seasons is also home to the private nightclub Desiree, which is open to hotel guests. *2800 Pennsylvania Ave., NW, 20007, tel. 202/342–0444 or 800/332–3442. 197 rooms, including 30 suites. Facilities: 24-hr room service, 2 restaurants, bar, nightclub, health club with pool, multilingual staff, valet parking. AE, CB, DC, MC, V.*

**Expensive** **Georgetown Inn.** With an atmosphere like a gentlemen's sporting club of 80 years ago, the inn recreates the intimacy and quiet of a small European hotel. The architecture is red-brick and 18th-century in flavor, appropriate to its setting. This is the home of the Georgetown Bar & Grill, whose bar is particularly renowned for lavish appetizers. Traditionally furnished rooms, in apple-green or pink color schemes, are un-hotellike. *1310 Wisconsin Ave. NW, 20007, tel. 202/333–8900 or 800/424–2979. 95 rooms, including 10 suites. Facilities: room service 7 AM–11 PM, restaurant, bar, access to exercise classes, valet parking. AE, CB, DC, MC, V.*

**Key Bridge Marriott.** Situated just across the Potomac from Georgetown, the Key Bridge Marriott in Arlington provides a room away from it all. The hotel is a short walk across the Key Bridge to Georgetown and sits near the Rosslyn Metrorail station, which provides easy access to Washington's major sites. Many rooms have a view of Washington, as does the rooftop restaurant. The rooms were redecorated in 1988 in contemporary decor. You can swim from the indoor to the outdoor pool via an underwater connection; when it gets cold, the portal is closed, and guests can stay wet in the interior section. At times there is noisy air traffic over the hotel. *1401 Lee Hwy., Arlington, VA 22209, tel. 703/524–6400 or 800/228–9290. 558 rooms, including 20 suites. Facilities: 24-hr room service; 2 restaurants; 2 bars; health club with Universal weights, stationary bikes, indoor-outdoor pool; valet service; beauty salon; shops; parking. AE, CB, DC, MC, V.*

**Moderate**  **Georgetown Dutch Inn.** Tucked away on a side street in Georgetown, this modest 25-year-old hotel has a homey ambience and a few clients who stay for months at a time. The small lobby is decorated with 18th-century touches; rooms have family-room-style furnishings. All have a sofabed in the living room and a walk-in kitchen. Some bedrooms lack windows. Nine suites are built on two levels, with the bedrooms upstairs. *1075 Thomas Jefferson St. NW, 20007, tel. 202/337–0900. Facilities: room service noon–11 PM, restaurant, access to health club, free parking. AE, CB, DC, MC, V.*

★ **Georgetown Marbury Hotel.** A small, country-style hotel in the midst of the city's liveliest neighborhoods, the red-brick Marbury feels far removed from the hubbub. Those who value total quiet may want to request one of the 40 rooms underground; the only windows in these rooms face a hallway that has the appearance of a narrow lane. Other rooms have views of the C&O Canal or busy M Street. A colonial theme predominates; rooms have low ceilings and country cotton prints. A downstairs restaurant is incongruously decorated in a safari theme. Opened in 1981, the hotel is popular with Europeans, sports figures, and devotees of Georgetown. *3000 M St. NW, 20007, tel. 202/726–5000 or 800/368–5922. 164 rooms, including 9 suites. Facilities: room service 7 AM–10:30 PM, 2 restaurants, 2 bars, outdoor pool, access to health club, valet parking. AE, CB, DC, MC, V.*

## Southwest

**Expensive**  **Loew's L'Enfant Plaza.** After a day of tramping through the museums on the nearby Smithsonian Mall, families return here to collapse and, during the warmer months, take a dip in the inviting rooftop pool. Loew's is an oasis of velvet and chintz in L'Enfant Plaza, a concrete collection of office buildings with underground shops that is DC's version of Brasilia. Travelers with government business stay here, too, in close proximity to several agency headquarters and just down the street from Capitol Hill. Each room has a fully stocked liquor cabinet and a refrigerator. Service is friendly. *480 L'Enfant Plaza SW, 20024, tel. 202/484–1000 or 800/223–0888. 372 rooms, including 22 suites. Facilities: 24-hr room service, 3 restaurants, 2 bars, outdoor pool, health club, parking. AE, CB, DC, MC, V.*

**Inexpensive**  **Channel Inn.** This informal establishment on an inlet of the Potomac offers views of bobbing boats and tranquil parkland across the water. Within walking distance of Arena Stage and a 15-minute walk away from the Mall, the Channel Inn still

seems far-removed from official Washington. The L'Énfant
Plaza subway stop is about a 15-minute walk away; buses are
also nearby. Air traffic can be noisy during the daytime. All
rooms have a balcony or deck area and separate vanity area; 37
have a river view. At press time, renovations were under way.
*650 Water St. SW, 20024, tel. 202/554–2400 or 800/368–5668.
100 rooms, including 2 suites. Facilities: room service 6:30 AM–
11 PM, restaurant, bar, coffee shop, outdoor pool, free parking.
AE, CB, DC, MC, V.*

## Upper Connecticut Avenue

**Very Expensive**  **Sheraton Washington Hotel.** A veritable city on a hill, this is
Washington's largest hotel. It consists of an "old town"—a
1920s red-brick structure that used to be an apartment
building—and the modern sprawl of the new, convention-
ready, main complex. The 250 rooms and the public areas of the
10-story old section were renovated in 1988; they are furnished
traditionally in soft colors and have large closets. Rooms in the
nine-year-old new section are contemporary, with chrome and
glass touches. Most rooms have a good view. The courtyard is
graced by a modernistic fountain; the hotel also has an airy
atrium and plush, sunken seating-areas galore. Pastry chef
Wolfgang Friedrich has a carry-out shop on the premises:
Calorie-watchers beware. The hotel is close to the National Zoo
and just a few yards from the Woodley Park Metrorail station.
*2660 Woodley Rd. NW, 20008, tel. 202/328–2000 or 800/325–
3535. 1,505 rooms, including 124 suites. Facilities: 24-hr room
service, 4 restaurants, 2 bars, nightclub, health club with Universal weights and stationary bikes, 2 outdoor pools, baby-
sitting service, parking. AE, CB, DC, MC, V.*

**Expensive**  **Omni Shoreham Hotel.** You're in good company when you check
★  in at this grand, 1930s Art Deco–Renaissance hotel. The
Beatles stayed here on their first U.S. tour. John Kennedy
courted Jackie in the Blue Room cabaret, where Judy Garland,
Marlene Dietrich, and Maurice Chevalier once appeared. Resembling an old-time resort, this hotel overlooks Rock Creek
Park and its jogging and bike paths. In back is the pool, where
you can look out to a sweeping lawn and woods beyond. Adding
to the '30s tropical-resort atmosphere are mock bamboo furnishings in the entrance area and doormen wearing pith
helmets during the warmer months. The rooms are large and
light-filled. Some have fireplaces; half overlook the park. Co-
medienne Joan Cushing holds forth in the Marquis Lounge (the
Blue Room is now a meeting room). The loyal staff takes your
stay personally. Situated in a fairly quiet area, the Omni is
close to the Adams Morgan neighborhood, Dupont Circle, and
the National Zoo. *2500 Calvert St. NW, 20008, tel. 202/462–
8775 or 800/834–6664. 770 rooms, including 50 suites. Facilities: room service 6 AM–11 PM, 2 restaurants, bar, snack
counter, cabaret, outdoor pool, 3 lighted tennis courts, shuffle-
board court, horseshoe pits, half-size basketball court, shops,
art gallery, parking. AE, CB, DC, MC, V.*

**Inexpensive**  **Days Inn Connecticut Avenue.** An alternative for those who prefer to stay away from the downtown hustle and bustle, this
Day's Inn is on a wide avenue in a largely residential area. A
subway line close by provides quick transportation to the National Zoo (two stops away) and all of Washington's major
attractions. The University of the District of Columbia is next

door. Rooms have standard hotel furnishings and may be small. A complimentary continental breakfast is provided in the lobby. There are several cafés nearby. *4400 Connecticut Ave. NW, 20008, tel. 202/244–5600. 155 rooms, including 5 suites. Facilities: free parking. Room service expected to be available by early 1990. AE, DC, MC, V.*

**Hotel Windsor Park.** Directly across from the Chinese Embassy, in the residential Kalorama neighborhood, the Windsor Park offers small, immaculate rooms furnished in hotel moderne. It is close to Dupont Circle, the National Zoo, and major convention hotels. *2116 Kalorama Rd. NW, 20008, tel. 202/483–7700 or 800/247–3064. 44 rooms, including 5 suites. AE, CB, DC, MC, V.*

★ **Kalorama Guest House.** Really great-grandma's house in disguise, this inn consists of four turn-of-the-century townhouses: three on a quiet street in the Adams-Morgan neighborhood and one in residential Woodley Park. The Kalorama's comfortable atmosphere is created by dark wood on the walls; hand-me-down antique oak furniture; traditional, slightly worn upholstery; brass or antique wooden bedsteads; and calico curtains at the windows. Magazine illustrations, sheet music, and family photos from the 1890s and early 1900s decorate the walls. The coffee pot is always on, the staff is knowledgeable and friendly, and guests have the run of each house, its front parlor, and the areas where complimentary breakfast is served. Rooms range from large to tiny; none have phone or TV. The inn in Adams-Morgan is steps from one of Washington's most interesting neighborhoods, containing a riot of boutiques and ethnic restaurants. The Woodley Park inn is near the National Zoo and the Metro. The Kalorama is a good value for budget-minded travelers in search of atmosphere. *1854 Mintwood Place NW 20009, tel. 202/667–6369; and 2700 Cathedral Ave. NW 20008, tel. 202/328–0860. 50 rooms, including 5 suites; 30 with private bath. AE, DC, MC, V.*

★ **Normandy Inn.** A small, European-style hotel on a quiet street in the exclusive embassy area of Connecticut Avenue, the Normandy is near restaurants, the National Zoo, and some of the most expensive residential real estate in Washington. The rooms are standard and functional, but comfortable. A complimentary continental breakfast is served. *2118 Wyoming Ave. NW, 20008. 202/483–1350 or 800/424–3729. 74 rooms, including 10 suites. Facilities: room service 7–11 AM, underground parking. AE, MC, V.*

## West End/Foggy Bottom

Very Expensive **Park Hyatt Washington.** A notable collection of modern art adorns this three-year-old hotel in the West End. The interior of its main level is built of stone and polished marble, and guests walk on carpeting so thick it almost bounces. Bronzes, chinoiserie, and a fortune teller at tea in the main-floor lounge are a few of the Old-World touches that offset the spareness of the hotel's design. The rooms are a blend of traditional and contemporary elements and contain reproductions of Chinese antiques from Washington museum collections. Fruit and cookies are provided in each room. A special touch, unique in the city, are the upholstered benches along the rear wall of the elevators. The staff has a "never say no" policy, and cars left overnight are washed. *1201 24th St. NW, 20037, tel. 202/789–1234 or 800/228–9000. 224 rooms, including 132 bedroom* *suites. Facilities: 24-hr room service; restaurant; outdoor café (in season); bar; health club, with indoor pool, Jacuzzi, and Nautilus equipment; beauty salon, valet parking. AE, CB, DC, MC, V.*

★ **Watergate Hotel.** The internationally famous Watergate, its distinctive sawtooth design a landmark along the Potomac, completed a $14 million renovation in 1988 and is now offering guests a taste of old-English gentility. Scenic murals and a portrait of Queen Elizabeth contribute to the effect. The rooms here are among the largest in Washington. All have live plants or fresh flowers, many have balconies, and most have striking river views. The Jean-Louis restaurant has the only two-star Michelin chef in the United States. The hotel is accustomed to serving the world's elite, but it also welcomes vacationing families and couples on getaway weekends. Part of the exclusive Watergate apartment-and-commercial complex, the hotel is next door to the Kennedy Center and a short walk from Georgetown. *2650 Virginia Ave. NW, 20037, tel. 202/965–2300 or 800/424–2736. 237 rooms, including 160 suites. Facilities: 24-hr room service; 2 restaurants; 2 bars; health club with weights, stationary bikes, steam room, sauna, and indoor pool; complimentary limousine service to Capitol Hill or downtown, valet parking. AE, CB, DC, MC, V.*

★ **Westin Hotel.** Just steps from Georgetown, Rock Creek Park, and the Kennedy Center, this hotel is a modern interpretation of a French village. Set around a courtyard, the Westin is filled with modern interpretations of Gallic elegance, with a soupçon of Italian classicism. The opening scenes of the movie *Broadcast News* were filmed in the ballroom area. Built in 1985, the Westin offers bright, airy, traditionally furnished rooms decorated in greens, blues, and burnished oranges. Each room is supplied with terry-cloth bathrobes and a minibar. About a third of the rooms have a view of the central courtyard. The hotel's informal restaurant, the Bistro, has the flavor of 19th-century Paris and contains an antique mahogany bar. The state-of-the-art health club includes rowing machines, a cross-country ski simulator, treadmills, Nautilus equipment, a lap pool, and a café. The hotel is steps from Georgetown, Rock Creek Park, and the Kennedy Center. *2401 M St. NW, 20037, tel. 202/429–2400 or 800/228–3000. 416 rooms, including 8 suites. Facilities: 24-hr room service, 2 restaurants, bar, café, beauty salon, valet parking. AE, CB, DC, MC, V.*

**Expensive** **Embassy Suites.** The hodgepodge of decorative details and cinderblock construction suggest the hanging gardens of Babylon reconstructed in a suburban shopping mall. In the atrium, waterfalls gush, tall palms loom, and plants drip over balconies. Classical columns are mixed with plaster lions and huge Asian temple lights. Ducks swim in the lagoon, and a white rabbit capers nearby, to the delight of children and many grown-ups. Businesspeople flock to the hotel during the week, but it is also ideal for families. Each suite, furnished in neo–art deco, has two remote-control TVs, as well as a wet bar, microwave, coffee-maker, and queen-size sofabed. Complimentary cocktails and cooked-to-order breakfast are served in the atrium. The Italian restaurant, Vivande, has received favorable reviews. Situated in a fairly quiet enclave in the West End, Embassy Suites is within walking distance of Georgetown, the Kennedy Center, and Dupont Circle. *1250 22nd St. NW, 20037, tel. 202/857–3388, 800/EMBASSY, or in Canada 800/458–5848. 318* *suites. Facilities: room service 11–11; restaurant; health club with weight-lifting equipment, treadmills, indoor pool, and sauna; parking. AE, CB, DC, MC, V.*

**Guest Quarters.** All of the units in these two all-suite hotels in Foggy Bottom have a fully equipped walk-in kitchen, minibar, dishwasher, and sofa sleeper. The staff is small and so are the lobbies, but the rooms, decorated in a combination of traditional and contemporary decor, are well-furnished and comfortable. The two-bedroom suites have a table that seats eight, which is good for family dinners as well as business conferences. The New Hampshire Avenue location has an outdoor rooftop pool (a great spot for viewing fireworks on July 4th). Both hotels are close to the Kennedy Center, Georgetown, and George Washington University. *801 New Hampshire Ave. NW, 20037, tel. 202/785–2000 or 800/424–2900; and 2500 Pennsylvania Ave. NW, tel. 202/333–8060 or 800/424–2900. Together, 224 suites. Facilities: room service, access to health club, pool (New Hampshire Ave.), library (Pennsylvania Ave.). AE, CB, DC, MC, V.*

**River Inn.** Just entering its second decade, the River Inn is a member of the highly rated Potomac Hotel Group, which also operates the similar St. James and One Washington Circle hotels nearby. This small, all-suite hotel is steps from Georgetown, George Washington University, and the Kennedy Center. On the premises is the highly rated River Inn restaurant. The best views are from the 14 Potomac Suites, each of which has a full walk-in kitchen. The lobby is sleek and contemporary, but the room furnishings are homey and modest. This is a popular spot with parents of George Washington University students. *924 25th St. NW, 20037, tel. 202/337–7600 or 800/424–2741. 127 suites. Facilities: room service 6:30 AM–11 PM, restaurant, use of outdoor pool at One Washington Circle and health club at the St. James Hotel. AE, DC, MC, V.*

**Wyndham Bristol Hotel.** This hotel doesn't offer much in the way of views, but the location is excellent: Located midway between the White House and Georgetown, the Wyndham is a favorite place for movie and theater people because the Kennedy Center is just a few blocks away. The rooms here are quiet, although the building is bordered on two sides by major thoroughfares. The hotel looks as if it belongs to someone who collects Chinese porcelain: A whole cabinet-full greets guests on arrival in the small, quiet lobby. The rest of the hotel, created in 1984 from an apartment building, is English in decor; each room has a butler's table. *2430 Pennsylvania Ave. NW, 20037, tel. 202/955–6400, 800/822–4200, or in Canada 800/631–4200. 240 rooms, including 22 suites. Facilities: room service 7:30 AM–10:30 PM, 2 restaurants (with seasonal outdoor café), bar, access to health club, valet parking, garage. AE, CB, DC, MC, V.*

**Inexpensive** **Howard Johnson Kennedy Center.** This 10-story lodge offers HoJo reliability in a location close to the Kennedy Center, the Watergate complex, and Georgetown. Rooms are clean, and each has a refrigerator. *2601 Virginia Ave. NW, 20037, tel. 202/965–2700 or 800/654–2000. 192 rooms. Facilities: room service 6 AM–11 PM, restaurant, rooftop pool, free parking. AE, CB, DC, MC, V.*

# 8 The Arts and Nightlife

# The Arts

*by John F. Kelly*

Washingtonians no longer balance a chip on their shoulders when it comes time to discuss sophisticated entertainment. In the last 20 years this cultural backwater has been transformed into a cultural capital. The Kennedy Center is a world-class venue, home of Mstislav Rostropovich's National Symphony Orchestra and host to Broadway shows, ballet, modern dance, opera, and more. Several art galleries present highly regarded chamber music series. The service bands from the area's numerous military bases ensure an endless supply of martial music of the John Philip Sousa variety as well as rousing renditions of more contemporary tunes. At the other end of the spectrum, Washington was the birthplace of hardcore, a socially aware form of punk rock music that has influenced young bands throughout the country. Go-go—infectious, rhythmic music that mixes elements of rap, rhythm and blues, and funk —is touted as the next big thing to come out of the capital city.

Friday's *Washington Post* "Weekend" section is the best guide to events for the weekend and the coming week. The *Post's* daily "Guide to the Lively Arts" also outlines cultural events in the city. The *Washington Times* "Weekend" section comes out on Thursday. The free weekly *City Paper* hits the streets on Thursday and covers the entertainment scene well. You might also consult the "City Lights" section in the monthly *Washingtonian* magazine.

Any search for cultured entertainment should start at the **John F. Kennedy Center for the Performing Arts** (New Hampshire Ave. and Rock Creek Parkway NW). On any given night America's national cultural center may be hosting a symphony orchestra, a troupe of dancers, a Broadway musical, *and* a comedic who-done-it. In other words, America's national cultural center has a little of everything. The Kennedy Center is actually four stages under one roof: the **Concert Hall,** home park of the National Symphony Orchestra; the 2,200-seat **Opera House,** the setting for ballet, modern dance, grand opera, and large-scale musicals; the **Eisenhower Theater,** usually used for drama; and the **Terrace Theater,** an intimate space designed by Philip Johnson that showcases experimental works and chamber groups. For information call 202/467–4600 or 800/444–1324.

**Tickets**  Tickets to most events are available by calling or visiting each venue's box office.

**Metro Center TicketPlace** sells half-price, day-of-performance tickets for selected shows; a "menu board" lists available performances. Only cash is accepted for same-day tickets; cash and credit cards may be used for full-price, advance tickets. *12th and F streets NW, tel. 202/TICKETS. Open Tues–Fri. noon–4, Sat. 11–5. Tickets for Sunday performances sold on Saturday.*
**TicketCenter** (202/432–0200 or 800/448–9009) takes phone charges for events around the city. No refunds, exchanges, or cancellations.
**Ticketron** (1101 17th St. NW, tel. 202/659–2601) is a computerized ticket service with outlets around the city, including many in Woodward & Lothrop stores.

## Theater

**Commercial Theaters and Companies**

**Arena Stage** (6th St. and Maine Ave. SW, tel. 202/488–3300). The city's most respected resident company (now in its 40th season), the Arena was the first theater outside New York to win a Tony award. It presents a wide-ranging season in its three theaters: the theater-in-the-round Arena, the proscenium Kreeger, and the cabaret-style Old Vat Room.

**Ford's Theatre** (511 10th St. NW, tel. 202/347–4833). Looking much the way it did when President Lincoln was shot at a performance of *Our American Cousin*, Ford's is host mainly to musicals, many with family appeal. Dickens's *A Christmas Carol* is presented each winter.

**National Theatre** (1321 Pennsylvania Ave. NW, tel. 202/628–6161). Destroyed by fire and rebuilt four times, the National Theatre has operated in the same location since 1835. It presents pre- and post-Broadway shows.

**Shakespeare Theatre at the Folger** (201 East Capitol St. SE, tel. 202/546–4000). Four plays—three by the Bard and another classic from his era—are presented each year in this replica of an Elizabethan inn-yard theater, reminiscent of Shakespeare's Globe.

**Warner Theater** (13th and E streets NW, tel. 202/626–1050). Opened in 1924, the Warner is downtown's sole survivor from the days of vaudeville and the movie palaces. The 2,000-seat theater is home to Broadway touring shows, dance recitals, and pop acts as disparate as Little Feat and Patti LaBelle. At presstime the theater was undergoing a restoration scheduled to be completed sometime in 1990.

**Small Theaters and Companies**

Washington's small theaters and companies long labored in obscurity, spread out over the District, often performing in churches and other less-than-ideal settings. Fans of independent theater have been encouraged recently by the development of what many regard as the District's own off-Broadway: a five-block section of 14th Street NW that in the last few years has become home to almost a half dozen alternative stages. Other fledgling theaters are located near Dupont Circle.

**American Playwrights Theatre** (1742 Church St. NW, tel. 202/232–1122). As the name implies, this small theater presents works by well-known and little-known American writers. Readings of works in progress allow audiences to watch a play's development.

**Gala Hispanic Theatre** (1625 Park Rd. NW, tel. 202/234–7174). This 13-year-old company produces Spanish classics as well as contemporary and modern Latin American plays in both Spanish and English.

**Horizons Theatre** (1401 Church St. NW, tel. 202/342–5503). Recently relocated to Washington's burgeoning 14th Street theater district, Horizons presents what it describes as "theater from a woman's perspective."

**Olney Theatre** (2001 Rte. 108, Olney, MD, tel. 301/924–3400). Musicals, comedies, and summer stock are presented in this converted barn, an hour from downtown in the Maryland countryside.

**Source Theatre** (1835 14th St. NW, tel. 202/462–1073). The 107-seat Source Theatre presents established plays with a sharp satirical edge and modern interpretations of classics. Each July and August Source hosts the Washington Theater Festival, a celebration of new plays, many by local playwrights.

**Studio Theatre** (1333 P St. NW, tel. 202/332–3300). An eclectic season of classic and off-beat plays are presented in this 200-seat theater.

**Woolly Mammoth** (1401 Church St. NW, 202/393–3939). Unusual, imaginatively produced shows have earned this company good reviews.

## Music

Orchestra **The National Symphony Orchestra** (tel. 202/785–8100). The season at the Kennedy Center extends from September to June. During the summer, the NSO performs at Wolf Trap and presents concerts on the West Terrace of the Capitol on Memorial Day and Labor Day weekends and on July 4th. One of the cheapest ways to hear—if not necessarily see—Mstislav Rostropovich and the NSO perform in the Kennedy Center Concert Hall is to get a $5 "obstructed view" ticket.

Concert Halls **D.A.R. Constitution Hall** (18th and D sts. NW, tel. 202/638–2661). Constitution Hall was the home of the National Symphony Orchestra before the Kennedy Center was built. It still hosts visiting performers, from jazz to pop to rap.

**John F. Kennedy Center for the Performing Arts** (New Hampshire Ave. and Rock Creek Parkway NW). (*See* above.)

**Merriweather Post Pavilion** (tel. 301/982–1800). An hour north of Washington, in Columbia, Maryland, Merriweather Post is an outdoor pavilion with some covered seating. It plays host in warmer months to big-name pop acts.

**National Gallery of Art** (6th St. and Constitution Ave. NW, tel. 202/737–4215). Free concerts by the National Gallery Orchestra, conducted by George Manos, as well as performances by outside recitalists and ensembles, are held in the venerable West Building's West Garden Court on Sunday evening from October to June. Most performances highlight classical music, though April's American Music Festival often features jazz.

**Smithsonian Institution** (tel. 202/357–2700). An amazing assortment of music—both free and ticketed—is presented by the Smithsonian. Some highlights: American jazz, musical theater, and popular standards are performed in the National Museum of American History's Palm Court. In the third-floor Hall of Musical Instruments, musicians periodically perform on historic instruments from the museum's collection. The Smithsonian's Resident Associate Program (tel. 202/357–3030) offers everything from a cappella groups to Cajun zydeco bands, many of which perform in the National Museum of Natural History's Baird Auditorium. In warm weather performances are held in the courtyard between the National Portrait Gallery and the National Museum of American Art.

**Wolf Trap Farm Park** (1551 Trap Rd., Vienna, VA, tel. 703/255–1860). Just off the Dulles Toll Road, about one-half hour from downtown, Wolf Trap is a national park dedicated to the performing arts. On its grounds is the **Filene Center,** an outdoor theater that is the scene of pop, jazz, opera, ballet, and dance performances each June through September. The rest of the year, the intimate, indoor **Barns at Wolf Trap** hosts folk and acoustic acts.

Choral Music **Choral Arts Society** (tel. 202/244–3669). Now in its 25th year, this 180-voice choir performs a varied selection of classical pieces at the Kennedy Center from September to April. Three Christmas sing-alongs are scheduled each December.

Choral and church groups frequently perform in the impressive settings of the **Washington Cathedral** (tel. 202/537–6200) and the **National Shrine of the Immaculate Conception** (tel. 202/526–8300).

**Chamber Music** **Corcoran Gallery of Art** (17th St. and New York Ave. NW, tel. 202/638–3211). Hungary's Takacs String Quartet and the Cleveland Quartet, playing on matched sets of Amati and Stradivarius string instruments owned by the gallery, are among the groups that appear in the Corcoran's Musical Evening Series. Concerts are followed by a reception with the artists.

**Folger Shakespeare Library** (201 East Capitol St. SE, tel. 202/544–7077). Now in its 13th season, the Folger Shakespeare Library's internationally acclaimed resident chamber-music ensemble regularly presents a selection of instrumental and vocal pieces from the medieval, Renaissance, and baroque periods, during a season that runs from October to May.

**Phillips Collection** (1600–1612 21st St. NW, tel. 202/387–2151). The long, panelled music room of gallery founder Duncan Phillip's home is the setting for Sunday afternoon recitals from September through May. Chamber groups from around the world perform; May is devoted to performing artists from the Washington area. Arrive early for the 5 PM concerts.

**Performance Series** **Armed Forces Concert Series.** From June to August, service bands from all four branches of the military perform nightly, Sunday through Friday evenings, on the West Terrace of the Capitol and at the Sylvan Theater on the Washington Monument grounds. The traditional band concerts include marches, patriotic numbers, and some classical music. The bands often perform at other locations throughout the year. *For information: Air Force, tel. 202/767–5658; Army, tel. 703/696–3399; Navy, tel. 202/433–2525; Marines, tel. 202/337–9393.*

**Carter Barron Amphitheater** (16th St. and Colorado Ave. NW, tel. 202/485–9666). On Saturday and Sunday nights from mid-June to August this lovely, 4,250-seat outdoor theater in Rock Creek Park plays host to pop, jazz, gospel, and rhythm and blues artists such as Chick Corea, Nancy Wilson, and Tito Puente.

**District Curators** (tel. 202/783–0360). An independent organization, District Curators sponsors adventurous contemporary performers from around the world. Past artists have included Laurie Anderson, Philip Glass, the World Saxophone Quartet, and the Japanese dance troupe Sankai Juku.

**Fort Dupont Summer Theater** (Minnesota Ave. and F St. SE, tel. 202/485–9666). The National Park Service presents national and international jazz artists at 8:30 on Friday and Saturday evening from mid-June to August at this outdoor theater. Past performers at the free concerts have included Wynton Marsalis, Betty Carter, and Ramsey Lewis.

**Sylvan Theater** (Washington Monument grounds, tel. 202/485–9666). Service bands from the four branches of the military perform at this outdoor theater from mid-June to August every evening except Wednesday and Saturday. On Wednesday there's dancing to big-band and swing music.

**Washington Performing Arts Society** (tel. 202/393–3600). An independent nonprofit organization, WPAS books high-quality classical music, ballet, modern dance, and some drama into halls around the city. Most of the shows—ranging from the

Harlem Boys Choir to Leonard Bernstein conducting the Vienna Philharmonic—are held at the Kennedy Center. The **Parade of the Arts** series features shows with family appeal.

## Opera

**Mount Vernon College** (2100 Foxhall Rd. NW, 202/331–3467). The college's intimate Hand Chapel is the setting for rarely produced chamber operas each fall and spring.

**Opera Theater of Northern Virginia** (tel. 703/549–5039). The three operas in this company's season are sung in English and produced at an Arlington, Virginia, community theater. Each December the company presents a one-act opera especially for young audiences.

**Summer Opera Theater Company** (Hartke Theater, Catholic University, tel. 202/526–1669). This independent professional company mounts two fully staged productions each July and August.

**Washington Opera** (tel. 202/822–4757 or 800/87–OPERA). Seven operas—presented in their original languages with English supertitles—are performed each season (November to March) in the Kennedy Center's Opera House and Eisenhower Theater.

## Dance

**Dance Place** (3225 8th St. NE, tel. 202/269–1600). This studio theater, now in its 10th season, annually hosts a wide assortment of modern and ethnic dance.

**Joy of Motion** (1643 Connecticut Ave. NW, tel. 202/387–0911). A dance studio by day, Joy of Motion is the home of several area troupes, including Michelle Ava and Company (jazz and modern dance), JazzArt (jazz), and the Dupont Alley Dance Company (teenage performers).

**Mount Vernon College** (2100 Foxhall Rd. NW, tel. 202/331–3467). An emerging center for dance in Washington, this women's liberal arts college presents eight dance companies a year—three in the fall, five in the spring. Past participants in the dance series have included the troupes of Robert Small, Nancy Meehan, and Gus Solomons, Jr.

**Smithsonian Resident Associate Program** (tel. 202/357–3030). National and international dance groups often perform at various Smithsonian museums.

**The Washington Ballet** (tel. 202/362–3606). In October, February, and May this contemporary ballet company dances selections from the works of such choreographers as George Balanchine and Paul Taylor, mainly at the Kennedy Center. Each December, the Washington Ballet presents *The Nutcracker*.

## Film

Washington has a wealth of first-run movie theaters, in the city and in nearby suburbs:

**The AMC Union Station 9** (Union Station, tel. 202/842–3751) on Capitol Hill features nine screens and validated, three-hour parking at an adjacent parking lot. Closer to downtown are **Cineplex Odeon's West End 1–4** (23rd and L streets NW, tel. 202/293–3152) and **West End 5, 6, 7** (23rd and M streets NW, tel.

202/452–9020). The art deco **Cineplex Odeon Uptown** (3426 Connecticut Ave. NW, tel. 202/966–5400) boasts a single huge screen, Dolby sound, and a wonderful balcony. Other first-run movie theaters are clustered near Dupont Circle, in Georgetown, and around upper Wisconsin Avenue.

Several Washington theaters screen revivals and foreign, independent, and avant-garde films.

**The American Film Institute** (Kennedy Center, tel. 202/785–4600, 4601). More than 700 different movies—including contemporary and classic foreign and American films—are shown each year at the American Film Institute's theater in the Kennedy Center. Filmmakers and actors are often present to discuss their work.

**The Biograph** (2819 M St. NW, recorded information tel. 202/333–2696). Washington's home for alternative cinema, the Biograph presents a mixture of first-run and repertory domestic and foreign films that have in common "their position out of the mainstream."

**The Key** (1222 Wisconsin Ave. NW, tel. 202/333–5100). This four-screen theater specializes in foreign films and presents an annual animation festival.

**The Hirshhorn Museum** (tel. 202/357–2700) and the **National Archives** (tel. 202/523–3000). These museums on the Mall often show little-known, unusual, or experimental films.

**Filmfest DC**, an annual citywide festival of international cinema, takes place in late April and early May. For information, write Box 21396, Washington, DC 20009 or call 202/789–7000.

# Nightlife

Washington's bars and nightclubs cater to a wide spectrum of customers, from proper political appointees to blue-collar regulars in from the suburbs. Many night spots are clustered in a few key areas, simplifying things for the visitor who enjoys bar-hopping. Georgetown, in northwest Washington, leads the pack with an explosion of bars, nightclubs, and restaurants on M Street east and west of Wisconsin Avenue and on Wisconsin Avenue north of M Street. A half dozen Capitol Hill bars can be found on a stretch of Pennsylvania Avenue between 2nd and 4th streets SE. There is another high-density nightlife area around the intersection of 19th and M streets NW. Located near the city's lawyer- and lobbyist-filled downtown, this neighborhood is especially active during happy hour.

As for music, Washington audiences are catholic in their tastes and so are Washington's music promoters. That means you can hear funk at a rock club, blues at a jazz club, and calypso at a reggae club. And it means big-name acts often perform at venues that also book Broadway shows and other nonmusical forms of entertainment. The music listings below are an attempt to impose order on this chaos. Your best bet is to consult Friday's "Weekend" section in the *Washington Post* and the free, weekly *City Paper*. It's also a good idea to call clubs ahead of time to find out who's on that night and what sort of music will be played.

## Bars and Lounges

**Brickskeller.** A beer lover's mecca, this is the place to go when you want something more exotic than a Bud Lite. More than 500 brands of beer are for sale—from Central American lagers to U.S. microbrewed ales. Bartenders oblige beer-can collectors by opening the containers from the bottom. *1523 22nd St. NW, tel. 202/293–1885. Open Mon.–Thurs. 11:30 AM–2 AM, Fri. 11:30 AM–3 AM, Sat. 6 PM–3 AM, Sun. 6 PM–2 AM. AE, CB, DC, MC, V.*

**Champions.** Walls covered with jerseys, pucks, bats, and balls, and the evening's big game on the big-screen TV, leave little doubt that this popular Georgetown establishment is a sports-lover's bar. Ballpark-style food enhances the mood. *1206 Wisconsin Ave. NW, tel. 202/965–4005. Open Mon.–Thurs. 5 PM–2 AM, Fri. 5 PM–3 AM, Sat. 11:30 AM–3 AM, Sun. 11:30 AM–2 AM. In the evening, shirts with collars are required. One-drink minimum Fri. and Sat. after 10 PM. AE, MC, V.*

**The Dubliner.** Snug, panelled rooms; thick, tasty Guinness; and nightly live entertainment are the main attractions at Washington's premier Irish pub. You don't have to be Irish to enjoy it, as scores of staffers from nearby Capitol Hill attest. *520 North Capitol St. NW, tel. 202/737–3773. Open Mon.–Thurs. 11 AM–2 AM, Fri. 11 AM–3 AM, Sat. 7:30 AM–3 AM, Sun. 7:30 AM–2 AM. AE, CB, DC, MC, V.*

**F. Scott's.** Elegant art deco surroundings and dancing to music from the '30s and '40s make this upper-Georgetown night spot popular with older, well-dressed Gatsbys and Daisys. *1232 36th St. NW, tel. 202/342–0009. Open Mon.–Thurs. 6 PM–2 AM, Fri. and Sat. 6 PM–3 AM. AE, CB, DC, MC, V.*

**Food for Thought.** Lots of Birkenstock sandals, natural fibers, and activist conversation give this Dupont Circle lounge and restaurant (vegetarian and organic meat) a '60s coffeehouse feel. Nightly folk music completes the picture. *1738 Connecticut Ave. NW, tel. 202/797–1095. Open Mon.–Thurs. 11:30 AM–11:30 PM, Fri. 11:30 AM–12:30 AM, Sat. noon–12:30 AM, Sun. 5 PM–11:30 PM. AE, CB, DC, MC, V.*

**Gallagher's Pub.** This mildly Irish bar is a restful haven for those eager to avoid the crush of Georgetown. Some of Washington's most heartfelt acoustic music can be heard at the Sunday night open mike. *3319 Connecticut Ave. NW, tel. 202/686–9189. Open Mon.–Thurs. 5 PM–2 AM, Fri. 5 PM–3 AM, Sat. noon–3 AM, Sun. noon–2 AM. AE, CB, DC, MC, V.*

**Hawk 'n' Dove.** A friendly neighborhood bar in a neighborhood coincidentally dominated by the Capitol building. Regulars include political types, lobbyists, and well-behaved Marines (from a nearby barracks). *329 Pennsylvania Ave. SE, tel. 202/543–3300. Open Sun.–Thurs. 10 AM–2 AM, Fri. and Sat. 10 AM–3 AM. AE, CB, DC, MC, V.*

**Sign of the Whale.** The best hamburger in town is available at the bar in this well-known post-Preppie/neo-Yuppie haven. *1825 M St. NW, tel. 202/223–4152. Open daily 11 AM–2 AM. AE, CB, DC, MC, V.*

## Cabarets

**Chelseas.** Four nights a week this Georgetown restaurant features cabaret-style musical comedy, straight comedy, and the political comedy of the Capitol Steps, a group of current and former Hill staffers. After that, it's dancing to top Latin bands. *1055 Thomas Jefferson St. NW, tel. 202/298–8222. Shows Wed.– Sat. 6 PM–10 PM. Ticket charge. Reservations suggested. AE, MC, V.*

**d.c. space.** Dinner theater, poetry readings, film screenings, and other avant-garde events are held at this artists' hangout near the old Patent Office building. Times and shows vary, so call for schedule. *433 7th St. NW, tel. 202/347–4960. Reservations required. Ticket charge and minimum. AE, MC, V.*

**Gross National Product.** The titles of a few past shows should give you an idea of what this irreverent comedy troupe is up to: "BushCapades: An Administration on Thin Ice," "Man Without a Contra," and "The Phantom of the White House." GNP, which the *Washington Post* has compared to the original cast of "Saturday Night Live," performs at the Bayou in Georgetown. *3135 K St. NW, tel. 202/783–7212. Show Sat. 7:30. Ticket charge. Reservations suggested. No credit cards.*

**Marquee Cabaret.** Funnylady Joan Cushing assumes the character of quintessential Washington insider "Mrs. Foggybottom" and, with a small cast, pokes fun at well-known political figures in satirical skit and song. *Omni-Shoreham Hotel, 2500 Calvert St. NW, tel. 202/745–1023. Shows Thurs.–Sat. 9 PM. Ticket charge. Reservations required. AE, CB, DC, MC, V.*

## Comedy Clubs

**Comedy Cafe.** Local and national comics appear at this club in the heart of downtown. Thursday is open-mike night; on Friday and Saturday, the pros take the stage. *1520 K St. NW, tel. 202/638–JOKE. Shows Thurs. and Fri. 8:30 and 10:30; Sat. 7:30, 9:30, and 11:30. Cover charge. AE, CB, DC, MC, V.*

**Garvin's Comedy Club.** This club features top acts and is affiliated with the dozen or so Garvin's up and down the east coast. *1335 Greens Ct. NW (L Street between 13th and 14th streets NW), tel. 202/726–1334. Shows Tues.–Thurs. 8:30; Fri. 8:30 and 10:30; Sat. 7:30, 9:30, and 11:30. Cover charge. Reservations required. AE, DC, MC, V.*

**Garvin's Comedy Club at Phillips Flagship.** Garvin's has just started serving up comedians at this popular Washington seafood restaurant. *900 Water St. SW, tel. 202/726–1334. Shows Fri. and Sat. 8:30 and 10:30. Cover charge. Reservations required. AE, DC, MC, V.*

**Garvin's Comedy Club at the Ramada Inn.** The final jewel in Garvin's triple crown of comedy is in this suburban Virginia hotel. *I-395 and Seminary Rd., Alexandria, VA, tel. 202/726– 1334. Shows Fri. 9, Sat. 8:30 and 10:30. Cover charge. Reservations required. AE, DC, MC, V.*

## Acoustic/Folk/Country

**Birchmere.** The best place in the area to hear acoustic folk and bluegrass acts is in an unpretentious suburban strip shopping center. Favorite sons the Seldom Scene are Thursday-night regulars. Audiences come to listen, and the management politely insists on no distracting chatter. *3901 Mt. Vernon Ave., Alexandria, VA, tel. 703/549–5919. Open Tues.–Sat. 7 PM– 11:30 PM. MC, V.*

**Country Junction.** A suburban Maryland hotel lounge is the scene of country dance lessons followed by country and swing dancing. DJs spin records, except on Thursdays, when country bands perform. *11410 Rockville Pike, Rockville, MD, tel. 301/ 231–5761. Open daily 7 PM–1 AM. Cover charge Thurs.–Sat. AE, MC, V.*

**Dylan's.** There's a different type of music nearly every night at this Georgetown restaurant-cum-club; most groups fall into the light rock and acoustic folk categories. *3251 Prospect St. NW, tel. 202/337–0593. Open daily 11 AM–2 AM. Cover charge on weekends. AE, MC, V.*

## Dance Clubs

**Cities.** A varied crowd dances to international disco in this Adams-Morgan club. Every few months the decor changes to reflect another part of the world, right down to the signs on the restroom doors. *2424 18th St. NW, tel. 202/328–7194. Open Wed. and Thurs. 9:30 PM–2 AM, Fri. and Sat. 9:30 PM–3 AM. Cover charge. AE, DC, MC, V.*

**Dakota.** On Wednesday and Sunday the crowd at this popular multilevel Adams-Morgan club is predominantly gay. The rest of the week Dakota attracts a diverse crowd eager to dance or to eat at its highly rated restaurant, Montana. *1777 Columbia Rd. NW, tel. 202/265–6600. Open Sun.–Thurs. 7 PM–2 AM, Fri. and Sat. 7 PM–3 AM. No jeans or sneakers. Cover charge. AE, MC, V.*

**Fifth Column.** A trendy, well-dressed crowd waits in line to dance to the latest releases from London and Europe on three floors of this converted bank. Avant-garde art installations change every four months. *915 F St. NW, tel. 202/393–3632. Open Tues.–Thurs. and Sun. 9 PM–2 AM, Fri. and Sat. 9 PM–3 AM. Cover charge. AE, MC, V.*

**Kilimanjaro.** Deep in ethnically diverse Adams-Morgan, the Kilimanjaro specializes in "international" music from the Caribbean and Africa. Every Thursday there's a local reggae band, and international artists often perform on Sunday. *1724 California St. NW, tel. 202/328–3838. Open Mon.–Thurs. 5 PM–2 AM, Fri. 5 PM–4 AM, Sat. 6 PM–4 AM, Sun. 6 PM–2 AM. Cover charge. MC, V.*

**Tracks.** A gay club with a large contingent of straight regulars, this warehouse-district disco has one of the largest dance floors in town and stays open late. *1111 1st St. SE, tel. 202/488–3320. Open Mon. and Tues. 6 PM–2 AM, Wed. and Thurs. 6 PM–4 AM, Fri. 6 PM–5 AM, Sat. 6 PM–6 AM, Sun. noon–4 AM. Cover charge Wed.–Sun. after 9 PM. No credit cards.*

**The Vault.** There is beat-heavy disco on the first floor, more laid-back tunes upstairs, and downstairs there's the cozy security of the actual vault that gives this dance-club-in-a-bank its name. *911 F St. NW, tel. 202/347–8079. Open Wed.–Thurs. and Sun. 9 PM–2 AM, Fri. and Sat. 9 PM–3 AM. Cover charge. AE, MC, V.*

## Jazz Clubs

**Anton's 1201 Club.** A recent addition to the Washington restaurant and music scene, this supper club books headline artists like Peggy Lee, Jack Jones, and Mel Torme. *1201 Pennsylvania Ave. NW, tel. 202/783–1201. Shows Tues. and Wed. 8:30, Thurs.–Sat. 8:30 and 10:45. Cover charge. AE, CB, DC, MC, V.*

**Blues Alley.** The restaurant turns out Creole cooking, while cooking on stage are such nationally known performers as

Sarah Vaughan and Ramsey Lewis. You can come for just the
show, but those who come for a meal get better seats. *Rear 1073
Wisconsin Ave. NW, tel. 202/337–4141. Open Mon.–Thurs. 6
PM–midnight, Fri. and Sat. 6 PM–2 AM. Shows at 8 and 10, plus
midnight shows Fri. and Sat. Cover charge and $2 food/drink
minimum. AE, CB, DC, MC, V.*

**One Step Down.** Low-ceilinged, intimate, and boasting the best
jazz jukebox in town, this small club books talented local artists
and the occasional nationally known act. *2517 Pennsylvania
Ave. NW, tel. 202/331–8863. Open Mon.–Fri. 10 AM–2 AM, Sat.
and Sun. noon–2 AM. AE, CB, DC, MC, V.*

**219 Basin Street Lounge.** Across the Potomac in Old Town Alexandria above the 219 Restaurant, jazz combos perform in an
attractive Victorian-style bar. *219 King St., Alexandria, VA,
tel. 703/549–1141. Open Sun.–Thurs. 8:30 PM–12:30 AM, Fri.
and Sat. 9 PM–1 AM, Sun. jazz brunch 1 PM–6 PM. Cover charge.
AE, MC, V.*

## Rock, Pop, and Rhythm and Blues Clubs

**The Bayou.** Located in Georgetown, underneath the Whitehurst Freeway, the Bayou is a Washington fixture that showcases national acts on weeknights and local talent on weekends.
Bands cover rock in all its permutations: pop rock, hard rock,
soft rock, new rock, and classic rock. Tickets are available at
the door or through TicketCenter. *3135 K St. NW, tel. 202/333–
2897. Open daily 8 PM–2 AM. Cover charge. No credit cards.*

**Club Soda.** The room and dance floor are tiny, but this is one of
the best places in town to hear cover bands perform consistent-
ly accurate oldies music (Wednesday through Sunday). A DJ
spins the real thing next door. *3433 Connecticut Ave. NW, tel.
202/244–3189. Open Sun.–Thurs. 5 PM–2 AM, Fri. and Sat. 5
PM–3 AM. Cover charge on weekends. MC, V.*

**d.c. space.** Early in the evening this downtown artists' bar features cabaret shows. After that, bands take the small stage and
treat the casually dressed audience to punk, new wave, and
various other interesting musical forms. *433 7th St. NW, tel.
202/347–4960. Open Mon.–Thurs. 11:30 AM–2 AM, Fri. 11:30
AM–3 AM, Sat. 6 PM–3 AM. Cover charge. AE, MC, V.*

**Grog and Tankard.** A college-age crowd downs cheap pitchers
of beer while listening to exuberant local bands in this small,
comfortably disheveled night spot. *2408 Wisconsin Ave. NW,
tel. 202/333–3114. Open Mon.–Thurs. 4 PM–2 AM, Fri. 4 PM–3
AM, Sat. noon–3 AM, Sun. noon–2 AM. Cover charge after 8 PM.
AE, MC, V.*

**Ibex.** On Wednesday and Thursday the well-known DJ Kool
spins dance records at this three-floor uptown club. Local go-go
phenoms Rare Essence appear on Wednesday, Chuck Brown
and the Soul Searchers on Sunday. National rhythm-and-blues,
pop, and jazz acts perform on Friday and Saturday. *5832 Georgia Ave. NW, tel. 202/726–1800. Open Wed.–Sun. 9 PM–4 AM.
Cover charge. AE.*

**9:30 Club.** This trendy club in the center of Washington's old
downtown books an eclectic mix of local, national, and international artists, most of whom play what used to be known as
"new wave" music (from the Fleshtones, Guadalcanal Diary,
and Robyn Hitchcock, among others). The regulars dress to be
seen, but visitors won't feel out of place. Get tickets at the door
or through Ticketron. *930 F St. NW, tel. 202/393–0930. Open*

*Tues. 8 PM–2 AM, Wed.–Thurs. 4 PM–2 AM, Fri. 4 PM–3 AM, Sat.
9 PM–3 AM. Cover charge. No credit cards.*

**The Roxy.** An unassuming club that understands that a cold
beer and a hot band are usually more important than fashionable decor. Local and national acts appear four nights a week;
there's reggae every Saturday. *1214 18th St. NW, tel. 202/296–
9292 (concert line). Open Wed.–Sat. 8:30 PM–2 AM. Cover
charge. AE, MC, V.*

**Twist & Shout.** A suburban-Maryland American Legion hall is
the perfect setting for homegrown music: rockabilly, blues,
boogie woogie, Cajun zydeco, and plain old rock-and-roll. *4800
Auburn Ave., Bethesda, MD, tel. 301/681–8536. Open Fri. and
Sat. 9 PM–1 AM. Cover charge. No credit cards.*

# 9 Excursions

# Tour 1: The C & O Canal and Great Falls

## Introduction

Michael Dolan, a DC native, is a freelance editor and writer. A frequent contributor to the *Washingtonian*, the *City Paper*, and other publications, Dolan is also the author of *A.M.D.G.*, a novel set in the capital.

In the 18th and early 19th centuries, the Potomac river was the main transport route between Cumberland, Maryland, one of the most important ports on the nation's frontier, and the seaports of the Chesapeake Bay. Tobacco, grain, whiskey, furs, iron ore, timber, and other commodities were sent down the Potomac from Cumberland to the ports of Georgetown and Alexandria, which served as major distribution points for both domestic and international markets.

Although it served as a vital link with the country's western territories, the Potomac did have some drawbacks as a commercial waterway: Rapids and waterfalls along the 190 miles between Cumberland and Washington made it impossible for traders to navigate the entire distance by boat. Just a few miles upstream from Washington, the Potomac cascaded through two such barriers—the breathtakingly beautiful Great Falls and the less dramatic but no less impassable Little Falls.

To help traders move goods between the eastern markets and the western frontier more efficiently, 18th-century engineers proposed that a canal with a series of elevator locks be built parallel to the river. The first such canal was built at the urging of George Washington, who actually helped found a company just for this purpose. In 1802, after 17 years of work, his firm opened the Patowmack Canal on the Virginia side of the river.

In 1828 Washington's canal was replaced by the **Chesapeake & Ohio Canal,** which had been dug along the opposite shore. The C & O stretched from the heart of Washington to Cumberland. Starting near what is now the intersection of 17th Street and Constitution Avenue NW (the public restroom there was originally a lockhouse), the C & O moved barges through 75 locks.

Ironically, the C & O Canal began operation the same day as the Baltimore & Ohio Railroad, the concern that eventually put the canal out of business. The C & O route to the west nevertheless did prove to be a viable alternative for traders interested in moving goods through the Washington area and to the lower Chesapeake. During the mid-19th century, the canal boats carried as many as one million tons of merchandise a year. The C & O Canal stopped turning a profit in 1890 but remained in business until 1924, when a disastrous storm left it in ruins. Ownership then shifted to the B & O Railroad, which sold the canal to the federal government in 1938 for $2 million. In 1939 the canal became part of the National Capital Parks System.

In the 1950s a proposal to build a highway over the canal near Washington was defeated by residents of the Palisades, a neighborhood that overlooks the waterway. The battle was won when a prominent resident, Supreme Court Justice William O. Douglas, invited journalists to join him on a seven-day walk from Washington to Cumberland in order to draw attention to the canal's unique blend of natural beauty and historic interest. Douglas succeeded, and since 1971 the canal has been a national park, providing Washingtonians and visitors with a window into the past and a marvelous place to pursue recreational activities.

The twin parks of **Great Falls**—on either side of the river 13 miles northwest of Georgetown—are also now part of the National Park system. The 800-acre park on the Virginia side is a favorite place for outings for local residents and is easily accessible to tourists. The steep, jagged falls roar into a narrow gorge, providing one of the most spectacular scenic attractions in the East.

## Escorted Tours

A tour of the visitors center and museum at **Great Falls Park** (tel. 703/285–2966) in Virginia takes 30 minutes. Staff members conduct special tours and walks year round. Visitors are encouraged to take self-guided tours along well-marked trails, including one that follows the route of the old Patowmack Canal.

On the Maryland side, the old **Great Falls Tavern** (tel. 301/299–2026) serves as a museum and headquarters for the rangers who manage the C & O Canal. During warm weather, replica mule-drawn boats carry visitors along this stretch of the canal; similar trips also begin in Georgetown. History books and canal guides are on sale at both parks as well as at many bookstores in the District.

## Getting Around

**By Car**   To reach the Virginia side of Great Falls Park, take the scenic and winding Route 193 (exit 13 off Route 495, the Capitol Beltway) to Route 738, and follow the signs. It takes about 25 minutes to drive to the park from the Beltway. You can get to the Maryland side of the park by following MacArthur Boulevard from Georgetown or by taking exit 41 off the Beltway, following the signs to Carderock.

**By Foot, Canoe,**   The C & O Canal Park and its towpath are favorite destinations
**or Bicycle**   for joggers, bikers, and canoeists. The towpath has only a slight grade, which makes for a leisurely ride or hike. Most recreational bikers consider the 13 miles from Georgetown to Great Falls an easy ride; there's only one short stretch of rocky ground near Great Falls where bikers need to carry their cycles. You can also take a bike path that parallels MacArthur Boulevard for much of the distance to the Maryland side of the park. Storm damage has left parts of the canal dry, but many segments remain intact and navigable by canoe. You can rent canoes or bicycles at **Fletcher's Boat House,** just upriver from Georgetown (*see* Exploring, below). In winter the canal sometimes freezes solid enough to allow for ice skating; during particularly hard freezes it's possible to skate great distances along the canal, occasionally interrupting your stride for short clambers around the locks.

## Exploring

*Numbers in the margin correspond with points of interest on the C & O Canal and Great Falls map.*

This tour moves from Georgetown northwest along the Potomac to Great Falls Park. The Canal itself is worth a day's stroll or ride.

❶ The towpath along the canal in **Georgetown** passes traces of that area's industrial past, such as the Godey Lime Kilns near the mouth of Rock Creek, as well as the fronts of numerous houses dating to 1810. From April through October mule-drawn barges leave for 90-minute trips from the Foundry Mall on Thomas Jefferson Street NW, half a block south of M Street. No reservations are required for the public trips. *For information, tel. 202/472-4376. For group reservations and rates, tel. 202/653-5844. Cost: $4 adults, $3 senior citizens, $2.50 children under 12.*

❷ **Fletcher's Boat House** (4940 Canal Rd. NW, tel. 202/244-0461) rents canoes and bicycles and sells fishing tackle and D.C. fishing licenses. Fishermen often congregate here to try their luck with shad, perch, catfish, striped bass, and other freshwater species. Fletcher's opens at 5:30 AM, stops renting equipment at 5, and during warm weather closes at 7:30 PM. During the coldest months of the year Fletcher's shuts down.

❸ **Chain Bridge**—named for the chains that held up the original structure—links the District with Virginia. The bridge was built to enable cattlemen to bring Virginia herds to the slaughterhouses located along the Potomac on the Maryland side. During the Civil War the bridge was guarded by Union troops stationed at earthen fortifications located along what is now Potomac Avenue NW. The Virginia side of the river in the area around Chain Bridge is known for its good fishing and narrow, treacherous channel. Not far from the walkway that leads down to the C & O towpath on the Maryland side is one of the few active beaver dams in the nation's capital.

❹ **Glen Echo** (5801 Oxford Dr., tel. 301/492-6246), founded as part of the Chautauqua movement of the late 19th century, is a charming village of Victorian houses, including the home of Red Cross founder Clara Barton, which has been preserved as a monument to her career and as an example of American building style. The Chautauqua center at Glen Echo later saw use as an amusement park; it now houses an arts and cultural center that frequently hosts dances and folk festivals. For scheduling information, check the free weekly *City Paper.*

**Glen Echo Park** (MacArthur Blvd. and Goldsboro Rd., tel. 301/492-6282) is noted not only for its whimsical architecture but for its splendid and still-functioning carousel. From late spring to early fall a quarter buys a trip into the past, complete with music from a real calliope.

❺ **Great Falls Tavern,** on the Maryland side of Great Falls Park, features displays of Canal history and a platform from which to view the Falls. On the canal walls are "rope burns" caused by decade upon decade of friction from barge lines. Half a mile west a flood marker shows how high the Potomac can go—after a hurricane in 1972 the river crested far above the ground where visitors stand. Canal barge trips start here between April and October *Park, tel. 301/299-2026. Open 9-dusk. Tavern and museum, tel. 301/299-3613. Open Wed.-Sun. 9-5.*

❻ The Virginia side of **Great Falls Park** offers the best views of the gorge of the Potomac, as well as trails leading past the old

# C&O Canal and Great Falls

Georgia Ave.

16th St.

Rock Creek Park

Military Rd.

Connecticut Ave.

Wisconsin Ave.

DISTRICT OF COLUMBIA

Wisconsin Ave.

Georgetown ❶

❷ Fletcher's Boat House

Whitehurst Freeway

Arlington Blvd.

Wilson Blvd.

Lee Hwy.

Military Rd.

N

River Rd.

Massachusetts Ave.

Wisconsin Ave.

Goldsboro Bradley Blvd.

❸ Chain Bridge

Glebe Rd.

Lee Hwy.

VIRGINIA

Chain Bridge Rd.

Kirby Rd.

Bradley Blvd.

River Rd.

MARYLAND

Clara Barton Pkwy.

George Washington Memorial Pkwy.

George Washington Memorial Pkwy.

❹ Glen Echo

Kirby Rd.

Old Dominion Dr.

Westmoreland St.

Georgetown Pike

Dolley Madison Blvd.

Balls Hill Rd.

Great Falls St.

Great Falls Access and Toll Rd.

Seven Locks Rd.

Bradley Blvd.

Persimmon Tree Rd.

Macarthur Blvd.

Capital Beltway

Washington Dulles Access and Toll Rd.

Lewisville Rd.

South Glen Kentsdale Rd.

Bells Mill Rd.

Brickyard Rd.

Potomac River

Old Dominion Dr.

Spring Hill Rd.

River Rd.

❺ Great Falls Tavern

❻ Great Falls Park

Georgetown Pike

Leigh Mill Rd.

Stoney Creek

Leesburg Pike

2 miles

3 km

0

Patowmack Canal and among the boulders and forests lining the edge of the falls. Horseback riding is permitted—maps are available at the visitors center—but you can't rent horses in the park. Swimming and wading are prohibited, but there are fine opportunities for fishing (Virginia, Maryland, or D.C. licenses are required for anglers 16 and older), rock climbing (climbers must register at the visitors center beforehand), and white-water kayaking (*below* the falls only, and only by experienced boaters). From peaks beside the river and from several manmade platforms you can watch helmeted kayakers and climbers test their skills against the river and the rocks. As is true all along this stretch of the river, the currents are deadly. Despite frequent signs and warnings, each year some visitors dare the water, and lose. It's best to keep away from even the most benign-looking ripple. *Tel. 703/759–2169. Open daily 9 AM until dark. Closed Christmas. Parking fee: $3.*

# Tour 2: Mount Vernon, Woodlawn, and Gunston Hall

## Introduction

Long before the capital city was planned, the shores of the Potomac had been divided into plantations by wealthy traders and gentleman farmers. Even though most traces of the Colonial era were obliterated as the capital grew in the 19th century, several splendid examples of plantation architecture remain on the Virginia side of the Potomac just 15 miles or so south of the District. The three mansions described in this section can easily be visited in a single day: **Mount Vernon,** one of the most popular sites in the area, was the home of George Washington; **Woodlawn,** the estate of Washington's grand-daughter; and **Gunston Hall,** the home of George Mason, patriot and author of the document on which the Bill of Rights was based. Spread out on hillsides overlooking the river, these estates offer a look into a way of life long gone.

## Escorted Tours

**Tourmobile** offers trips to and from Mount Vernon. Tours depart daily at 10 AM, noon, and 2 PM from Arlington Cemetery and the Washington Monument. Reservations must be made in person one hour before departure. Advance sales for next-day tickets begin at 2 PM. *Tel. 202/554–7950. Cost: $14.25 adults, $6.57 children. 2-day combo tickets good for Mount Vernon and several sites in Washington: $22.50 adults, $10.75 children.*

**Gray Line Tours** runs half-day trips to Mount Vernon and Old Town Alexandria. Buses depart at 9 AM from Union Station. *Tel. 202/386–8300. Cost: $18.*

## Getting Around

**By Car** To get to Mount Vernon from the Capitol Beltway (Route 495), take exit 1 onto the George Washington Memorial Parkway, and follow the signs. From downtown Washington, cross into

Arlington on either the Key Bridge or Memorial Bridge, and drive south on the George Washington Memorial Parkway toward National Airport. Proceed past the airport and through Alexandria straight to Mount Vernon. The trip from Washington takes about a half hour.

To reach Woodlawn and Gunston Hall from Mount Vernon, continue south on the George Washington Parkway to Route 1. The entrance to Woodlawn is straight across from the exit; to reach Gunston Hall, turn left and follow the signs.

**By Subway or Bus**  You can get to Mount Vernon from the District by using the Metro and bus service. During rush hours (7 to 9 AM and 4:30 to 6:30 PM), get on a Yellow Line train headed south to Huntington, debark at National Airport, and catch the 11-P bus to Mount Vernon. Don't forget to pick up a transfer when you're boarding the train. The fare is $1.40 with transfer, $1.70 without. During non-rush hours, take the train to Huntington and catch the 11-H bus; the fare is 45 cents with transfer, 80 cents without.

**By Boat**  An especially pleasant way to travel down the Potomac is to cruise on the ***Spirit of Mount Vernon,*** which makes the trip from Washington to the plantation twice daily from mid-March through October (Boats leave from Pier 4 (6th and Water streets SW, tel. 202/554–8000).

**By Bicycle**  An asphalt bicycle path leads from the Virginia side of Memorial Bridge (adjacent to the Lincoln Memorial), past National Airport, and through Alexandria all the way to Mount Vernon. The trail is steep in places, but a biker in moderately good condition can make the 23-mile trip in less than two hours. Bicycles can be rented at several locations in Washington (*see* Biking in Chapter 5).

## Exploring

*Numbers in the margin correspond with points of interest on the Mount Vernon, Woodlawn, and Gunston Hall map.*

**Mount Vernon**  **Mount Vernon** and the surrounding lands had been in the Washington family for nearly 90 years by the time George inherited it all in 1761. Before taking over command of the Continental Army, Washington was a yeoman farmer, directing the management of the 8,000-acre plantation, of which more than 3,000 acres were under cultivation. He also oversaw the transformation of the main house from an ordinary farm dwelling into what was for the time a grand mansion. His improvements resulted in a dwelling more suited to his status as Founding Father. Even though his plans were ambitious, Washington was a thrifty homeowner: When he replaced a plain stairway with one made of black walnut, he recylced the old stairs, installing them between the second and third floors of the expanded house.

The main house, with its red roof, is elegant though understated. The exterior is made of yellow pine painted and coated with layers of sand—"rusticated," in the language of the day—to resemble white-stone blocks.

The inside of the building is more ornate, especially the formal receiving room with its molded ceiling decorated with agricultural motifs. Throughout the house you'll find other, smaller symbols of the owner's eminence, such as a key to the main por-

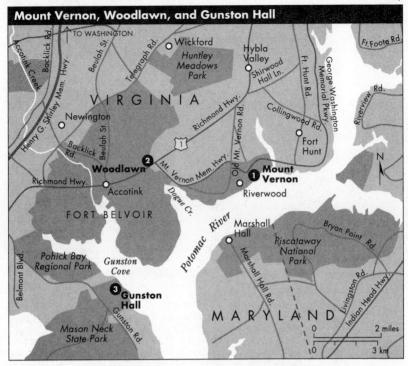

## Mount Vernon, Woodlawn, and Gunston Hall

tal of the Bastille, presented to Washington by the Marquis de Lafayette, Washington's Presidential chair, and a case of traveling wine bottles. Small groups of visitors are ushered from room to room, each of which is staffed by a guide who describes the furnishings and answers questions.

The real (often overlooked) treasure of Mount Vernon is the view from around back: Beneath a 90-foot portico (George Washington's contribution to the language of architecture) the home's dramatic riverside porch looks out on an expanse of lawn that slopes down to the Potomac. In springtime the view of the river (a mile wide at the point at which it passes the plantation) is framed by the blossoms of wild plum and dogwood. Ships of the U.S. and foreign navies always salute when passing the house.

Tours of the sprawling grounds are self-guided. Visitors are free to visit the plantation workshops, the kitchen, the carriage house, the gardens, reconstructions of the slave quarters, and down the hill toward the boat landing, the tomb of George and Martha Washington. Among the souvenirs sold at the plantation are stripling boxwoods that began life as clippings from bushes planted in 1798, the year before Washington died. *Tel. 703/780–2000. Open Mar.–Oct. 9–5, Nov.–Feb. 9–4. General admission: $5 adults; $4 senior citizens 62 and older; $2 children 6 to 11 accompanied by adults. Regular group admission (minimum 20 paid admissions): $4.50 adults; $3.50 senior citizens; $2 children 6 to 11. Youth and student group ad-*

*mission (minimum 12 paid admissions): $2 grades 1 through 12; $2 chaperons (1 per 10 students; additional chaperons $4.50). A limited number of wheelchairs is available at the main gate. The tour of the house and grounds takes about two hours.*

**Woodlawn** Three miles south of Mount Vernon on Route 1, **Woodlawn** Plan-
❷ tation occupies a piece of ground that was originally part of the
Mount Vernon estate; even today you can see the red roof of
Washington's home from Woodlawn. The house at Woodlawn
was built for Washington's step-granddaughter, Nellie Custis,
who married his favorite nephew, Lawrence Lewis. (Lewis had
come to Mount Vernon from Fredericksburg to help the General manage his five farms.)

The Lewises' home, completed in 1805, is noteworthy from an
architectural standpoint. It was designed by William Thornton, who drew up the original plans for the Capitol. Like Mount
Vernon, the Woodlawn house is made wholly of native
materials, including the clay for its bricks and the yellow pine
used throughout the interior.

In the tradition of Southern riverfront mansions, Woodlawn
has a central hallway that provides a cool refuge during the
summer. At one corner of the passage is a bust of George Washington, set on a pedestal so that the crown of the head is at
6'2"—Washington's actual height. Elsewhere is a music room
with a ceiling two feet higher than any other in the building,
built that way to improve the acoustics for the harp and clavi-
chord recitals that the Lewises and their children enjoyed.

After Woodlawn passed out of the Lewis family's hands it was
owned by a Quaker community, which established there a
meetinghouse and the first integrated school in Virginia. Subsequent owners included the playwright Paul Kester and
Senator and Mrs. Oscar Underwood of Alabama. The property
was acquired by the National Trust for Historic Preservation
in 1957.

Also on the grounds of Woodlawn is the **Pope-Leighey House,**
designed by Frank Lloyd Wright and built in 1940. The structure originally stood in nearby Falls Church, Virginia; it was
rescued from the path of a highway and moved to the Woodlawn
grounds in 1964. Wright's modernist design in cypress, brick,
and glass offers a peculiar counterpoint to the Georgian
stylings of Woodlawn. It is not to every taste, but it *is* an architectural education. *Woodlawn, 3 mi. straight down the GW
Parkway from Mount Vernon, tel. 703/780–4000. Open daily
9:30–4:30. Tours every half hour. Last tour at 4 PM. Admission:
$5 adults, $3.50 students and senior citizens, children under 5
free. An $8 combination ticket also covers admission to the
Pope-Leighey House.*

**Gunston Hall** Unlike Mount Vernon, **Gunston Hall,** 15 miles away in Lorton,
❸ is rarely crowded with visitors. This was the home of a lesser-
known George: George Mason, gentleman farmer, captain of
the Fairfax militia and author of the Virginia Declaration of
Rights. Mason was one of the framers of the Constitution but
refused to sign the final document because it did not prohibit
slavery, adequately restrain the powers of the federal government, or include a bill of rights.

Completed in 1759, Gunston Hall is built of native brick, black walnut, and yellow pine. The architectural style of the time demanded absolute balance in all structures. Hence the "robber" window on a second-floor storage room and the fake door set into one side of the center hallway. The house's interior, with its carved woodwork in styles from Chinese to Gothic, has been meticulously restored, with paints made from the original recipes and with carefully carved replacements for the intricate mahogany medallions in the moldings.

The formal gardens are famous for their boxwoods, some of which were planted in the 1760s and have now grown to be 12 and 14 feet high. In Mason's day boxwood was used as a garden border because its acrid smell repelled deer. The grounds may look familiar, since the last scene in the 1987 movie *Broadcast News* was filmed here, by the gazebo.

To reach Gunston Hall, turn south on Route 1 from Woodlawn and follow the highway 7 miles, then turn left and follow the signs. The tour takes 45 minutes to an hour. *Tel. 703/550–9220. Admission: $3 adults, $2.50 senior citizens, $1 children 6 to 15. Open daily 9:30–5, grounds 9:30–4. Last tour at 4:30.*

# Tour 3:
# Fredericksburg, Virginia

**Introduction**

Situated on land once favored by Indian tribes as fishing and hunting ground, this compact city near the falls of the Rappahannock River figured prominently at crucial points in the nation's history, particularly during the Revolutionary and Civil wars. Just 50 miles south of Washington on I-95, Fredericksburg is today a popular day-trip destination for history buffs. In fact it rivals Alexandria and Mount Vernon for Washington-family associations. The town's 40-block **National Historic District** contains more than 350 original 18th- and 19th-century buildings, including Mary Washington's home, James Monroe's law office, the Rising Sun Tavern, and Kenmore, the magnificent 1752 plantation home of George Washington's sister. The town is a favorite with antique collectors, who enjoy cruising the dealers' shops along Caroline Street.

Although its site was visited by explorer Captain John Smith as early as 1608, the town of Fredericksburg wasn't founded until 1728. Established as a frontier port to serve nearby tobacco farmers and iron miners, Fredericksburg took its name from England's crown prince at the time, and the streets still bear names of members of his family: George, Caroline, Sophia, Princess Anne, Hanover, William, and Amelia.

George Washington knew Fredericksburg well, having grown up just across the Rappahannock on Ferry Farm. He lived there from age 6 to 16, and the legends about chopping down a cherry tree and throwing a coin across the Rappahannock—later mythologized as the Potomac—go back to this period of his life. In later years Washington often returned to visit his mother at the home he bought for her on Charles Street.

Fredericksburg prospered in the decades after independence, benefitting from its location midway along the 100-mile path between Washington and Richmond, an important intersection of railroad lines and waterways. When the Civil War broke out in 1861, Fredericksburg became the linchpin of the Confederate defense of Richmond and, as such, the inevitable target of Union assaults. In December, 1862 Union forces attacked Fredericksburg in what was to be the first of four major battles fought in and around the town. In the battle of Sunken Road, Confederate defenders sheltered by a stone wall at the base of Marye's Heights mowed down Union soldiers by the thousands as they charged across the fields on foot and on horseback.

By war's end, the fighting in Fredericksburg and in battles at nearby Chancellorsville, the Wilderness, and Spotsylvania Court House had claimed more than 100,000 dead or wounded. Fredericksburg's cemeteries hold the remains of 17,000 soldiers from both sides. Despite heavy bombardment and house-to-house fighting, however, much of the city remained intact, and the historic district today contains many fine examples from the period.

A walking tour through the town proper takes three to four hours; battlefield tours each can take that long. The short hop across the Rappahannock to Chatham House is well worth it, if for no other reason than that the site offers a splendid view of all of Fredericksburg.

## Escorted Tours

**The Fredericksburg Department of Tourism** (706 Caroline St., tel. 703/373–1776 or 800/678–4748) offers a booklet that includes a short history of Fredericksburg and a self-guided tour covering 29 sites. Also available from the visitors center is a booklet outlining 3-, 9-, and 20-mile bike tours (bike rentals are not available).

**The Historic Fredericksburg Foundation** offers group tours of the city (904 Princess Anne St., tel. 703/371–4504; 3-hour tour $35, or $20 for school groups; each additional hour $10 per guide).

**Heritage Guide Service** arranges group tours of the city as well as of battlefields and other historic sites in the area. Advance reservations are required. Contact Tour Coordinator (706 Caroline St., Fredericksburg, VA 22401, tel. 703/373–1776).

## Getting Around

By Car  To get to Fredericksburg from the District, take I-95 south to Route 3, turn left, and follow the signs. The drive takes about 60 minutes one way, except during rush-hour.

By Train  **Amtrak** trains bound for Fredericksburg depart three times daily from Washington's Union Station (tel. 202/484–7540 or 800/872–7245). The Fredericksburg railroad station is near the historic district (Caroline St. and Lafayette Blvd.) A round-trip ticket from Washington costs $15–$20.

By Bus  **Greyhound** (tel. 202/565–2662) and **Trailways** (tel. 202/737–5800) depart several times a day from Washington to Fredericksburg. The average round-trip price is $18. Buses stop at a

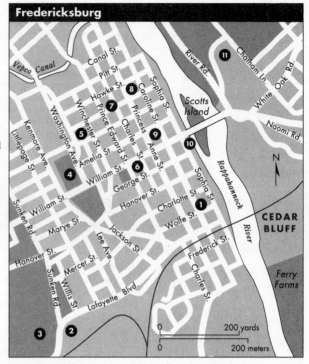

Fredericksburg

station on alternate Route 1, about 2 miles from the center of town; cabs are available there.

## Exploring

*Numbers in the margin correspond with points of interest on the Fredericksburg map.*

**1** The **Fredericksburg Visitor Center** offers booklets and pamphlets on local history, information on restaurants and lodging, and a slide show that orients visitors to the city. Also available at the center are parking passes, good for designated spots in 2-hour zones, and Hospitality Passes ($12) to six city attractions. The center is in a structure that was built in 1824 as a residence and confectionary; during the Civil War it was used to hold prisoners of war. *706 Caroline St., tel. 703/373-1776. Open daily 9-5, extended summer hours. Closed Christmas and New Year's Day.*

**2** At the **Fredericksburg Battlefield Visitor Center** you can learn about Fredericksburg's role in the Civil War by attending the succinct, informative slide show and then moving on to displays of soldiers' art and battlefield relics. The center offers tape-recorded tour cassettes and maps showing how to reach hiking trails at the nearby Wilderness, Chancellorsville, and Spotsylvania Courthouse battlefields (all within 15 miles of Fredericksburg). Just outside the Center is Sunken Road, where on December 11 to 13, 1862, General Robert E. Lee led his troops to a bloody but resounding victory over Union forces

attacking across the Rappahannock; 18,000 men from both
sides died in the clash. Much of the stone wall that hid Lee's
sharpshooters has been rebuilt, but 100 yards from the visitors
center part of the original wall looks out on the statue *The Angel of Marye's Heights*, by Felix de Weldon. This memorial
honors Sergeant Richard Kirkland, a South Carolinian who
risked his life to bring water to wounded foes; he later died at
the Battle of Chickamauga. *Lafayette Blvd. at Sunken Rd., tel.
703/373–6122. Open daily 9–5, extended summer hours.
Closed Christmas and New Year's Day.*

❸ The **National Cemetery** is the final resting place of 15,000 Union casualties, most of whom were never identified. *Lafayette
Blvd. at Sunken Rd. Open daily sunrise to sunset.*

❹ The **Confederate Cemetery** contains the remains of more than
2,000 soldiers (most of them unknown) as well as the graves of
generals Dabney Maury, Seth Barton, Carter Stevenson, Daniel Ruggles, Henry Sibley, and Abner Perrin. *Entrance at 1100
Washington Ave., near the corner of Washington Ave. and
Amelia St. Open dawn to dusk.*

❺ **Kenmore** was the home of Fielding Lewis, a patriot, plantation
owner, and brother-in-law of George Washington. (Lewis sacri-
ficed much of his fortune to operate a gun factory that supplied
the American forces during the Revolution.) Kenmore's plain
exterior belies the lavish interior; these have been called some
of the most beautiful rooms in America. The plaster moldings
in the ceilings are outstanding and even more ornate than
Mount Vernon's. Of equal elegance are the furnishings, which
include a large standing clock that belonged to Mary Washington. Across the street are fine examples of Victorian architecture and a monument to Mary Washington, as well as the entrance to the Confederate cemetery. After the 60-minute tour
visitors to Kenmore are served cider and gingerbread made according to a Washington family recipe. *1201 Washington Ave.,
tel. 703/373–3381. Admission: $4 adult, $2 student, $3.20
group adult, 45¢ group student. Open Mar.–Nov., daily 9–6;
Dec.–Feb., Mon.–Sat. 10–4, Sun. 1–4. Closed Dec. 24, 25, 31,
and Jan. 1.*

❻ The **James Monroe Museum and Memorial Library** is the tiny
one-story building where the man who was to be the fifth president of the United States practiced law from 1787 to 1789. In
this building are many of Monroe's possessions, collected and
preserved by his family until this century, including a mahogany dispatch-box used during the negotiation of the Louisiana
Purchase and the desk on which Monroe signed the doctrine
named for him. *908 Charles St., tel. 703/373–8426. Open daily
9–5. Admission: $2.50 adult, 50¢ student, $2 group adult, 40¢
group student. Closed Thanksgiving, Dec. 24, 25, 31, and
Jan. 1.*

**Time Out**  Stop for a gourmet sandwich or a slice of quiche at the **Made in
Virginia Store Deli** (101 William St., tel. 703/371–2030). Do not
skip the rich desserts.

❼ On Charles Street is the modest white **home of Mary Washington.** George purchased it for her in 1772, and she spent the last
17 years of her life there, tending the charming garden where
her boxwood still flourishes and where many a bride and groom
now exchange their vows. Displays include many of Mrs. Wash-

ington's personal effects, as well as period furniture and a box-wood garden that includes plants she herself started. Local residents bought and preserved the house to keep it from being dismantled and taken to the Chicago World's Fair. *1200 Charles St. Admission: $2.50 adult, 50¢ student, $2 group adult, 40¢ group student. Open Mar.–Nov., daily 9–5; Dec.–Feb., daily 10–4. Closed Thanksgiving, Dec. 24, 25, 31, and Jan. 1.*

In 1760 George Washington's brother Charles built as his home **⑧** what became the **Rising Sun Tavern,** a watering hole for such pre-Revolutionary patriots as the Lee brothers, Patrick Henry, Washington, and Jefferson. A "wench" in period costume leads the tour without stepping out of character. From her perspective you watch the activity—day and night, upstairs and down—at this busy institution. In the tap room you are served spiced tea. *1306 Caroline St. Admission: $2.50 adult, 50¢ student, $2 group adult, 40¢ group student. Open Mar.–Nov., daily 9–5; Dec,–Feb. daily 10–4. Closed Thanksgiving, Dec. 24, 25, 31, an Jan. 1.*

**⑨** The **Hugh Mercer Apothecary Shop** offers a close-up view of 18th- and 19th-century medicine. It was established in 1771 by Dr. Mercer, a Scotsman who served as a brigadier general of the Revolutionary Army (he was killed at the Battle of Princeton). General George S. Patton of World War II fame was one of Mercer's great-great-great grandsons. Dr. Mercer might have been more careful than most other Colonial physicians, yet his methods will make you cringe. A costumed hostess will explicitly describe amputations and cataract operations. You will also hear about therapeutic bleeding and see the gruesome devices used in Colonial dentistry. This is an informative if slightly nauseating look at life two centuries ago. *1020 Caroline St. at Amelia St., tel. 703/373–3362. Admission: $2.50 adult, 50¢ student, $2 group adult, 40¢ group student. Open Mar.–Nov., daily 9–5; Dec.–Feb. daily 10–4. Closed Thanksgiving, Dec. 24, 25, 31, and Jan. 1.*

**⑩** The **Old Stone Warehouse** once overlooked a landing on the Rappahannock. Besides the function implied by its name, the four-story building has been used as a granary, brewery, arsenal, morgue (during the First Battle of Fredericksburg), and curing house for salt fish. The ceiling beams still show scars from Civil War bombardments. *Sophia St. at William St. Admission free. Open Sun. 1–4.*

**Time Out** Built in 1772 and reportedly haunted by the ghosts of several past residents (including President Chester A. Arthur's wife), **Chimneys Tavern** (623 Caroline St., tel. 703/371–9229) is now a restaurant serving regional specialties. Try the rack of lamb with tarragon, or veal Virginia—veal topped with Smithfield ham and backfin crabmeat. There's an extensive wine list.

**⑪** **Chatham Manor** is a fine example of Georgian architecture, built between 1768 and 1771 by William Fitzhugh on a site overlooking the Rappahannock and the town of Fredericksburg. Fitzhugh, a noted plantation owner, frequently hosted such luminaries of his day as George Washington and Thomas Jefferson. During the Civil War, Union forces commandeered the house and converted it into a headquarters and hospital. President Abraham Lincoln visited to confer with his generals; Clara Barton and the poet Walt Whitman tended the wounded.

After the war the house and gardens were restored by private owners and eventually donated to the National Park Service. Concerts often are held here during the summer. *Chatham Ln., Stafford County (take William St. across the bridge and follow signs approx. ½ mile). Admission free. Open daily 9–5; extended summer hours. Closed Dec. 25 and Jan. 1.*

# Index

# Personal Itinerary

**Departure** *Date*

*Time*

**Transportation**

**Arrival** *Date*    *Time*

**Departure** *Date*    *Time*

**Transportation**

**Accommodations**

**Arrival** *Date*    *Time*

**Departure** *Date*    *Time*

**Transportation**

**Accommodations**

**Arrival** *Date*    *Time*

**Departure** *Date*    *Time*

**Transportation**

**Accommodations**

*Personal Itinerary*

**Arrival** *Date*      *Time*

**Departure** *Date*      *Time*

**Transportation**

**Accommodations**

**Arrival** *Date*      *Time*

**Departure** *Date*      *Time*

**Transportation**

**Accommodations**

**Arrival** *Date*      *Time*

**Departure** *Date*      *Time*

**Transportation**

**Accommodations**

**Arrival** *Date*      *Time*

**Departure** *Date*      *Time*

**Transportation**

**Accommodations**

## Addresses

Name

Address

Telephone

Name

Address

Telephone

Name

Address

Telephone

Name

Address

Telephone

Name

Address

Telephone

Name

Address

Telephone

Name

Address

Telephone

Name

Address

Telephone

Name

Address

Telephone

Name

Address

Telephone

Name

Address

Telephone

Name

Address

Telephone

Name

Address

Telephone

Name

Address

Telephone

# Fodor's Travel Guides

## U.S. Guides

Alaska
Arizona
Atlantic City & the
  New Jersey Shore
Boston
California
Cape Cod
Carolinas & the
  Georgia Coast
The Chesapeake Region
Chicago
Colorado
Disney World & the
  Orlando Area

Florida
Hawaii
Las Vegas
Los Angeles, Orange
  County, Palm Springs
Maui
Miami,
  Fort Lauderdale,
  Palm Beach
Michigan, Wisconsin,
  Minnesota
New England
New Mexico
New Orleans

New Orleans (Pocket
  Guide)
New York City
New York City (Pocket
  Guide)
New York State
Pacific North Coast
Philadelphia
The Rockies
San Diego
San Francisco
San Francisco (Pocket
  Guide)
The South

Texas
USA
Virgin Islands
Virginia
Waikiki
Washington, DC

## Foreign Guides

Acapulco
Amsterdam
Australia, New Zealand,
  The South Pacific
Austria
Bahamas
Bahamas (Pocket
  Guide)
Baja & the Pacific
  Coast Resorts
Barbados
Beijing, Guangzhou &
  Shanghai
Belgium &
  Luxembourg
Bermuda
Brazil
Britain (Great Travel
  Values)
Budget Europe
Canada
Canada (Great Travel
  Values)
Canada's Atlantic
  Provinces
Cancun, Cozumel,
  Yucatan Peninsula

Caribbean
Caribbean (Great
  Travel Values)
Central America
Eastern Europe
Egypt
Europe
Europe's Great
  Cities
France
France (Great Travel
  Values)
Germany
Germany (Great Travel
  Values)
Great Britain
Greece
The Himalayan
  Countries
Holland
Hong Kong
Hungary
India,
  including Nepal
Ireland
Israel
Italy

Italy (Great Travel
  Values)
Jamaica
Japan
Japan (Great Travel
  Values)
Kenya, Tanzania,
  the Seychelles
Korea
Lisbon
Loire Valley
London
London (Great
  Travel Values)
London (Pocket Guide)
Madrid & Barcelona
Mexico
Mexico City
Montreal &
  Quebec City
Munich
New Zealand
North Africa
Paris
Paris (Pocket Guide)
People's Republic of
  China

Portugal
Rio de Janeiro
The Riviera (Fun on)
Rome
Saint Martin &
  Sint Maarten
Scandinavia
Scandinavian Cities
Scotland
Singapore
South America
South Pacific
Southeast Asia
Soviet Union
Spain
Spain (Great Travel
  Values)
Sweden
Switzerland
Sydney
Tokyo
Toronto
Turkey
Vienna
Yugoslavia

## Special-Interest Guides

Health & Fitness
  Vacations
Royalty Watching

Selected Hotels of
  Europe

Selected Resorts and
  Hotels of the U.S.
Shopping in Europe

Skiing in North America
Sunday in New York

*Help us evaluate hotels and restaurants for the next edition of this guide, and we will send you a free issue of Fodor's newsletter, TravelSense.*

**Title of this guide:**

**1 Hotel** ❑ **Restaurant** ❑ *(check one)*

Name

Number/Street

City/State/Country

Comments

**2 Hotel** ❑ **Restaurant** ❑ *(check one)*

Name

Number/Street

City/State/Country

Comments

**3 Hotel** ❑ **Restaurant** ❑ *(check one)*

Name

Number/Street

City/State/Country

Comments

**General Comments**

*Please complete for a free copy of TravelSense*

**Name**

**Number/Street**

**City/State/Zip**

# Business Reply Mail

*First Class*      *Permit Nº 7775*      *New York, NY*

*Postage will be paid by addressee*

## Fodor's Travel Publications

*201 East 50th Street*

*New York, NY 10022*